THE ROAD FROM RIO

Sustainable Development and the
Nongovernmental Movement
in the Third World

Julie Fisher

Foreword by THOMAS W. DICHTER

Westport, Connecticut
London

Library of Congress Cataloging-in-Publication Data

Fisher, Julie.
  The road from Rio : sustainable development and the non-
governmental movement in the Third World / Julie Fisher ; foreword
by Thomas W. Dichter.
    p.   cm.
  Includes bibliographical references and index.
  ISBN 0–275–94535–9 (alk. paper).—ISBN 0–275–94715–7 (pbk.: alk. paper)
  1. Non-governmental organizations—Developing countries.
  2. Sustainable development—Developing countries.   3. Economic development
projects—Developing countries.   4. Developing countries—Population.   I. Title.
  HC59.7.F548   1993
  338.9′009172′4—dc20   92–35339

British Library Cataloguing in Publication Data is available.

Library of Congress Catalog Card Number: 92–35339
ISBN: 0–275–94535–9
ISBN: 0–275–94715–7 (pbk.)

First published in 1993

Praeger Publishers, 88 Post Road West, Westport, CT 06881
An imprint of Greenwood Publishing Group, Inc.

Printed in the United States of America

(∞)™

The paper used in this book complies with the
Permanent Paper Standard issued by the National
Information Standards Organization (Z39.48–1984).

10 9 8 7 6 5 4 3 2

THE ROAD FROM RIO

Contents

Foreword

Development as a field of deliberate endeavor has not been around for very long, forty years at best. Yet it has become a large industry—a conservative estimate would be roughly $50 billion on an annual basis. Like any industry the development business has developed, willy nilly, its own social structures and internal cultures, a rapidly growing specialized lexicon (opaque to outsiders), layers of underlying values, and prevailing conceptual paradigms. Given the nature of the development endeavor—essentially to do deliberately what until the mid-twentieth century happened without conscious plan or direction—we should not be surprised that this astoundingly ambitious if not arrogant project has also generated considerable ideological froth since its beginnings.

While the ideological tensions of the development business have subsided somewhat in recent years, some of the habits that evolved around those tensions remain strong. One is a tendency to attach the leading hopes of the development business to different "informing ideas" (Basic Human Needs, Sustainable Development) and to attribute "magic bullet" characteristics to different actors, like NGOs (nongovernmental organizations). These fashions tend, interestingly, to last about a decade each. A second tendency is to leap fairly headlong into activating these ideas and actors without much research or reflection.

The great value of Julie Fisher's *The Road From Rio* is its demonstrable humbling effect on our industry's oversimplification of the NGO movement to date. It puts the movement squarely beyond fashion and ideology. The

depth and breadth of research behind this book and the consequent level
of detail is unprecedented in the growing literature on NGOs.

For while others have paid due heed to the heterogeneity of the NGO
movement, Fisher makes its diversity palpable. The first six chapters are as
thoroughly researched and fairminded a compendium of NGO diversity as
exists. Moreover, the author demonstrates to the reader that the movement's
diversity lies not only in function and typology but in its historical roots,
culture, and the nature of relationships between NGOs and their different
political, social, and economic contexts.

The danger in demonstrating such heterogeneity, of course, is to lose any
thread of connection in the face of the differences. *The Road From Rio*
does not permit this to happen. For NGOs, as Fisher demonstrates, by and
large share a common view of where to begin—at the grassroots. This is a
seemingly simple commonality, but one with powerful (and revolutionary)
implications, as the author suggests.

The audience for this valuable work could be anyone in the development
business or anyone interested in it. But there are two audiences for whom
this book is particularly valuable: (1) NGOs themselves, especially the
35,000 grassroots support organizations (GRSOs) that Fisher estimates are
in the world at present, and (2) the international donor community.

For the former, especially the many among them that are isolated, un-
derfunded, and unsung, this book is both an enormous encouragement and
stimulus. It says to them, "you are not alone." It reminds them that there
are no natural limits to what they can do. There is enough evidence in this
book to break down some key myths about NGO limits, among them that
NGOs are not good at scaling up, can only work at the grassroots, are poor
at articulating their lessons learned, cannot work at the policy level, and
above all do not reach significant numbers of people. As a stimulus, *The
Road From Rio* provides a compendium of ideas that may generate even
more creativity in a movement that Fisher's research demonstrates already
has a very high proportion of it.

At the same time that *The Road From Rio* can and should have a con-
fidence-building effect on thousands of NGOs, Fisher does not pull punches
about the challenges. While there is much promise, there are challenges a
plenty, and the movement is young in a young industry. Fisher doesn't say
it, but we are at the early stages of the movement. The "pickens" are
promising, but to date they remain slim. There are areas where NGOs do
less well than in others. GRSOs face vested-interest problems and important
issues of succession and leadership as they approach their second generation.
Most important, as the author points out, the full implications of sustainable
development are not yet understood or absorbed by most GRSOs, who form
the heart of the movement. Nor, I would add, are NGOs sufficiently aware
of the degree to which they are at the mercy of very large external forces

besides the obvious ones like lack of political stability, hostile politics, and failing economies, not to mention the weather. The concept of an enabling environment for NGOs is only now beginning to dawn on many, and the need to organize to promote such an environment is just beginning to be felt. NGOs do not see the extent to which their economic future may depend on legal and fiscal policies that are buried in the laws and tax structures of their host countries.

But it is perhaps the second audience, the international donor community, for whom this book is an absolute must. Increasingly, the large actors in the international donor community (the multilateral agencies like the World Bank and the bilateral agencies of the OECD nations) have come to form a new element in the political economy of the NGO movement. The hidden dangers for the NGO movement are considerable. While the major donors are genuinely committed to development, they are no less immune to their own political economy than the smaller, less-powerful NGOs. To a large extent, the major donors are beholden to their constituencies and covet their share of the budget as much as their competitors for a piece of the national or international pie. They have their territorial imperatives, and they face their own "use it or lose it" dilemma each budget cycle. And at the end of the day, they are rewarded as much for getting the money out the door as they are for promoting development. With the limelight and all its accompanying expectations shining more and more on NGOs this decade, the large donors are seriously interested in finding ways to work with them. They tend, naturally enough, to assume that what others say about NGOs is true—they need capacity building, they need funding, they need, in short, what the donors have to offer.

Fisher should be read as a polite caution to these donors that they must be very careful in accepting their own and others' assumptions about the movement. She reminds them that there is considerable organizational capacity, management savvy, and sophistication in the movement; that there is even a capacity for financial self-sufficiency. A great many NGOs, therefore, may not need what the donors want to give them. Most important, Fisher points to some central paradoxes that the donors may not be conscious of in looking to NGOs as the next solution to development's many dilemmas. First, much of what is vibrant about NGOs, especially GRSOs, is that they came up by themselves; they were not, for the most part, set up and started from the top or by someone else to act as their agent. At the same time, NGOs are not different from other organizations. Once begun they want to stay in business—thus, they are prone to take donations and grants without first asking whether it is in the best interests of development to do so. Secondly, as Fisher points out, the project of helping others in the end means that the helper must eventaully back away. This poker-like calculus (knowing "when to hold 'em and when to fold 'em") is an enormous challenge for the large donors. NGOs can be smothered by funds if they have no absorptive capacity; NGOs can likewise have the heart taken out of them if they become too formalized.

Finally, Fisher shows in Chapter 8 how truly complex the question of results is. How to evaluate, monitor, and measure what NGOs accomplish has only begun to be tackled.

The message for the donor community is: do not rush to judgement too quickly, either positive or negative, and consider a more light-handed approach to your involvement than has been your habit thus far. If that message gets across, this book will have done invaluable service to its subjects.

Thomas W. Dichter

Preface

The end of the Cold War has loosened the paralyzing grip of ideology on the world's resources and imagination. There is an emerging awareness that now the real problems confronting humanity can and must be addressed. Eastern Europe and the former Soviet Union are beginning to deal with economic stagnation and environmental catastrophes. In the United States there is growing discontent with politics as usual. With the United Nations Conference on Environment and Development (UNCED) held in Rio de Janeiro in June 1992, the global community took some tentative first steps toward dealing with the worldwide environmental crisis and advancing the cause of "sustainable development." Sustainable development can be defined as meeting the needs of the present without destroying resources that will be needed in the future. And, perhaps most remarkable of all, a nongovernmental revolution is already sweeping the Third World.

Unlike previous revolutions, it seeks not to violently overthrow and to replace existing governments but rather to challenge their inequitable and often repressive political monopoly by enlarging civil society. Since the early 1970s, more than a hundred thousand nongovernmental organizations (NGOs) have been founded in Asia, Africa, and Latin America by peasant women and professors, squatters and students, fisherfolk and unemployed intellectuals. Like some previous revolutionaries, nongovernmental activists target escalating poverty and the need for subjects to become citizens. Unlike previous revolutionaries, however, the nongovernmental movement challenges both the narrow scope and the top-down style of decision making about human needs rather than merely the identity or even the ideology of decision makers.

Yet even as people in the Third World organize themselves, and even as the threat of nuclear annihilation recedes, three horsemen of the global apocalypse remain. Poverty, population, and environmental degradation ride roughshod over the aspirations and hopes of people everywhere. In many countries these interrelated crises are beginning to fuse into a vicious downward spiral. Deforestation accelerates as a rising population finds itself less and less able to eke a living out of previously deforested land that is unsuitable for agriculture. Rivers polluted by factories that provide only a few jobs can no longer provide fish for anyone. Malnourished women, overburdened with childbearing, are among the poorest of the poor. Their children may not even survive to adulthood. The road from Rio, in other words, is a "steep and rocky path" that we must locate, construct, and somehow pull ourselves along if we are to survive without destroying the lives of future generations. Third World NGOs will be essential contributors to this process, provided their remarkable creativity is understood and supported.

With this book, I initiate a two-volume "appreciative inquiry" into the promise and realistic possibilities of a movement that is remarkably similar in Bangladesh and Bolivia, Mali and Malaysia, Colombia and the Cameroon.[1] Because of this similarity, the reader will have to put up with a certain amount of jumping around from continent to continent and country to country. The trade-off for avoiding this would have been to weaken the strong argument that NGOs are a truly global trend. It is my hope that the mini case studies set apart from the flow of text will provide more in-depth information on particular organizations.

This volume focuses on those NGOs with the greatest potential impact on sustainable development, as well as on the relationships between different types of NGOs. The next volume will focus on the relationships between NGOs and governments, their potential impact on political development, and their relationships with foreign donors.

My interest in voluntary activism in the Third World really began thirty years ago in Chile, where I spent a semester studying the Christian Democratic Party. I was, of course, fascinated by the idealism and lower-class support of a dynamic political movement that was soon to culminate in the election of Eduardo Frei to the presidency in 1964. But I was also intrigued by the squatter neighborhood organizations and groups of street vendors that joined the party to gain access to potential political leaders. And I spent time in squatter settlements, where middle-class students and housewives were beginning to provide assistance to neighborhood organizations.

During the next two decades I married, reared two children, wrote a doctoral dissertation about the squatter neighborhood organizations in

Latin America, taught a seminar at Connecticut College entitled Politics of Third World Development, and began to do consulting assignments in the Third World. Then, in 1986, I attended the annual meeting of the Latin American Studies Association in Boston. I heard Brian Smith, then at MIT, talk about the indigenous intermediate level nongovernmental organizations that had developed all over the Third World beginning in the 1970s. And I met the late Mario Padron, the inspired organizer and leader of DESCO, a Peruvian grassroots support organization. The three of us had lunch together, and I knew then that I wanted to understand this new intellectual movement and its connections with the grassroots organizations I had studied in my thesis and observed in the Third World. That afternoon, three Latin American political scientists who might have been revolutionaries only a few years before talked about the need to meld "liberal democratic values" with social justice through the growth of "civil society." And that discussion set the stage for the second volume of this study.

I have chosen to take a comprehensive look at the nongovernmental movement in the Third World instead of comparing it in two or three countries. In doing so, I recognize that I am taking the risky path of having to accept judgments that lack corroboration and of sometimes foregoing analytical rigor. I have done so because many people have already written about a few countries, and I saw a need to pull all this information together and to develop some consistent ways of looking at and defining institutions that are cross-nationally similar. I also believe that this worldwide phenomenon, like the proverbial elephant, cannot be fully appreciated by analyzing only a piece of it.

My deepest thanks for psychological support and intellectual insight go to my husband and editor-in-chief, Richard Peck, without whom I could not have written this book. My parents, David and Frances Hawkins, my sons, Tom and Scott Fisher, my stepson David Peck, and my step-daughters Su, Linda, and Penni Peck provided continuing support and encouragement. My father also contributed his knowledge of political philosophy. Phil and Phyllis Morrison read and critiqued parts of the manuscript. Linda Peck, a real pro at desktop publishing, is responsible for the tables. My friend and walking companion, Francine Caplan, was good at listening to my frustrations. Dr. John Seashore read several chapters and contributed the original and precise political insights of a pediatric surgeon. My friend Emily Morrison became a one-woman clipping service for the book. Philip Coombs contributed indirectly by helping me hone my professional skills during the early 1980s. Dr. Norman Uphoff of Cornell University read the draft manuscript and contributed valuable insights. Brad Gray and my other colleagues at the Yale University Program on Non-Profit Organizations provided me with a forum for presenting my findings and obtaining feedback. Guy Gran provided me with helpful bibliographical assistance. In addition to the many people from the Third World and the United States who I interviewed, I want to acknowledge the special support, contributions, and encouragement of Tom Dichter, Brian Smith, Jane Vella, and Brian Truman.

NOTE

1. The phrase has been used by David Cooperrider of Ohio State University.

Selected Acronyms

ADAB	Agricultural Development Agencies of Bangladesh
AID	Agency for International Development (United States)
AIDSEP	Inter-Ethnic Association for the Development of the Peruvian Rainforest
ANAI	Association of New Alchemists (Costa Rica)
ASINDES	Associacion de Entidades de Dessarrollo ey de Servicion No Gubernamentales de Guatemala
AVARD	Association of Voluntary Agencies in Rural Development (India)
AVDs	village development associations (Senegal)
BINGOs	big NGOs (Indonesia)
CCHR	Coordinating Council for Human Rights (Bangladesh)
CET	Center for Education and Technology (Chile)
CIDOB	Center for Indigenous Peoples in Eastern Boliva
COLUFIFA	Committee to Fight for the End of Hunger in Senegal
CONGAD	Council of NGOs Supporting Development (Senegal)
FAO	Food and Agriculture Organization (United Nations)
FAVDO	Forum of African Voluntary Development Organizations

FEMUC	Federation of Peasant Women (Honduras)
FONGS	Federation of NGOs of Senegal
FOV	Federation of Voluntary Organizations (Costa Rica)
FUNDAEC	Foundation for the Application and Teaching of Science (Columbia)
FUNDASAL	Salvadoran Foundation for Development and Low Cost Housing
GONGOs	government sponsored NGOs
GRO	grassroots organization
GRSO	grassroots support organization
IAF	Inter-American Foundation
IAs	Interest Associations
ILO	International Labour Organization
INGO	International Nongovernmental Organization
IPPF	International Planned Parenthood Federation
LA	local administration
LDAs	local development associations
LG	local government
LINGOs	little NGOs (Indonesia)
NGOs	nongovernmental organizations
OEPs	popular economic organizations (Chile)
ORAP	Organization of Rural Associations for Progress (Zimbabwe)
PQLI	Physical Quality of Life Index
PRADAN	Professional Assistance for Development Action (India)
PRAXIS	The Training Program for Social Action and Research (Mexico)
PVOs	Private Voluntary Organizations (United States)
SAM	Sahabat Alam Malaysia
SEWA	Self-Employed Women's Association (India)
SIX S	Association Se Servir de la Saison Seche en Savane et au Sahel (Making Use of the Savannah and the Sahel in the Dry Season)
TNS	Technoserve (United States)
UNDP	United Nations Development Program
UNICEF	United Nations Children's Fund
WALHI	Indonesian Environmental Forum

THE ROAD FROM RIO

1

The Politics of Development

To be sure, one wants to know what the most probable outcomes are. They represent baselines to work from and indicate what is most likely to result if nothing new or different is done. The challenge in development work is how to make possible outcomes that are deemed desirable somehow more probable.

Uphoff, 1992:229.

It is often said that human beings only change under the most terrible of circumstances. Today in the Third World the connection between catastrophe and human ingenuity is being dramatically and extensively confirmed. Asians, Africans, and Latin Americans suffer from an almost endless list of ills. Yet millions of people in these continents are working through hundreds of thousands of nongovernmental organizations (NGOs) to survive and build a better life for themselves and their children.

Since World War II the absolute number of the poor in the Third World has increased dramatically as improvements in public health produced declines in death rates without concomitant declines in fertility. However, it took a newer crisis, global environmental degradation, to begin to drag poverty and population to center stage.

American awareness of global environmental issues increased dramatically during the sweltering summer of 1988, as speculation mounted that the symptoms of global warming had begun. And the burning of the Amazon, dramatized on television, began to link "ecophobia" to what was happening in the Third World. Then, in November 1989, Chico Mendez, an independent Brazilian rubber tapper who had organized his fellow *fazendeiros* to save the forest, was murdered.

The Gordian knot being tied ever tighter around humanity's future is still only on the periphery of public awareness, however. This knot is tied from three ominous strands—poverty, environmental degradation, and the population explosion. In the 130 years between 1850 and 1980 Africa lost 60 percent of its forest cover, and the pace is escalating with increasing population. Haiti, once known as the "Pearl of the Antilles," has become a barren wasteland. Despite reforestation efforts, only half of tree seedlings survive because Haitian peasants are so destitute that they cut down and sell whatever they can find.

The international response to the poverty/environment connection has been positive if still seminal. Prime Minister Gro Brundtland of Norway headed an international commission in 1987 that greatly enhanced international public and governmental awareness of the need for a rapid and extensive proliferation of "sustainable development" strategies, defined as development in the present that does not destroy the resources needed for future development. And in an increasing number of Third World communities people are learning to recycle waste, build solar cook stoves, and plant fruit trees rather than cut down forests.

By June 1992, with the convening of the United Nations Conference on Environment and Development in Rio, the connections between sustainable development in the developed and developing world were finally becoming the focus of global debate. Several weeks before the conference opened a *Business Week* cover story pointed out that environmentally sensitive technologies could actually promote rather than retard economic growth everywhere. In Europe, the Business Council for Sustainable Development was aggressively pursuing the need for government policies to penalize polluters and promote energy-efficient technologies. And a World Bank economist, Lawrence H. Summers, generated controversy by arguing that it might be cheaper for the developed countries to pursue aggressive policies to reduce Third World poverty and its terrible environmental consequences than to significantly reduce global warming through reducing greenhouse gases.

There is less international dialogue on the connections between poverty, environmental devastation, and the population explosion, however, despite the projected doubling of the world's population to 10 billion by the year 2040. The Rio Conference, held in June 1992, did little to alter this situation. (See Exhibit 1.1.) As many people will be added to the world population in the decade of the 1990s as were on the planet in 1900; 90 percent of them in the Third World, and 90 percent of those in urban areas. Without massive increases in the availability of choices for women and family planning, even "sustainable development" strategies will break down.

Before 1980 the United States was the largest single contributor to family planning in the Third World, and people talked openly about the perils of the population explosion. The more recent reticence to confront the global population issue is tied both to the rightward pull of the U.S. antiabortion

Exhibit 1.1
The Results of Rio

The centerpiece of the formal results of the Rio Conference is Agenda 21. By focusing on developmental and environmental issues in an integrated fashion, Agenda 21 fundamentally alters both the international agenda and the public debate. Agenda 21 also addresses the reverse flow of resources from developing countries and connects this issue to sustainable development. It commits the developed countries to providing 0.7 percent of GNP for Official Development Assistance (ODA) and proposes a restructuring of the Global Environmental Facility that would expand its scope and accessibility.

Agenda 21 also combines two strands of development action: one strand that focuses on improving the access of the poor to resources and the other that deals with the management of natural resources. The major groups of detailed programs deal with land, water, and biotic management in developing countries. Within each group are elaborate, detailed discussions of such issues as the development and conservation of forest resources. The discussion links the international conventions already negotiated on ozone layer depletion to other environmental problems.

The Commission on Sustainable Development, charged with monitoring Agenda 21, will be the focal point of intergovernmental decision making in the years ahead. Its sucessful implementation will depend on cross-cutting program areas. In some cases, the specific details outlined in the agreement are sufficient to begin implementation immediately, but in other cases, such as the impact of population on sustainable development, much more work will be required. "When historians put UNCED in perspective, they may highlight the paradox between the cardinal importance of the human population factor in most of the issues UNCED was addressing, and the remarkable reluctance to address this factor in the UNCED documentation. The political reasons for this are well known" (Blackburn, 1992).

UNCED's most dramatic outcome was the nongovernmental networking that occurred under the aegis of the parallel Global Forum. Over 20,000 participants representing 9,000 organizations from 171 countries, in addition to 9,000 journalists and 450,000 visitors, attended the sessions. Although over 350 meetings were formally scheduled, there were an estimated 1,000 organized substantive discussions held over the 14 days of the Forum. According to the Centre for Our Common Future (1992), the results of this "information overload" will take years to assess.

---

movement and to the leftward tug of a "politically correct" cultural sensitivity that, ironically, can skip over the views of Third World women.

Few commentators of any persuasion in the United States have focused on the contribution of the developed countries to the population crisis. The United States, with only 5 percent of the world's population, uses 25 percent of its nonrenewable resources. Thus, a 1 percent increase in the U.S. population may have as dramatic an impact on the destruction of nonrenewable resources as a 3 percent growth rate in a poor country.

Also neglected in the political dialogue in the developed countries is an understanding of the macro dimensions of the economic crisis further accelerating the downward spiral of environmental destruction. The Third World loses almost 6 percent of its gross domestic product every year to debt repayment. In fact, after subtracting foreign assistance, investments, and new loans, many Third World countries are experiencing a reverse flow of resources to developed countries totaling $60 billion a year.[1] Crushing debt also has a devastating impact on natural resources. Since 1983 developing nations have exported $50 billion in resources annually. Yet farming, fishing, forestry, and mining account for more than two-thirds of employment and 50 percent of export earnings. If these trends continue, twenty-three of thirty-three countries that exported tropical timber in 1985 will have totally destroyed their forests by the year 2000.

For their part, Third World governments spend over $180 billion a year on their military establishments.[2] In northeast Brazil, semifeudal land tenure systems force the poor into the Amazon, even as government policy shifts away from a tax system that promoted deforestation. Few Third World governments, even those that promote family planning, understand the crucial connection between educating women and lowering family size. In fact, the combination of massive corruption, entrenched interests, and overwhelming poverty makes it unlikely that even well-intentioned governments will be able to achieve sustainable development.

The seminal global institutions that are beginning to emerge around the need for sustainable development only highlight the inadequacy of governments in the developed as well as the developing world. Although the European Community has become a global environmental leader, the Bush administration succeeded in scuttling the mandatory provisions of the treaty to stabilize greenhouse gas emissions before the Rio meeting even began. Global change, in other words, demands political change on the national and local level that will be difficult everywhere.

THE EMERGENCE OF NONGOVERNMENTAL ORGANIZATIONS (NGOs)

Fortunately, the nongovernmental organizations founded in the Third World in recent years are already implementing sustainable development and are increasingly challenging and sometimes changing government policy. Confronted by catastrophic changes in their own lives, people in Asia, Africa, and Latin America are organizing their own communities in partnership with committed professionals. In doing so they are inventing alternatives to a dismal human future.

As awareness of the impending catastrophe grows, activists in developed countries will need to draw strength and inspiration as well as warning signals from the Third World. Yet most Americans and Europeans are not even dimly aware of this promising trend. "Northern" governments have traditionally responded to conditions in the Third World by aiding governments or through promoting the interests of multinational corporations. The spread of NGOs is a real turning point, yet foreign donors are only beginning to be aware of the potential of bottom-up initiatives.

While it is true that urban services are collapsing in Latin America, it is also true that in São Paulo alone 1,300 neighborhood improvement associations have planted gardens, recycled garbage, and built over thirty-three kilometers of street gutters. Deforestation in Nepal contributes to flooding in Bangladesh, yet a growing number of environmental organizations work at the grassroots level in both countries. Starvation continues on a massive scale in parts of Africa, but there are now more than 700 African "technology institutions," 137 of which are working on agricultural tools and implements.[3] With increased numbers of women of child-bearing age the population explosion will continue even as fertility begins to decline in the Third World. Yet, low-cost family planning and health care methods, pioneered in the 1970s in Asia, demonstrated that voluntary organizations can have an impact on government policies affecting millions of people.

The rapid growth of the voluntary, nonprofit, "third" or independent sector in the Third World centers on what Berg (1987:38) calls the "twin challenges of empowerment and development." In Asia, Latin America, and, more recently, in Africa, this organizational explosion is creating a partnership between some of the best- and least-educated people in each society as intellectuals and technically trained professionals seek out and work with grassroots village and neighborhood groups.

This partnership defines the parameters of two major types of NGOs. Beginning in the 1970s, the availability of foreign assistance provided idealistic young professionals with an alternative to dead-end government jobs or migration to the developed countries. They were able, instead, to create thousands of grassroots support organizations (GRSOs) concerned with development, environment, the role of women, and primary health care. GRSOs are nationally or regionally based development assistance organizations, usually staffed by professionals, that channel international funds to grassroots organizations (GROs) and help communities other than their own to develop. There are at least 30,000 to 35,000 active grassroots support organizations in the Third World. Although some GRSOs are "counterparts" to international NGOs (INGOs) from the developed countries, the vast majority are indigenous. In addition to building linkages with GROs, GRSOs are also uniting with each other.

GROs are locally based groups that work to improve and develop their own communities through communitywide or more-specific memberships, such as women or farmers.[4] Although many have been promoted and stimulated by GRSOs, they have also become more active on their own. Faced with the deterioration of their environment and the increasing impoverishment of the 1980s, both traditional and newly created GROs are organizing horizontal networks among themselves. In some cases they have created GRSOs from below by hiring their own expertise.

An African chief explained that the drought "has become a weapon for us. With abundance, each one worked for himself. We have discovered plants that grow more rapidly. Hunger has become a teacher that has forced us to think."[5] The daily struggle for survival ensures that this is not just a phenomenon of traditional elites, however. Schneider (1985:168), who spent two years visiting nineteen countries, attributes this "astounding aptitude for adaptation" to the activism of followers as well as leaders.

Despite the growing importance of GROs, which Durning (1989) estimates to be in the hundreds of thousands, the acronym NGO is often assumed to be synonymous with grassroots support organizations. As used here, NGO is defined more broadly to include not only GRSOs but also GROs, GRO networks, and networks of GRSOs involved in development.[6]

NGOs, even broadly defined, do not comprise the entire voluntary "third" or "independent" sector in the Third World. Yet they have extended its boundaries and contributed to its dramatic growth. The rise of NGOs has led some traditional service organizations such as hospitals or charities to assume new grassroots support functions. Traditional kinship or burial societies at the community level are also getting involved in development.

Increasing numbers of international conferences and the spread of personal computers have accelerated the momentum of this organizational proliferation. Never before have local organizations been so able to communicate with each other—both nationally and internationally.

NGOs AND POLITICAL EMPOWERMENT

Whatever the economic and environmental impact of NGOs in the immediate future, their long-term impact will depend upon changes in the inequitable political and economic structures that dominate most Third World countries. Without political change, NGOs will remain isolated and threatened. Yet NGOs that promote political empowerment at the local level can also begin to erode those same structures. This occurs, for example, when women who have already organized microenterprises speak out for the first time in village council meetings. At the national level, vested interests can be undermined by scientists working for GRSOs who convince officials to stop supporting an environmentally destructive project.

The challenges posed by the poverty-population-environment crisis are daunting precisely because social and economic advances must become politically as well as environmentally sustainable. Although it would be naive to assume that everything can be achieved at once, there are powerful potential connections between political, social, and sustainable economic development that are being pursued consciously if not always simultaneously by NGO activists. They possess a remarkably widespread commitment to the notion that political empowerment from below can untie the negative connections that now sustain poverty.

For all of the rhetorical commitment to "popular participation" and "bottom-up development" among development professionals, few official donors or international nongovernmental organizations (INGOs) have been willing to commit time and thought to who is doing what where in a particular country. Projects are still initiated without regard to whether GROs or GRSOs are active in a particular region. Partnerships with GRSOs are, as we shall see in Volume 2, increasingly common but are often established with the best-known organizations, which may or may not be doing the best job of grassroots organizing. And the subtle assumption that "capacity building" is a one-way street is still widespread. While I cannot provide an institutional road map of the Third World, it is my hope that this two-volume study will encourage international development professionals to collaborate more closely with their GRSO and GRO colleagues to map NGOs in the countries where they work.

IMPLEMENTING SUSTAINABLE DEVELOPMENT

This two-volume study focuses primarily on the ability of the nongovernmental movement in the Third World to *implement* sustainable development at the local level and, ultimately, to contribute to its implementation at the national level through political development. This volume deals with GROs, GRSOs, their networks, and their ability to work together. Volume 2 concentrates on the relationship of NGOs to governments and to outside donors and assesses the potential for NGOs to promote sustainable development in the wider political and international arena. There are many references to sustainable development strategies and projects described throughout these volumes, and Chapter 5 focuses more specifically on the environmentally and economically sustainable activities of GRSOs. Nonetheless, the central question, addressed at the end of each chapter, is whether NGOs are institutionally and politically sustainable in the long run and whether, therefore, they will be able to make a major contribution to the worldwide crisis of poverty, environmental degradation, and population growth.

A major difficulty in assessing this intertwined phenomenon of organizational and informational growth and exchange is that while it has produced a substantial body of knowledge about particular organizations and movements, the vast majority of NGOs remain isolated or even invisible. The organizational proliferation occurring in many countries has left academics and development practitioners struggling to catch up with a new reality. In 1985, the Club of Rome estimated that "Southern" NGOs "may involve as many as 60 million people in Asia, 25 million in Latin America, and 12 million in Africa."[7] Since then, the environmental movement has grown rapidly and become involved in sustainable development, networking has accelerated, and more-traditional voluntary organizations are undertaking grassroots support activities.

Another major difficulty in assessing what is happening is the need to tread a fine line between what one African community activist called the "luxury of pessimism" and excessive optimism that overestimates NGO capacity or underestimates the magnitude of the tasks confronting them. Despite the inadequacy of individual written accounts of NGOs, I believe the cumulative effect of existing research, including field observations, can contribute to some valid initial assessments of NGOs, to be explored in chapters 7 and 8.

What is the magnitude and power of this quiet revolution? Relative to what was there before, an organizational explosion is occurring in the Third World. Relative to the magnitude of the sustainable development task, this is a revolution stumbling through its early stages. NGOs are making inroads but are still far from overthrowing the old order of poverty and inequality.

The next section outlines the role of NGOs within the broader voluntary or independent sector. This is followed by a discussion of the formidable political barriers to change on the macro level. The chapter concludes with an introduction to the political impact of NGOs and a brief outline of the two volumes.

NGOs AND THE INDEPENDENT SECTOR

Scholars argue about what to call everything left over after the government and private business sectors are defined. Brown and Korten (1989:5) point out that the term *voluntary sector* implies that shared values rather than political or economic imperatives motivate the utilization of resources. However, the term also tends to imply the use of volunteers. Volunteers are not always a hallmark of the sector, even in developed countries. In the Third World, some GRSOs are composed entirely of paid staff, although they may work with volunteers from GROs.

The term *third sector*, developed by Waldemar Nielsen (1979) is somewhat confusing unless one already knows that government is the first sector and private business the second. It also accentuates the leftover characterization of the sector. As scholarly controversy over what organizations belong in this sector has increased, the term has become less prevalent.

Although the term *nonprofit sector* is useful for developed countries, it does not encompass the complex reality of institutional development in the Third World today. Cooperatives, for example, promote projects benefitting an entire community in addition to making profits for their members. They often have very broad member/ownership, share common values, and provide services at cost.[8] Water users' associations and work-sharing groups are based on in-kind economic contributions. Even GRSOs, which are nonprofit, converge with and build on the growing vitality of the underground or informal part of the business sector described by Hernando De Soto (1989) in *The Other Path*.

Indeed, the growth of the informal economy and the emergence of NGOs are like two great organizational wellsprings bubbling up from below, both based on demands for autonomy and a strengthening of civil society. Although the informal economy and what we shall call the independent sector are not identical, they overlap, with a joint potential for enhancing both economic and institutional sustainability. Both challenge the state and its "mercantilist" interrelationships with the formal part of the business sector.[9] Both have outgrown the confines of the left-right continuum, combining, albeit in different combinations, radical notions such as land reform, broad-based ownership, and the economic emancipation of women with an understanding of the generative power of small business and the market system.

The relationships between informal economic activity and the independent sector do not resemble those between nonprofits and the *formal* part of the business sector in either the Third World or the developed countries. Nonprofit organizations such as the Grameen Bank in Bangladesh are literally promoting thousands of small businesses as their principal activity.[10] Sometimes this overlap provokes controversy. For example, Andre Eugene Ilboudo, a GRSO leader from Burkina Faso, says that "in the villages where we work people argue about whether [community owned] restaurants should be profitable."[11]

The term *independent sector* has the further advantage of encompassing both autonomy and shared values. What is included in the independent sector? Anheier (1990:34) points out that it differs not only between the developed and developing countries but also within each continent and sometimes within one country. Definitions can be based on legal statutes or national accounts. They may also be residual (whatever is not governmental or business), and boundaries can, therefore, vary considerably.[12] Perhaps Douglas's (1983) observation that the sector unites market flexibility with the production of public goods comes closest to being a cross-nationally relevant description.

Even though NGOs dominate the new institutional landscape in the Third World, a number of traditional organizations also belong to the independent sector. Although the broader boundaries of the sector are outside the scope of this book, it is important to understand the wider if less populated terrain within which NGOs develop.

What organizational functions are included in the independent sector in the Third World? Some parameters are as relevant in the Third World as in the developed countries. For example, charitable or community devel-

opment activities of religious organizations are included but their sacra-
mental activities are generally not. However, in addition to the blurred
distinction between for-profit and not-for-profit activities in the Third
World, there are other differences in the two contexts. Some definitions
relevant to the developed countries exclude "member serving" activities of
community organizations. Yet the community kitchens developed by GROs
in Lima and Santiago feed thousands of people and are simultaneously
meeting individual and collective needs.[13]

Many organizations that are a part of the independent sector in the Third
World are not included in this book. Among these are arts organizations,
professional associations, traditional charities, and private universities and
hospitals. Although all of these are technically nongovernmental organizations, the term NGO is increasingly used to describe development organizations. Moreover, NGOs are proliferating much more rapidly than other
nonprofit organizations in most countries and are inspiring them to undertake grassroots support activities and become NGOs. Hospitals are developing programs of primary health care outreach. People interested in theater
are using it to teach villagers about clean water or agriculture. Churches,
particularly in Africa, are increasingly involved in grassroots support. Universities support development research, including field activities. Professional associations, particularly professional women's associations, are
helping people organize to obtain legal rights or build housing. And traditional charities, foundations and general membership associations in some
countries are evolving into GRSOs. The Girl Guides in Sri Lanka, for example, are promoting microenterprises.

The potential political impact of NGOs is greater in the Third World
than in the developed countries. In the United States, local and national
governments remain the major political arena where demands surface, issues
are debated, and decisions are made, even though voluntary organizations
often step in where governments fear to tread. In most of the Third World
it is not just that governments may be ineffective or corrupt, it is also that
they are often irrelevant to the most crucial political issues confronting
society. To understand the potential role of NGOs in political development,
we need to understand the political context within which they emerge. In
so doing we will begin to understand why they have emerged at all.

MONOPOLIES OF POWER

What are the major political barriers to sustainable development in the
Third World? In most countries today "politics" reflects competition or
collaboration among economically powerful elites. Whether regimes are
characterized as rightist authoritarian, leftist authoritarian, or oligarchic
democracies, power monopolies at the top have traditionally formed a kind
of political superstructure. Organski (1965) described this power monopoly

as a "syncratic alliance" uniting traditional agrarian interests too strong to be destroyed with a modernizing industrial elite. In exchange for obtaining the political support of agrarian interests, powerful urban sectors agree not to disturb the semifeudal conditions of the countryside. Thus, industrialists might theoretically favor a minimum agricultural wage to expand peasant purchasing power, but their political commitments to landowners prevent them from supporting it.

In Latin America and parts of Asia, large landowners represent the rural side of this coalition, whether they leave land idle or own large commercial plantations. A succession of Indian governments, for example, despite socialist rhetoric, have failed to break with powerful rural elites. Although Organski's description may be less relevant to Africa, Scarritt (1986:88) points out that support from those with wealth and power "is almost always more important to political decision makers than support from other classes." African money changers and intermediate brokers tend to enforce tributary rather than productive relationships between classes.[14]

This basic explanation of the political barriers to Third World development should not be understood as an all-inclusive theory. There are many variations and some exceptions to this theme that need to be taken into account. There is much that it does not explain. In many Third World countries, the military becomes a third party to this alliance, even though officers may be of humble origin and may even replace agrarian elites. In some countries the poor are stratified into classes as well. Political monopolies are now being challenged by civil wars and ethnic violence as well as by democratization and the rise of NGOs. But the concept of power monopolies helps unlock the complexities of politics and its relationship to development. It also helps define the political limits that constrain even the more complex and industrialized of the developing countries.[15]

Such power monopolies have made it difficult for broad-based national political parties to develop or for pressure groups to emerge at the local level, even in some of the more democratic Third World countries. Syncratic political systems, despite frequent, violent changes in regimes, do, however, develop certain political capacities. These include, according to Almond and Powell (1966), the coercive capacity to discourage or repress peasant discontent, the symbolic capacities needed to appear to improve conditions through massive public works or distraction through military adventurism, the distributive capacity to improve the welfare of favored groups of urban workers, and the extractive capacity to obtain resources from rural areas through patron-client networks. These capacities often enable governments that perpetuate inequality to survive. For example, most Third World governments derive a relatively small percentage of their revenues from income taxes, and even income taxes are often regressive. Other sources of income such as land are not taxed.

Syncratic coalitions are not limited to authoritarian regimes. They define the pattern of political power in many countries that alternate between military and civilian rule and are also a means of maintaining upper class power in such "oligarchical democracies" as Chile before 1964 or Colombia today. Oligarchical democracies resemble competitive constitutional regimes in that potential opposition groups are free to organize, while power monopolies remain politically dominant. Similarly, the new democracies such as the Philippines that began to emerge during the 1980s overthrew dictatorial regimes without necessarily defeating narrowly based power monopolies.

In Mexico, well along in the process of both industrialization and the development of local and national political institutions, "syncratic politics" has apparently reached both its limits and its most advanced and perhaps precarious stage. The syncratic coalition, maintained through the official Party of Revolutionary Institutions (PRI) has for many years adaptively included urban labor as a way of not having to deal with rural unemployment and poverty. The rural landowners in the coalition are not Mexico's original aristocracy, but the new rich who bought up the failed *ejidos* after the long term disintegration of the land reform of the 1930s. After 1985, however, the PRI's strategy began to unravel in the industrialized provincial cities of northern Mexico with challenges to the automatic election of their candidates. The PRI's margin of slightly over 50 percent in the 1988 elections was the lowest in six decades of uninterrupted rule, and even those results are under suspicion since the television projections were abruptly halted at midnight on election night when it began to look as if the opposition was going to win.

The absence or breakup of the syncratic coalition is not a sufficient condition for political, economic, and social development to be able to reinforce each other, but it is clearly a necessary one. Adelman and Morris (1982) point out that land reforms in South Korea, Taiwan, Singapore, and China were an essential precondition to economic growth without simultaneous deterioration in income distribution. Reforms, of course, had to be followed by productivity investments in the redistributed resource through technical assistance and agricultural credit.

Under what conditions has so general a phenomenon as the syncratic coalition failed to develop or been destroyed? In a few countries, fortuitous historical circumstances prevented the emergence of this coalition during the period of incipient industrialization. When Japan relinquished her colonial hold on Taiwan at the end of World War II, the Nationalists, who had failed to achieve land reform in China, had a political incentive to break the power of the large Taiwanese landowners. In addition, the Japanese overlords, intent on creating a rice basket for their own population, had introduced high-yielding Ponlai rice, increased productivity through education and technical assistance, and established over 400 agricultural credit cooperatives that left the new smallholders well prepared to produce for themselves and helped preclude the rise of a new class of large landowners.

Taiwan's early emphasis on agriculture, which continued after World War II, set the stage for a massive economic takeoff in the 1960s.[16]

The syncratic coalition never really developed in Costa Rica. Despite its name, Costa Rica had little gold and became a backwater of the Spanish colonial system. Because few Spanish aristocrats settled there, a class of peasant smallholders developed. Relative equity in land ownership increased with a gradual land reform initiated in the early 1960s. At that time approximately 100 families owned plantations of over 6,000 acres. Today there are only 38 families with such large holdings.[17] Costa Rica is also the only long-term constitutional democracy in Central America.

The historical weakness of the syncratic coalition at the national level often coexists, however, with powerful local interests. In India, the British allied themselves with large rural landowners and British commercial interests. This alienated the emerging Indian commercial class, who allied themselves with the peasants. Barrington Moore (1966:354) argued that "This may be judged a decisive contribution toward the eventual establishment of a parliamentary democracy on Indian soil." The power of landowners, however, remains a major barrier to Indian development in local rural areas and continues to define the limits of agricultural policy at the national level.[18]

The syncratic alliance can also be weakened or destroyed by revolutions. Among the non-Marxist examples is the Bolivian revolution of 1952. Although led by middle-class civilians, the revolutionary base expanded rapidly once the reformers achieved power, as peasants seized large estates and forced the pace of land reform to accelerate. Bolivia has had a succession of military and civilian governments since that time, but a new syncratic coalition has not reemerged in part because the revolution weakened the landed aristocracy and in part because urban industrial interests were not very powerful at the time of the revolution.

When Marxist regimes came to power in the past, they also destroyed the syncratic coalition, usually with speed and finality. But by placing the political system in a kind of deep freeze soon after taking over and utilizing patterns of top-down control inherited from their predecessors, Marxist leaders such as Fidel Castro, Ho Chi Minh, and Mao Tse-tung arbitrarily limited the creative use of such political innovations as grassroots organizations to enhance feedback and improve the effectiveness of social and economic development. The political evolution of Marxist societies is beyond the scope of this book, yet their decline and demise underlines the long-term futility of replacing political monopolies with other political monopolies.

Deliberate top-down policies to promote and strengthen intermediate institutions among lower- and middle-class groups are another means of countering the syncratic alliance. Such policies are, in a sense, more politically radical and courageous than ordinary attempts by revolutionary or nationalist elites to control or mobilize mass participation. Because such policies involve a measure of trust and the willingness to promote institutions that could turn against a regime in the future, they are hardly common, but have occurred in the Third World.

In Venezuela, the Betancourt presidency (1958–63) resulted in significant advances in such social indicators as literacy and infant mortality and also led to a dramatic change in Venezuela's political culture. Oil revenues were used creatively to buy off the military. The regime encouraged the transformation of peasant leagues that were based on a patron-client system into more-independent political organizations that were provided with agricultural credits. The urban poor, urban middle class, and certain carefully chosen industrialists were also brought into the policy process, particularly when structural changes such as land reform were at stake. These groups did not always support the Betancourt regime or its successors but they did acquire a stake in the civilian political system. The old military-industrial rural alliance that had supported former regimes was crowded out by new entrants to the political system, supported from above.[19]

The Venezuelan experience depended not only on creative leadership but also on a unique configuration of forces. The Venezuelan oligarchy was weakened by internecine conflict that began in the nineteenth century, and Betancourt had the advantage of significant oil revenues. The fate of other short lived reformist regimes in Latin American history is testimony to the syncratic coalition's more typical ability to lash back.[20]

Since most Third World countries lack both favorable historical circumstances and exceptional leadership, the proliferation of NGOs may provide the only possible, albeit long-run, way of undermining power monopolies. Unfortunately, NGOs may be co-opted by governments or smothered by local elites.

The dilemma, in other words, is weighing the evidence of power creation from below against the leaden mass of social and economic privilege maintained by political repression. A number of case studies demonstrate that empowerment of the poor can loosen the grip of local elites such as landowners and moneylenders.[21] And such attempts are spreading in the Third World, propelled by worsening poverty and environmental collapse. But where and how fast is this process occurring? Is it spreading to surrounding communities? How long will it take before a critical mass of political power can begin to redress the balance against a power monopoly at the top without a violent revolution and the emergence of a new power monopoly? These are difficult questions, which we begin to address in the next section and discuss more fully in Volume 2.

THE POLITICAL IMPACT OF NGOs

The profoundly political implications of NGOs are evident from the history of the Salvadoran village of Tenancingo. In 1987 both the government troops and the guerrillas attacked the village and killed many of its people. A GRSO called the Salvadoran Foundation for Development and Low Cost Housing (FUNDASAL) helped villagers replant fields bombed by the Salvadoran air force and organized the villagers to remain neutral and to demand that both sides stay out. Politics, as it is usually understood, had not even provided physical security. Yet FUNDASAL successfully organized the entire village into a third political force. FUNDASAL's director alleged that neither side wanted neutral development to succeed because success would undermine their political messages.[22]

Even governments not at war usually fail to understand the rather obvious idea that community members and outsiders working together can accomplish more than strictly top-down efforts. Although NGOs have had some influence on government professionals, islands of capacity within particular ministries are still surrounded by a vast ocean of self-serving behavior.

NGOs that overcome political obstacles and succeed in influencing government policy still confront a seemingly endless list of ills stemming from the underlying issues of poverty, environmental degradation, and the population explosion. Among these are ethnic violence, political instability, corruption, lack of education and health care, and now, AIDS. Against these enemies GROs and GRSOs often use empowerment methodologies such as the processes of *conscientizacao* or consciousness raising developed by Paulo Freire, coupled to knowledge about health and family planning, resource preservation, and learning to become a conscious economic participant. Training is not always accompanied by job creation, however, although an estimated half of the Third World's active population is underemployed or unemployed. Given the dimensions of the population explosion, GRSOs specializing in family planning need to bound ahead just to stay even. With half a billion people in the Third World chronically malnourished and prey to parasitic disease that saps their energy, it is not hard to understand why James Grant of UNICEF has described development as a "discretionary activity."

Sustainable development is, in other words, a tough, complicated activity requiring enormous persistence, continual learning, and adaptation as well as resources and a certain amount of luck. As the Swiss entrepreneur who created the European Business Council for Sustainable Development argues, "We are at the foot of a steep and rocky path" and it may take generations before development is reconciled with nature.[23]

Although NGO proliferation has achieved social and economic gains in some local spaces, its long-run social, economic, and environmental impact, given the dimensions of the crises confronting the Third World, is hard to envision. What *is* already evident is the impact of this quiet revolution on grassroots politics. People organizing their own communities are supported by GRSOs that "have made the political choice for social change and justice, but have also chosen democracy; thus the importance they assign to notions such as self-government and democracy in their relations with the popular sectors."[24] As a kind of entering wedge, this process can get going in many communities despite the dominant monopolies of political power that constrain development. The economic and social impact of NGOs is, therefore, likely to be indirect, through its impact on local or national politics.

The short-run impact of grassroots organizing will also depend on political context. In countries such as Costa Rica, where power has been shared rather equitably for many years, the growth of the independent sector will probably strengthen this tendency. In India, where pluralism interacts with inequity, development organizations and grassroots political movements are weighing in against existing power monopolies and providing alternatives to opposition political parties, although the vast population and sheer weight of patron-client relationships slows down their impact.[25] In other countries there has as yet been little apparent change at the top despite the growth of the independent sector. And in most of the Middle East, GROs tend to play traditional social or religious roles and GRSOs have been slow to develop.

Despite these variations, however, there are signs in many countries that NGOs may be able, sooner or later, to achieve the kind of critical mass needed to erode if not overcome power monopolies. The process often begins with ties between government professionals and local communities. In Bolivia, as early as the 1970s, even as cocaine dealers were controlling the apex of governmental power, farsighted individuals in the Ministry of Education were hiring peasants as educational consultants. These peasant leaders had started their own "development theaters" to teach their communities about such topics as improving agricultural output or boiling water for drinking. In more recent years NGOs have begun to involve thousands of people in political advocacy. A Brazilian congressman recently told an official U.S. visitor that legislation against deforestation of the Amazon had been passed not because of international pressure or because congress understood the Greenhouse Effect but because it was facing intense, organized pressure from Brazil's environmental movements and horizontal networks of Indian tribes.[26]

The breakup of the syncratic coalition is, therefore, a necessary but insufficient condition for sustainable development. The evidence to be presented, in these volumes, however, suggests that *a gradual undermining of narrow political monopolies by an expanded independent sector in the Third World can have a more profound impact on sustainable development than did the accidental weakening or deliberate destruction of the political power of the ruling elites in some countries in the past.*

Institutional development has long been considered important to the overall progress of a country. What is happening today, however, has the potential to be tied more closely to socioeconomic results because the institutions that are emerging are specifically concerned with local development and national development policies, not just the advancement of an ideology or economic interest. The extreme dimensions of the global crisis further promotes the logic of a "fit" between sustainable development on the one hand and sustainable institutional/political development on the other. It has also pushed NGOs to the forefront of understanding what is in the common interest.

As public interest groups, GRSOs are proliferating more rapidly than are traditional interest groups such as federations of land owners or labor unions, even though some GRSOs may conceal hidden agendas.[27] GROs are also proliferating, although some, such as water users' associations, are more likely than others to combine public with private functions. Despite these complexities, political theorists such as Neumann (1950:58) have long recognized the importance of the public-private distinction. "The task of political theory [is] ... the determination of the degree to which a power group transcends its particular interest and advocates ... universal interests."

NGOs at the cutting edge of empowerment and development are also among the first to raise major environmental issues with global implications. Several years before the Brundtland Commission made its recommendations on "sustainable agriculture," the Forestry Association of Botswana was helping GROs plant trees and improve the economic viability of woodlots, in cooperation with the government of Botswana.[28]

NGO proliferation also increases opportunities for interactions with governments and thus advances the larger and longer-term process of political development. Although we focus on political development in Volume 2, it is in one sense the theme of the entire discussion. *Political development can be defined as an interactive public decision making and learning process, based on power creation and dispersion, within and between governmental and nongovernmental groups. This process leads to increasing individual and group autonomy from below and more responsiveness from above.*

NGOs are, in part, the product of the very system they now challenge. The deliberate attempt to exclude the public from narrow political coalitions has been coupled to an unprecedented expansion of mass education and the creation of an educated middle class. The failure of governments to even begin to meet the escalating challenges of sustainable development has vastly widened the gap between reality and what people believe to be possible.

In assessing this nongovernmental movement, two caveats should be kept in mind. The first is the difficulty in actually seeing what is happening. NGOs are often ahead of their time as well as their country, and their impact, while discernable, may not be visible for many years. Honduras adopted a land reform law in 1962 that has fallen far short of its goals. Yet according to Victor Meza, director of a private research center in Tegucigalpa, "Whatever land reform successes have been achieved in Honduras happened because this country developed a very well-organized peasant movement ... The bureaucracy doesn't respond to their petitions, so they organize takeovers of unused or underused land. They use illegal methods to achieve a legal goal."[29]

The second difficulty is being able to assess the relationship between old elites and new forces on the local as well as national levels. Whether old elites remain dominant or are successfully challenged remains problematical in any given situation. An analysis of 150 Third World case studies produced a "nil correlation" between GRO effectiveness and situations of social stratification.[30] In other words, inequality and repression sometimes inhibit organization and sometimes promote it. The degree to which outsiders (GRSOs or International NGOs) can tip the balance and promote local organization in the absence of local initiative is also unclear. Once local leadership emerges, however, it often sustains itself by what Brown and Korten (1989:9) call "self-reinforcing escalation." Yet even regional GRO networks organized from below can be subject to burnout when confronted by determined repression or internal dissension.

Although worsening conditions further enhance the likelihood that local organizations will be created and will attract popular support, political monopolies are enormously resilient. Many parts of the Third World seem to be poised between the persistence of old power structures and the development of new organizations not yet able to effectively challenge them.

The interwoven texture of this tapestry about to be examined is perhaps its most interesting feature in country after country. In the chapters that follow, I shall try to shed more light on the complexities and wide variations in its texture and color as well as design. Chapter 2 is about the spread and significance of GROs, and Chapter 3 focuses on their horizontal networks. Chapters 4 and 5 deal with GRSOs in general and, more specifically, with those specializing in economic development, environment, and population. Chapter 6 focuses on GRSO networks. GRO and GRSO performance are the subjects of Chapter 7. Some patterns in the relationships between GROs and GRSOs, discussed in Chapter 8, appear to be particularly effective in promoting empowerment, acheiving sustainable development, and scaling out local efforts. The networks that GROs and GRSOs are establishing among themselves and with each other may presage their impact on national government power structures as well. The political impact of NGOs, a major theme of Volume 2, is already evident in some countries.

NOTES

1. Joseph Van Arendonk, United Nations Population Fund, February 28, 1991.

2. In 1991 the World Bank and the International Monetary Fund announced that they would no longer ignore military expenditures in determining whether governments obtain loans. See Mathews, 1991.

3. Cordoba-Novion and Sachs, 1987.

4. James (1982) suggested that the indigenous voluntary sector be divided into two large groups: organizations in which contributions coincided with beneficiaries and those in which they are two distinct groups.

5. Pradervand, 1988, p. 12.

6. The World Bank includes GROs as well as GRSOs in the NGO category, since the former have "ends beyond those which are strictly economic, particularly social equity" (Salmen and Eaves, 1989:61). The Inter-American Foundation, which also includes both, used GSO for grassroots support organization. Since I have chosen the self-explanatory term "GRO" rather than the IAF's "base organization," I decided GRO and GSO would be confusing.

To add to the confusion, GRSOs are also called Southern NGOs, IPVOs (indigenous private voluntary organizations), PDAs (private development associations), DAOs (development assistance organizations), VOs (voluntary organizations), VDOs (voluntary development associations), and NGDOs (nongovernmental development organizations).

7. Borghese, 1987, p. 11.

8. Correspondence with Alan Fowler, December 1990. Cooperatives sponsored by governments straddle the government/private sector boundary rather than the private/independent sector boundary.

9. See De Soto, 1989. Jorgensen, Hafsi, and Kiggundu, 1986, describe this in terms of both government and market failure.

10. Nonetheless, individually owned businesses started by members of GROs can be considered part of the informal private sector. Industrial labor unions and formal business associations are part of the formal private sector, as in the developed countries.

11. Interview with Mr. Ilboudho, fall 1989.

12. Knapp and Kendall, 1990.

13. Diaz-Albertini, 1990; Anheier's (1990:373) religious distinction is particularly relevant to African churches. Korten (1990:96) argues, however, that GROs, by combining the state's power of threat, the economic power of private business and the integrative power of the independent sector constitute a fourth sector. Cooperatives do add the threat of explusion to their economic and integrative powers. GROs such as village councils however, do not usually engage in economic activities.

14. Hyden, 1983.

15. Barrington Moore (1966:423) developed a similar model from the history of the developed countries and noted that the coalition of landed aristocracy with the bourgeoisie constituted "and in some parts of the world still constitute the basic framework and environment of political action, forming the series of opportunities, temptations, and impossibilities within which political leaders have to act."

16. I am indebted to Roberta Lopez, a student of mine at Connecticut College in 1982, for this analysis.

17. Kinzer, 1987, p.5.

18. The introduction of miracle grains in Southeast Asia, therefore, increased local inequalities (Jacoby, 1972).

19. The idea of broadening the political base also seems to have occured to the Emir of Bahrain, who, like Betancourt, can count on ample financial resources. (Ibrahim, 1987a:1,14)

20. The Frei regime in Chile (1964–70) attempted to work with GROs but was unable to build a center-left coalition that could have precluded the rise of Allende and then Pinochet. The Allende regime (1970–73) alienated the middle class and was overthrown by a renewed syncratic coalition, unwilling to govern, as the syncratic coalition had before Frei, through constitutional democracy.

21. See, for example, Coombs, 1980, and Hollnsteiner, 1979.

22. LeMoyne, 1987, p. 4.

23. Smith, 1992, p.75.

24. Velarde, 1988, p. 17.

25. See Moen's (1991) field study of GRSOs in Tamil Nadu.

26. Interview with the speaker of the Connecticut House of Representatives, Irving Stolberg, 1988.

27. In contrast, public interest groups did not develop rapidly in Germany until the 1960s, long after interest groups developed. In the United States both types were active even in the nineteenth century, although public interest groups increased in the 1960s.

28. Cooperation for Development, 1987.

29. Kinzer (1987:5).

30. See Esman and Uphoff, 1984, p. 115.

2

Grassroots Organizations (GROs)

Nothing grows from the top down.

Atherton Martin

We shall organize, and it shall be our organization, not yours. But let us not name the baby before it kicks.[1]

The hardest thing is getting people to believe, because the politicians only promise.

Guillermo Voss,
president of an Argentine housing cooperative[2]

Grassroots organizations are also called *base groups*, *people's organizations*, or *local organizations*. However named, there is general agreement that they are locally based groups working to improve and develop their own communities either through communitywide or specialized memberships. Although this chapter focuses on GROs, the broader term *local organizations* will be used to include both GROs and other kinds of community groups such as burial societies or kinship organizations that are also accountable to members but are not focused on development.

Where do all these groups come from? How long have they existed? How many were originally founded by outsiders?

Although they are part of the independent sector, many GROs evolved from indigenous local governments that functioned in the absence of strong national authority.[3] Some tribal or village organizations were eclipsed but not replaced as more "modern" forms of governance emerged. A historical study of a Peruvian highland community found that the members of local organizations carried out thirty-seven major development projects including roads, schools, and irrigation ditches between 1895 and 1967.[4] With the failure of government to address poverty and environmental decline, new types of GROs are emerging and traditional organizations are redefining their roles.

Indigenous organizational knowledge is probably as important to human survival as time-honored agricultural techniques. Yet even development experts who try to build on indigenous technical knowledge assume that community organization resulted from outside intervention. "(T)he possibility of a self-perpetuating, completely indigenous model is not mentioned."[5] An alternative pitfall is the assumption, less common than a decade ago, that organizational behavior in the Third World is inevitably conditioned by patron-client relationships.[6]

Nor is the historical importance of local organizations to the development of the United States, Europe, and Japan always recognized. Women were active in the influential popular health movement in the United States in the 1830s and 1840s. During the same period the rural populist movement strengthened agricultural development through seed exchange societies. In Europe there were 25,000 rural cooperatives by 1937. In Japan, after the Meiji Restoration of 1868, farmer groups became an important component of technical progress.

This may be one reason why international nongovernmental organizations do not always explore the full implications of bottom-up development. At stake is the considerable difference between beneficiaries having a voice in projects initiated by outsiders and self-directed development supported by outsiders.

Although European NGOs have supported GRSOs for some time and American Private Voluntary Organizations (PVOs) are moving beyond their counterpart GRSOs, many development projects are still selected without reference to existing GROs. At worst, existing GROs are ignored. A Bolivian study written by Aymara Indians trained in anthropology concluded that although a dozen foreign development agencies had projects in northern Potosi, "none understood how the *ayllus* [traditional cooperative lineage systems] were organized or how it functioned ... at this moment the *ayllus* are being dismembered!"[7]

Other donors create GROs and then set about the difficult task of empowering people from above. Even though some very capable GROs have been created by outsiders, it is no longer obvious that outsiders should organize areas where GROs do not exist. Outsiders willing to research the spread of GROs and their networks, on the other hand, can acquire new opportunities for "accompanying the poor."[8]

One reason that GROs are sometimes ignored by official donors and INGOs is that there are few available assessments of their numbers and patterns of growth. Before describing the history and taxonomy of GROs, let us review the few estimates of their numbers.

COUNTING GROs

An important caveat in reviewing statistics about GROs is the realization that many estimates include organizations that exist only on paper. Data on numbers of organizations that at one time or another have registered with governments are probably substantially inflated. On the other hand, there are many organizations, particularly those linked to each other in regional grassroots movements, that have never officially registered themselves.

Durning (1989a:55) has estimated that "grassroots environmental and antipoverty groups probably number in the hundreds of thousands, and their collective membership in the hundreds of millions." This estimate is very rough, but probably not inflated. The estimates in Table 2.1 for just a few countries show why.

In Africa thousands of GROs are "the most significant driving force behind development" and have proliferated rapidly in recent years.[9] According to Ba (1990) the Inter-State Committee to Combat Drought in the Sahel (CLISS) estimates that numbers of GROs in the Sahel have been accelerating consistently, although not everywhere. The famine of 1984 and 1985, coupled with what Pierre Pradervand (1988) calls the "brutal disengagement of the state" acted as a spur to local organization.[10] A study of agricultural development in tribal areas of Zimbabwe concluded that nearly half of 500 randomly selected households were members of local agricultural associations.[11] On the other hand, there are fewer reports of GRO activity in other African countries such as Chad, Mauritania, the Central African Republic, and Niger.

Although there are few estimates of the numbers of GROs in Latin America, there is little doubt that their numbers have increased rapidly in recent years. A majority of the estimated 20,000 Latin American squatter settlements have created their own community organizations, for example.[12] A 1977 study of the Dominican Republic carried out by the Secretariat of Agriculture identified 1,116 registered but informal associations of small farmers that share labor or joint marketing. As of 1986, the number of GROs *not registered with the government* including women's groups and groups for unemployed youths was double that figure.[13] In Colombia there are over 700 public nonprofit community housing groups engaged in self-help housing. In Leon, Guanajuato, a Mexican industrial city of 700,000, 354 voluntary action groups have been identified.[14]

Village organizations are particularly widespread in Asia, and new kinds of organizations such as women's groups have emerged in many countries. Thousands of *pesantren* (rural Islamic boarding schools) in Indonesia are involved in local development activities. In the Philippines local water users' associations manage half of the irrigated land in the whole country. In India alone there were over 1,400 registered hand weavers cooperatives in 1986.[15]

Table 2.1
Counting GROs

Country	Date	Estimated # of GROs
Kenya	1980	5,000 GROs
	1989	15,000 - 20,000 GROs
	1991	26,000 GROs
Brazil	1989	1,000 community schools, 10,000 neighborhood associations, 100,000 Christian base organizations
	1990	4,000 rural unions
Peru	1990	1,500 community kitchens
Chile	1989	12,000 lower class membership organizations
Costa Rica	1989	6,000 neighborhood associations
Guatemala	1988	800 local development associations
India	1989	"tens of thousands"
Senegal	1987	1,000
Burkina Faso	1987	4,500 (2,500 officially recognized)
All Sahel countries	1990	12,000 - 15,000
Philippines	1989b	3,000 Christian base organizations

Sources: Fowler, 1990:7; Barkan and Holmquist, 1989:360; Gabriel Camara, presentation
at Interaction Forum, May 8, 1989; Harrazim, 1990:25; Barrig, 1990:78; Thompson, 1990:397; Checci, 1989:21; Ganuza, 1988; Ba, 1990:84; Durning, 1989b:69.

A large Bangladesh GRSO named PROSHIKA had organized over 20,000
GROs as of 1991, one-half of which were women's groups.[16]

GROs are not common in Northeastern India, Myanmar (Burma), and
the Asian Marxist countries. However, in China urban retail cooperatives
are often owned by the members of neighborhood associations. A handicraft
cooperative in Ho Chi Minh City organized by a 1972 graduate of the South
Vietnamese Institute of Administration started the first day care center in
the neighborhood and makes donations for neighborhood development.

According to the director "The government intermediaries are . . . not capable of managing us."[17] Yet the cooperative has smoothed its way into the confidence of local Communist party officials, and working conditions are better than in government owned enterprises.

GROs are also less common in the Middle East, perhaps because Koranic culture emphasizes the duty of the individual to assist Islamic charities, not the importance of organizing for social change. Esman and Uphoff (1984:97) surveyed 150 case studies of local organizations (GROs) and found only four from the Middle East in their "random walk" through the literature. Although they concede that this may merely reflect less coverage in English, other evidence supports their guess about the relative scarcity of GROs in the Middle East. Schneider (1985:34) argues that the religious character of the first European NGOs led to mistrust and fear among Arab Moslems.

On the other hand, hundreds of GROs that are not all connected with the *Intifada* are active on the West Bank. There are many small *ad hoc* committees in Gaza working on popular education and kitchen gardens. In Lebanon some 650 GROs emerged during the long civil war in the absence of government services.[18] One major study of local Egyptian organizations not engaged in development calls them "nuclei of potential development" that could change their character in the future.[19]

To understand the diversity and variety of GROs, I have selected two (out of many possible) ways of classifying them. The first classification relates to their origins, because an organization's history is important in understanding its character, its internal culture, and its relations with other organizational actors. The second classification, by role and function, centers on the potential impact of GROs on empowerment and development.

CLASSIFICATION BY ORIGIN

Although GROs are not an entirely new phenomenon and may have evolved from traditional organizations, they are often founded as new organizations within a community, either by community residents or by outsiders. Table 2.2 categorizes their origins as a kind of double continuum.

Clear categorization of GRO origins is difficult, since written accounts often ignore their history. Although the continuum in Table 2.2 categorizes origins, it may be more useful as a way of categorizing changing forms of local organizations over time. The tendency for local organizations to "shift from small concerns to larger social, economic and political concerns" noted by Thomson and Armer (1980:289) has accelerated in recent years. "Traditional organizations have not so much disappeared as hybridized, blended and built outward . . . there has been reorganization rather than organization at the grassroots."[20] The *Naams* of Burkina Faso, for example, originally acculturated young men into the tribe, but now elect leaders, attract new

Table 2.2
Age of Organization

Founded by:	Pre 1950 ——— ⟹ —— ⟹ 1950 —— ⟹ 1992 — ⟹	
INSIDERS	Traditional	New GROs founded by villagers
		New GROs founded by returning villagers
OUTSIDERS	GROs founded by missionaries, etc.	New organizations founded by INGOs, governments, etc.

members, and encourage crop diversification and sustainable development. Among the other traditional African groups involved in development are the M'botai of the Oulofs, the Walde of the Peulhs, the Kafo of the Mandinka, and the Tons of the Bambara.[21]

GROs may also be founded by local residents who return from urban areas or who have organizational experience provided by outsiders. New city dwellers often organize hometown associations and then return temporarily to help their village of origin. In Las Ollas, Panama, a rural consumer cooperative was founded by a young resident who had already been active in a local club organized by the Ministry of Agriculture.[22]

Undeniable as the relationship is between the birth of an organization and its subsequent history, indigenous groups often establish outside ties later. And the most capable groups initially organized by outsiders must, by definition, have become more autonomous.

Most of this chapter concerns new GROs. The next two sections, however, focus on the gradual evolution of traditional organizations into GROs as well as the role of early outsiders in this process.

Traditional GROs

Many GROs are descendents of much earlier ways of cooperating to achieve limited purposes. By the 1750s, tribes in what is now Tanzania were organizing informal work groups that dug irrigation canals, chased missing cattle, and extinguished fires.[23] In Trinidad and Tobago in 1947 there were 317 local "friendly societies" that offered sickness, maternity, and death benefits to their members, as well as traditional organizations that already resembled GROs.[24] A study of the Palau Islands in the Pacific in the 1940s found fifty active societies, organized by sex, age, and status.[25]

Ad hoc support networks tied to kinship and religion buttress the informal economy and minimize vulnerability during difficult times. One Tanzanian community has twelve separate organizations activated during emergencies.[26] Kinship organizations such as the *kafolu* in the Gambia allow strangers to belong as well and 10 percent of harvested food is given to the poorest people in a village.[27] These organizations also contribute in labor or money to the construction of local schools and bridges.

Although communal land ownership has been undermined by modernization, it still provides a basis for self-help. African land is often owned in common with the right to cultivate based on a decision of the village elders. In the Andean countries, cooperative labor arrangements date back thousands of years and provide a cultural basis for the development of GROs.[28] Local organizations have, for some time, focused on community improvements as well as shared agricultural labor. In 1967, 80 percent of the thirty-two local organizations in Mancos, Peru, were involved in community improvement.[29]

Although some types of local organizations, such as burial societies, may not take on development functions, even such apparently static organizations as Indian castes may be historically relevant to the development of GROs. Over the decades, the Nadar caste has built schools, colleges, libraries, and a cooperative bank that are now used by other castes.[30] By the late 1970s many caste associations, while still associated with maintaining power and status, had begun to work on economic and social problems. "Now that the old caste council leaders have retired, respect for age and familial status has declined and new leaders tend to be valued for their skills in coalition building across castes."[31]

In fact, the dominance of the caste system may be related to the subsequent spread of GROs and regional grassroots movements in India. By arguing that Western democracy grew out of the intermediate institutions of feudalism, Moore (1966:338) reinforced the notion that intermediate structures often precede autonomous or democratic functions in political development. The flip side of this insight is that outsiders should be careful about automatically ascribing positive values such as participatory democracy to local organizations.

Brown and Korten (1989:15), for example, argue that "people's organizations," including GROs and other local organizations such as burial societies, are for mutual benefit, are self-reliant, and have a democratic structure. This is a useful normative goal, and most GROs are, in my opinion, quite democratic. GROs should be distinguished from other local organizations, however, by their focus on development rather than by their internal political practices. A burial society may be internally democratic, yet have little impact on the community. A cooperative, on the other hand, could create jobs, even though it excluded the landless. It is also true that less democratic traditional organizations such as lineage systems may be appropriate to particular communities. Although democratic practices enhance impact, mutually beneficial activities may not always assist the larger community. Market women in West African cities, for example, often limit the number of their competitors or create artificial scarcities as they provide their own members with undeniable benefits.[32]

In some Asian countries GROs have been engaged in development for decades. In Nepal the central government was traditionally weak, and local organizations maintained irrigation systems, constructed roads, planted trees, and built schools. Community organizations in Thailand construct and maintain irrigation systems, flood control facilities, Buddhist temples, wells, ponds, roads, and bridges. They also manage welfare plans and insurance systems and are supported by youth clubs and credit cooperatives that operate markets, engage in cattle trading, and purchase land.[33] In Sri Lanka a wide range of community welfare societies, women's groups and water users' associations are organized around Buddhist temples.[34]

The Influence of Early Outsiders

Religious groups have had a complex, sometimes positive impact on local organizations for hundreds of years. During the sixteenth century, for example, a Spanish missionary bishop, Don Vasco de Quiroga, actually strengthened self-help traditions among the Puerepas Indians in Michoacan, Mexico.[35] In Kenya, by the late nineteenth century, missionaries were training teachers already supported by local communities and providing materials for communities to build schools.[36]

In India, agricultural colonies were initiated by Christian missionaries from the 1860s to the 1940s. By 1920 there were at least eighty-three of these throughout the country, and although some were run paternalistically, others sponsored schools, adult literacy classes, and credit cooperatives as an alternative to money lenders. By the 1950s the village of Martinpur (now in Pakistan) had no beggars and a literacy rate over 50 percent, although most of the original inhabitants had been members of the untouchable caste when the project began in 1898.[37]

While religious interventions ranged from participatory to paternalistic, early secular interventions were somewhat more focused on local community resources than were later international development projects promoted by international organizations or foreign governments. Among the oldest internationally sponsored rural development projects were those initiated in China in the 1920s by the rural reconstruction movement, a pioneer in integrated rural development through community organization.[38] Equally innovative was the work of the YMCA in India under Spencer Hatch, initiated in 1921 in Martandam, Travancore. Based on maximum use of local resources and technologies, it led to the development of marketing cooperatives, village libraries, and a village leadership training school.[39] Although this general approach did not take hold among "Northern" development professionals until much later, it was sustained by the Vicos project in Peru, initiated by Alan Holmberg, a Cornell University anthropologist, during the 1950s and 1960s.[40]

Among the most potentially powerful outsiders are those born in a community who return to found a new local organization. Although this phenomenon has become increasingly common in the Third World in recent years, there are historical precedents. Town improvement unions, founded in Nigeria in the late 1930s and early 1940s by young villagers who had studied abroad, gradually took over the functions of village councils.[41]

New GROs

Since the early 1970s traditional organizations have been joined by even greater numbers of new GROs. This organizational explosion has been fueled both by escalating demands from below and an increased supply of assistance from above. The interrelated impact of population growth, environmental degradation, and poverty, compounded by the macroeconomic decline of the 1980s, forced millions of people to organize themselves and demand change. Outside support, increasingly channeled through GRSOs, has further promoted local organizing.

The Demand Side. Natural and man-made disasters often lead to the creation of GROs. Village groups developed throughout Bangladesh in response to the massive 1975 floods caused by deforestation. The 1985 earthquake in Mexico City led to a dramatic increase in new urban GROs and a revival of existing organizations. In Colombia, many communities afflicted by violence and drug trafficking have organized security patrols, independent from local governments.

Deepening poverty is the most powerful organizer of GROs. As population and land pressures have worsened their plight, the poor of the Third World have begun to organize themselves. Nowhere was this more evident than in Africa, where thousands of GROs were organized in response to the droughts of 1973 and 1985. In Burkina Faso, for example, the traditional *Naam* youth groups have spread to new communities and have encouraged crop diversification and changes in food habits. They have constructed twenty-five maternity hospitals and are replacing the government in constructing pharmacies, schools, and village clinics.[42] In Senegal the village of Zom was nothing but bare rock in 1984. The local GRO added 30 centimeters of topsoil over three years and planted rice on village lands. After visiting Zom, Pradervand (1988:7) remarked that "never, having spent eleven years in Africa, had I encountered such determination." Tintam, a Malian village was devastated by drought in 1984 and ravaged by locusts in 1986. The village's twelve-year-old fruit trees died, one after the other. Yet the village assembly declared, "We are not discouraged. So long as there rests in us any energy, and that God has given us intelligence, we believe we can overcome our difficulties."

The African employment crisis has had a different kind of impact. Because so many African men have migrated to the cities, women have organized a majority of the GROs in the Sahel. Having to walk farther and farther for food, water, and firewood motivates women to do more than survive. In Kangoussema, Senegal women walk 70 kilometers round trip to sell their vegetables. The male president of a mixed group in Senegal was quoted as saying that "women organize themselves better, because they have more determination."[43] In Burkina Faso, the Naams groups have led to a virtual revolution in relations between the sexes, with activist women organizing microenterprises.

Trading rural poverty for the challenges of urban survival has for many years led squatters in Asia and Latin America to organize neighborhood improvement associations.[44] In Hyderabad and Bombay, women's community improvement organizations, called Mahila Mandals, are particularly active. Latin American neighborhood improvement associations are founded during the process of organized or accretive invasion of unoccupied land. They exist in a majority of the 20,000 or more Latin American squatter settlements and increased in number during the 1970s.[45] Moreira Alves (1984) has counted over 1,100 in São Paulo alone and estimates that there are thousands in Brazil.

Because governments often fail to provide squatter settlements with schools and urban services, neighborhood improvement associations frequently pirate nearby electric lines or lobby the city governments for common water taps. In Latin America these *juntas de vecinos* (neighborhood improvement associations) build schools, water taps, and organize garbage and transportation services.

Worsening economic conditions in recent years have pushed Latin American city dwellers to organize other types of GROs such as Parent Associations, "bench schools," child care centers, small producer cooperatives, vegetable gardens, and community kitchens. The economic crash of the early 1980s in Brazil "ignited mass mobilizations of all types."[46] Christian base communities rallied the homeless, and housewives coping with inflation of over 50 percent per month formed their own organizations. In Argentina, unemployment pushed thousands of city dwellers into informal work groups or labor cooperatives.[47]

In Lima there were 1,500 community kitchens averaging fifty members each by 1990. One hundred thousand people, mostly mothers, are organized into 7,000 *Vaso de Leche* (glass of milk) committees that work through community kitchens to distribute powdered milk donated by the EEC. They are organized into barrio, zonal, and district organizations that raise funds for other activities. According to Barrig (1990), few men are interested in these activities, and this has given the committees immunity from male-dominated local politics. Men are more active, however, in other GROs such as health committees, Christian base communities, and informal business associations.

Political repression can further fuel an explosion of GROs. In Asia, grassroots activists are consciously tying human rights to environmental rights.[48] Latin American dictatorships spawned thousands of women's organizations and human rights groups during the 1970s. Under the Pinochet dictatorship in Chile hundreds of urban *organizaciones economicas populares* (OEPs) emerged, including small factories, employment agencies, consumer and housing cooperatives, health and education groups, community kitchens, and alternative schools. Some were organized at the grassroots level and others were promoted by Catholic and secular GRSOs.[49]

Moreover, repression against GROs can backfire. The repression by the Colombian government of the National Association of Small Farmers provided their member GROs with organizational experience. Farmer's groups in Colombia are now engaged in everything from cooperative stores to environmental "green councils."[50]

Repression during civil wars can have a similar impact. In Afghanistan, tens of thousands of GROs were created by the resistance to provide social services. In El Salvador, GROs fell apart as refugees fled their homes, but new ones were continually being created in refugee communities by previous organizers. The resiliency of Salvadoran GROs was demonstrated after the November 1989 offensive. Two months after their offices were raided, most cooperatives and urban squatter organizations (as well as GRSOs) were back and functioning. Increasing conflict led to greater sophistication and more contacts with foreign diplomats, international organizations, and GRSOs.[51]

The Supply Side. The second force propelling GRO proliferation is the increasing supply of direct and indirect international financial support. International support from INGOs and official bilateral and multilateral donors has grown since the early 1970s, much of it channeled through GRSOs. Although no figures are available on Third World governmental support for GROs, ideologically diverse regimes have created and/or supported GROs as well, often with foreign assistance.

Private grants by INGOs from eighteen OECD countries increased from about $2.5 to $4.2 billion in constant dollars between 1979 and 1988.[52] Although international voluntary assistance is increasingly channeled through GRSOs to GROs, it has sometimes fueled the growth of GROs more directly. In Sierra Leone, for example, increased international assistance led to a dramatic growth of GROs. INGOs also create or reactivate GROs directly through their community organizers. Save the Children organized a network of women's clubs in Colombia to promote small enter-

prise development and health education, and Technoserve has provided
assistance for faltering agrarian reform cooperatives in Peru and El Salvador.[53]

Official European bilateral assistance has been partially channeled
through GRSOs and GROs for some time. The Inter-American Foundation
and the African Development Foundation, created by U.S. congressional
initiative, operate largely through funding GRSOs and GROs. The U.S.
Agency for International Development (AID) supports umbrella funding of
both GRSOs and GROs through GRSO consortia.

Because of the positive public image of international voluntary assistance,
official donors also work with INGOs in promoting institutional development. In some countries the long-term impact of such cooperation is already
visible. The Pan American Development Foundation established the Fundacion Dominicana de Desarrollo in the Dominican Republic over twenty-
five years ago to provide credit and technical assistance for GROs. The
Fundacion's program was then expanded with help from the Inter-American
Foundation and AID. "The end result of all these factors has been the
creation of a special climate where a highly successful program of one group
can ripple out and be replicated by many others, where private and public
agencies can enter into formal agreements to implement new development
methodologies together."[54]

Official multilateral organizations also provide financial support to
GROs. Between 1981 and 1987, in cooperation with AID, the World Bank
promoted the organization of 12,000 water users' associations in Pakistan.
In fiscal years 1991 and 1992, approximately 30 to 40 percent of newly
approved Bank projects included GROs or GRSOs.[55] UNICEF has provided
cereal mills to organized villages in Burkina Faso and has encouraged municipal governments in Lima and Rio de Janeiro to provide social services
through neighborhood improvement associations.

The impact of foreign support on GROs is not easy to assess. Large official
donors have been criticized, particularly in Africa, for linking GROs and
GRSOs to governments before they have attained the kind of sturdy autonomy that would allow them to achieve political influence without being
manipulated.[56] However, in the Philippines and Indonesia, AID has funded
some remarkably independent and creative GRSOs that are organizing thousands of GROs as well as having an impact on environmental policy.[57] Latin
American GRSOs cooperate with foreign donors but are verbally explicit
about their autonomy and the autonomy of the GROs with whom they
work.

Governments generally exert more top-down control than do international donors on the GROs they organize or support. The Marxist regime
in Ethiopia, for example, organized over 20,000 peasant associations. The
Egyptian government has co-opted many of the 10,000 or more autonomous

GROs through its support, and GROs organized by the Tunisian government often collapse when support is withdrawn.[58]

Governments also tend to ignore existing GROs in setting up their own, and are more likely than other outsiders to favor local elites, with predictable results. The Swanirvar movement in Bangladesh was organized after the 1975 floods to involve villagers in training civil servants and surveying village resources. However, officials rarely visited the villages and allowed local elites to assume leadership and monopolize benefits.[59] In Indonesia under Suharto, membership in the Village Unit Cooperatives was usually limited to wealthier farmers or those participating in government extension programs.[60] In Tanzania and Zimbabwe, "development associations" are often patronage resources for members of parliament.[61]

Yet some governments have been able to establish GROs and then promote their autonomy. The government of Botswana provides materials and technical assistance to "fence groups" dividing pasture from crop land. Because maintenance failure results in obvious damage, group responsibilities have been strengthened. The Small Farmer Development Program in Nepal increased the political influence of small farmers, even though wealthy farmers enjoyed higher income gains.[62]

GROs created by governments can also increase the likelihood that members will reorganize later.[63] The Colombian government began organizing rather paternalistic urban neighborhood organizations in the late 1950s. When the Rural Reconstruction Movement began working in Colombia in the 1960s, it found that cooperatives succeeded in 60 percent of the communities previously organized by the government or other outsiders, whereas the percentage of success in communities with no prior projects was only 29 percent.[64] In Indonesia officially sponsored hamlet-level organizations are cooperating with each other through the traditional village mass meetings, thus by-passing the official Village Unit Cooperatives.[65] Despite its deficiencies, even the Swanirvar movement in Bangladesh provided a forum for the disadvantaged to organize.

Similarly, Esman and Uphoff's (1984:155,166) broad literature search revealed that linkages between "local organizations" and governments can be effective. Local organizations are "better off with none . . . than with too much . . . [however] some involvement can be quite desirable as long as it does not become directive." Even more important, they found that organizations with no government ties did not perform any better than those with government connections and that no *locally established* organization had become totally dominated or "spoiled" by government connections. The Tanzanian government, for example, made enormous efforts to control village assemblies, but usually failed where local Christians were active.[66] However organized, GROs appear to have a stronger sense of identity than outsiders critical of government intervention assume.

Table 2.3
Local Actors in Third World Development

SECTORS	PROFIT	NONPROFIT
Government		Local Administration (LA)
		Local Government (LG)
Private	Private Business	
Independent		Local Development Associations (LDAs)*
	Pre-Cooperatives*	Interest Associations (IAs)*
	Cooperatives*	Grassroots Support Organizations (GRSOs)

Source: Adapted from Esman and Uphoff, 1984.
Note: Local Organizations (such as burial societies or kinship groups) that are purely member-serving are excluded from the independent sector/nonprofit category.
* GROs, which are all Membership Organizations (MOs) as well.

The most sustainable and potentially positive results of outside assistance stem from training or nonformal education. Internationally funded radio schools were important organizers of local action in Honduras.[67] One observer attributes the high density of GROs in Burkina Faso to the large number of INGO training programs initiated in the 1960s and 1970s. GROs are less pervasive in Mali, where there were few international training programs during those years.[68]

CESAO and INADES, two regional training institutes in West and Central Africa, have been laying the groundwork for self-help groups for three decades. They helped organize and train the first village groups in the Sahel in 1970–75 and the first horizontal networks of village groups in 1975–80. They also played a key role in training local organizers in Zaire.[69]

Although outside assistance has probably been a less powerful promoter of GROs than acute need, donors and even some governments have had a substantial impact on institutional development. Even attempts to control GROs from above have sometimes strengthened local autonomy.

CLASSIFICATION BY ROLE AND FUNCTION

To understand how GROs can be classified according to their role and functions, it helps to visualize the entire range of institutional actors who might function within a given Third World community (see Table 2.3). By using the term *local actor* we can get around the problem of several organizational levels or hierarchies and look specifically at their local roles.

Esman and Uphoff's (1984) distinction between Local Development Associations (LDAs) representing the whole community (such as village councils or neighborhood improvement associations) and interest associations (such as water users' or women's groups) is particularly useful. I have added the profit/nonprofit distinction to be able to include pre-cooperatives, cooperatives, and other community-based enterprises as grassroots membership organizations within the independent sector. Members of pre-cooperatives may not receive a strictly monetary profit, but they clearly receive an individual benefit from pooling their labor. In Chapter 1 it was argued that cooperatives can have a major impact on developing their own communities. Yet they clearly differ from nonprofit GROs, as well as from private businesses without members.[70]

GRSOs are included as "Service Organizations" in Uphoff's (1986) classification, but they are defined as charitable rather than development organizations. He places them in the private sector because, like businesses, they have clients instead of members. The term *voluntary sector*, used to convey a narrower range of activities based on unpaid, member contributions, is limited to GROs. Considering the broader developmental functions that have evolved in recent years it seems clear that service organizations (including GRSOs) belong with GROs in the independent sector just as they do in developed countries. In addition, development activities of both types of NGOs within a community are, by definition, interdependent.

The government sector includes local representatives of national government ministries (local administration, or LA) as well as local government (LG). For reasons of simplicity this table does not include local branches of political parties within what could be a "government and opposition" sector, although their competitive activities can be important in communities such as the Latin American squatter settlements.[71]

Local government and local administration are clearly distinguishable from membership organizations, since everyone living within their jurisdiction is subject to their authority. Yet all such categories have to be illustrative rather than rigid. Latin American *juntas de vecinos* have members, but often act as quasi-local governments and provide services beyond the reach of local authorities. The village forestry associations of South Korea could be considered arms of local administration, but since their leaders are elected by all household heads in a village they have characteristics of membership organizations as well.[72]

Categories of GROs also need to be somewhat fluid. Bolivian peasant unions combine the attributes of interest associations (IAs) and local development associations, since they construct schools, roads, and water systems.[73] In Andhra Pradesh, India, the 200 or more women's cooperatives founded since 1983 combine the attributes of interest associations and cooperatives.[74] In remote villages in Maharashtra, India, local development associations often evolve from women's groups.[75]

Nonetheless, many types of groups fall into the three major categories, to be described in more detail below.[76]

Local Development Associations

Local development associations are inclusive membership organizations engaged in community development. In their random but extensive sample of the literature on local rural organizations, Esman and Uphoff (1984:62) found that 19 percent of case studies concerned LDAs, 46 percent focused on interest associations, and 35 percent dealt with cooperatives. However, in urban areas of Latin America and parts of Asia, LDAs are more common than interest associations or cooperatives. Seventy-one of ninety-two specific squatter settlements studied in eleven Latin American countries had *juntas de vecinos*, and these neighborhood improvement associations continue to emerge with new squatter settlements.[77]

As multifunctional organizations, LDAs are founded where tasks are predictable, resources are available, and there is an assured supply of water. However, a serious crisis such as a flood or landslide can also create or reactivate LDAs. Both the focus and scope of local activity may also be significantly affected by outside assistance. For example, the traditional *cabildos* of the Sikuani tribe in Colombia are central to a health and water project being developed with assistance from the Inter-American Foundation, several Colombian GRSOs, and the regional health service.[78]

LDAs are often established in squatter settlements or remote villages lacking local governments and they often assume quasi-governmental powers. Neighborhood improvement associations in Latin America set aside public areas and adjudicate disputes between residents. In the Arab Republic of Yemen, a quasi-governmental role for LDAs has been officially sanctioned.[79]

Even taxation powers emerge as LDAs begin to evolve into local governments. In Yemen the LDAs collect a tithe on production. The Indonesian *subaks* assess fees in public meetings. *Juntas de vecinos* often levy dues shortly after a settlement is invaded and organized.

Some LDAs are dominated by elites and others are not. LDAs that reflect the social hierarchy of the community may be allied with local government or local administration against alternative organizations. The officers of the LDAs in Yemen are from prominent local families, although prior involvement in self-help activity has become a necessary qualification for leadership. In other cases, however, LDAs evolve out of "alternative" interest associations such as landless groups. In Mali, the *Kabala* (village associations) are run by women, and in Kenya the local women's groups are beginning to function more like LDAs than like women's interest associations. An early study (Hunter, 1974:68) of the Indian Panchayats was able to link organizational accomplishment to heterogeneous leadership because elites did not dominate everywhere.

Alternative LDAs can coexist in one community. The *Associations Villegeoises de Developpement* (AVDs) in Senegal do not usually cooperate with the official Local Development Committees controlled by local elites, although they work with youth and women's groups.[80] Some AVDs use mosque funds set up by migrants returning from cities. Others were organized by the youth movement of the UPS (Union Progressiste Senegalaise) party, but have become depoliticized to concentrate on development.

LDAs are often capable of substantial accomplishment. A group in San Francisco, Bolivia, with some help from a French NGO, built a 14-kilometer road by hand across a mountain to improve village marketing of fruit and vegetables.[81] More frequently, however, they carry out a wide range of less dramatic developmental activities over many years. Latin American *juntas de vecinos* represent the entire squatter settlement and engage in self-help as well as neighborhood defense against official reprisal. They also help squatters protect their property and preserve ownership records during periods of dictatorship and political chaos.[82]

With the exception of certain areas of Mexico and Brazil, most Latin American *juntas* are not dependently linked to patron-client networks, and even in Brazil the trend is away from clientage. These generally democratic organizations have succeeded in carrying out many self-directed development projects and in petitioning governmental authorities for municipal services. A fairly typical pattern is for an association to build a school and then petition the authorities for a teacher. Membership and participation statistics compare favorably to those of voluntary organizations in developed countries.[83]

In Yemen the LDAs evolved from informal village welfare associations and also have a substantial development record. One Yemeni LDA constructed 100 miles of road in difficult terrain and mobilized 1 million rials from members to match government funds.

The AVDs in Senegal build roads, plant trees, police wood cutting, and organize consumer cooperatives, clinics, and adult education programs. In Matan, 37 percent of the land is cultivated by AVDs as communal market gardens. AVDs also mediate intervillage rivalries.

Although traditional village councils are widespread in Asia, other types of LDAs have been promoted with outside assistance. Urban neighborhood organizations in Asia, in contrast to Latin America, were often organized or controlled by governments as of the early 1980s.[84] The Aga Khan foundation promotes village organizations in Bangladesh, India, and Pakistan (as well as Kenya) by offering a small project, such as an irrigation channel or linkage road, in exchange for the village agreeing to construct and maintain the project and save money on a regular basis.

Interest Associations

Interest associations are defined either by a single-development function
or by the type of person joining the group. They tend to be more exclusive
in membership than LDAs but may have more members than cooperatives.
Among traditional groups defined by function are water users' associations
and pastoralist organizations. More recently established types include village
health committees and parent groups that build and maintain schools.
Groups defined by personal attributes (women's groups, landless organizations, religious groups, and hometown associations) may be multifunctional.

Obviously, such distinctions begin to blur with increased mobilization.
Peasant associations and rural unions, for example, can have characteristics
of both functional and categorical groups. The Honduran Women's Peasant
Federation (FEMUC) unites 294 GROs in thirteen out of eighteen departments of the country and is cooperating with but maintaining its autonomy
from the male-dominated National Union of Peasants.[85] Nonetheless, the
general categories, described in more detail below, are a useful way of
beginning to understand the complexity and variety of interest associations.

Functional Interest Associations. GROs with a single functional interest
tend to be common in countries where soil and water are poor and tasks
are complex. In Botswana, for example, where such organizations are legion,
they manage catchment dams and dig and operate wells.[86] Where tasks are
difficult, people are often forced to create social organizations on their own,
and the "link between construction and operation" of irrigation or other
shared systems is "striking," according to Frances Korten (1986). Farmers
in Bali built a 2-kilometer tunnel through a mountain to bring water to
their fields.

Water users' associations are common in Indonesia, Pakistan, the Philippines, Sri Lanka, Thailand, Mexico, Peru, and Ecuador. Called *subaks* in
Bali, *zanjeras* in the Philippines, and *juntas de usuarios* in Latin America,
most operate under a traditional "water master" who has the trust of the
group and can adjudicate disputes.[87] Studies of strong associations in the
Philippines and Indonesia show that they have high ratios of leaders to
members, with responsibility for maintenance broken down into many parts,
based on the layouts of the irrigation canals.[88] *Galeria* organizations in
Mexico use traditional methods for tapping and conveying underground
water. According to Enge and Whiteford (1989), the methods were used by
the *ganat* organizations in ancient Persia.

Water users' associations are also promoted by outsiders. The World
Bank established 12,000 water users' associations in Pakistan between 1981
and 1987 that maintain irrigation channels, collect water charges, and promote agricultural extension.[89] A more innovative example is the Water
Council Movement, founded by Gram Gourav Pratishthan, a GRSO in a

drought-prone area of Maharashtra. Based on the success of an experimental farm, assistance is only provided for group irrigation plans, and the group must include the landless. Because the landless receive the same water share as members who own land, they acquire a bargaining chip within the organization. Water is shared on the basis of number of family members. Sugar cane cultivation, which requires a great deal of irrigation, is prohibited.[90]

Pastoralist societies often have strong nonhierarchical local organizations based on communal pasture ownership. In the Peruvian highlands, individual peasants own crop land, but pasture land is owned and managed in common. Small pastoral units in East Africa combine temporarily into local groups of several hundred people, and permanent territorial tribal groups of several thousand. During droughts, even the smallest units are dispersed to construct water storage areas, burn grass to promote nutritious shoots, and locate other natural resources. There are also procedures for sharing territory with nonmembers. Highland areas with more rainfall are treated as refuges for hardship years. Among the other highly skilled traditional coping mechanisms are the structuring of herds and the composition of species.[91]

Interest associations also form around educational objectives. Parent associations are common in squatter settlements in Santiago, Lima, and Panama City, for example.[92] In many areas of Peru, parent associations build and maintain schools and provide supplies since government educational investment is inadequate.

Village health committees are generally promoted by governments, GRSOs and INGOs. Particularly noteworthy are the village preventive health care and family planning groups initiated by several GRSOs in Thailand in the 1970s based on village health workers. Because of the high cost of health infrastructure, continued outside support is more essential for these groups than almost any other type of GRO. However, in Panama the strongest local health groups, particularly those organized in regional federations, continued to function effectively even as government support declined.[93]

Environmental associations have proliferated more recently than other functional IAs, although village forestry associations in South Korea managed over 2 million acres by 1978. Forest protection groups organized by Proshika, a Bangladesh GRSO, increased from 260 in 1986 to 1,944 as of 1991.[94] In Nepal, forestry associations have developed family-based user watchdog systems to protect forests.

The Village Forest Councils in India were spinoffs of Chipko, an environmental movement started by peasant women who lay down in front of bulldozers and hugged trees to save them from being uprooted. Like LDAs, environmental membership groups often operate as if they were local governments. As the line between development and environment blurs, a wide

range of GROs are taking on environmental activities. Brazilian neighborhood associations, for example, are assuming environmental responsibilities.[95] And in the Indian state of Kerala alone there are 7,300 GROs of all
types involved in tree planting.[96]

Categorical Interest Associations. Women's groups are not only the most
common type of categorical IA, they are probably the most rapidly proliferating type of GRO in the Third World. The International Women's Tribune Center in New York is the contact and referral office for over 6,000
groups in 160 countries.[97] As of 1985, Helmore (1985:15) estimated that
tens of thousands of women's projects were being carried out in the Third
World. In rural Brazil the growth of the women's movement has been
"explosive," according to Durning (1989:28)

In Africa, women's formal and informal organizations exist almost everywhere. In Ghana and Nigeria, where women's enterprise has a long history,
women have developed their own credit organizations.[98] In Kenya the
growth of the grassroots women's movement has been extraordinary. The
number of women's groups increased from an already significant 4,256 in
1980 to 16,000 in 1984, and to 20,000 by 1990. By 1984 membership
reached 600,000.[99] These groups have initiated many income-generating
projects and have also planted trees, coordinated literacy drives, and built
roads and bridges. Although the impetus for founding many groups was
the departure of husbands to the city for poorly paid jobs, some men remain
as coordinators, and membership is skewed towards older women. As with
all social movements, a number of the Kenyan women's clubs have fallen
prey to political divisions or the lack of time for volunteer labor, but the
overall organizational process continues.

Mother's Clubs in South Korea and Indonesia have been responsible
for successful family planning campaigns. They are also common in
Latin America, where they have a kind of instant cultural acceptability
that a more obvious "women's movement" might lack. Nonetheless,
such groups can radically change the way women think about themselves
and the way they act in their own communities. In the Sibundoy Valley
and in Guadalupe, Colombia many women had been afraid to leave their
houses and hung their heads in shyness during the first women's clubs
meetings organized by Save the Children. Within a few years, however,
they became valued contributors to family income and actively involved
in community activities and local development associations.[100] Brazilian
mother's clubs, created by the church in the 1960s, are now involved in
political mobilization on family planning and women's rights. Although
men rarely organize as fathers, family issues for women soon evolve into
political concerns.

Women's clubs are often supported, if not created by outsiders. In Colombia, both the National Coffee Growers Federation and Save the Children
have supported the evolution of women's groups from home economics

clubs to organizations managing revolving loan funds and providing their communities with health and literacy programs. But they also develop without outside assistance. In one remote village in Kenya women built their own clinic from thatch and mud to push the local hospital to send them a trained nurse midwife. They then raised money to build her a house as well as a more permanent clinic providing infant care and family services.

In South Asia, lower-class women are more directly involved with women's issues even when they are not involved with partisan politics.[101] Women's groups have mobilized around a number of notorious rape cases, dowry deaths, and bride burnings with the help of GRSOs such as the Grameen Bank and BRAC in Bangladesh and the Working Women's Forum in India.[102] In Pakistan, lower-class women are actively opposing the introduction of Sharia law, which halves the value of women's legal testimony, and the Hadood Ordinance, which does not differentiate between rape and adultery.

The success and spread of women's organizations seem to be exerting a centripetal pull on men in some communities. Women's dairy co-ops in Andhra Pradesh and Bihar are accepting more and more milk from male dairy farmers as the perception grows that they are more effective and honest than male-dominated cooperatives.[103] In Bolivia men are migrating to more-prosperous women's communities.

However, where women's participation in other kinds of GROs is high, women's organizations may become less important. In Venezuela, women are active in *juntas de vecinos*, and women's organizations are not particularly active in the squatter settlements. In the Huaral Valley in Peru, there were originally four women's groups within the Villa Hermosa Cooperative. Now that women have begun to become more active in the meetings of the cooperative, the women's groups are less active.[104]

Religious groups are a second type of categorical interest association. During the 1960s Catholic priests in Central America and Brazil were impressed with the way the poor survived by helping each other, and began organizing GROs, spurred on by liberation theologians who preached that God is on the side of the poor.[105] Like those in Central America, the estimated 80,000 Brazilian base communities are religious organizations grouping 40–1,000 people each, empowered to perform the sacraments in remote areas lacking priests and emphasizing internal democracy. But they also organize on issues such as land tenure.[106]

GRO activists in other countries also got their start in church programs. There are Catholic base communities, for example, in the Philippines and in Java. In Kenya, the development education program of the Catholic diocese of Machakos had organized 2,000 GROs with over 60,000 participants by the end of 1984 that were actively involved in tree planting, cooperatives, savings groups, water projects, enterprise development, and consumer shops. In northern Senegal a large federation of over 42,000 farmers (Amicale) gained the trust of the elders of the first village organized by building a mosque.[107]

Islamic GROs are more active in Indonesia than in the Middle East. It is estimated that there are more than 2,600 *pesantren* or Islamic boarding schools involved in community development on the island of Java alone. With roots in the anticolonial struggle dating back to the nineteenth century, *pesantren* began as antidotes to Western cultural values, but in recent years have developed social and economic programs supported by informal links to government officials and a network of intellectuals. *Pesantren* have also promoted Islamic and non-Islamic cooperatives.[108]

Hometown or provincial associations are a third type of categorical interest association. In Cairo, Caracas, and parts of Buenos Aires there are "provincial neighborhoods," whereas in other cities people from the same home town or province may be dispersed but still keep in contact. Hometown associations not only provide employment and housing help for new migrants, they also organize to provide assistance to their rural home towns.[109] During the 1973 and 1985 droughts in Senegal, the Regional Development Associations in urban areas exerted political pressure to insure distribution of grain to rural communities.[110] As we shall see in Chapter 8, some hometown associations evolve into active grassroots support organizations.

Pre-Cooperatives and Cooperatives

Pre-cooperatives and cooperatives are membership organizations that pool their private resources rather than allocating a public resource such as water or rangeland. Although they produce private goods and services, they have a larger ownership base than do other kinds of businesses and sometimes contribute facilities benefiting an entire community. The two most common types of traditional pre-cooperatives in the Third World are work groups and rotating credit associations. Borrower's groups, usually set up with GRSO or INGO assistance, are a more recently established type of pre-cooperative. Cooperatives can be classified as credit unions (savings and credit associations), consumer cooperatives, service cooperatives (providing input supply and marketing services to members) and production cooperatives (where land or other means of production are owned in common as well).

Pre-Cooperatives. Informal work groups cultivate one farmer's field one day and rotate to another member's property the next, usually on a seasonal basis. They may also hire out their services as a group, sharing the proceeds. In North Togo there are animal traction groups, for example. In Niger, according to Painter (1986), work groups are tied to traditional lineage systems, but in other African countries they may be organized around age sets. Work groups are also found in the Andean countries, where they are called *m'ita*, in Guatemala, where they are known as *kombit*, and in Indonesia where they are called *gotong royon*.[111]

In Africa alone, Cernea (1982:126) estimates that there are probably hundreds of different types of traditional economic organizations, including dancing societies that are vehicles for labor exchange. In Liberia there are at least nineteen different traditional patterns of shared labor differing in size, character, and reciprocal obligation. Since 1980 in Zimbabwe *mushandira pamwe* (working together) groups have, according to Bratton (1989:8) "contributed to a remarkable growth in agricultural productivity and output from the small farm sector." Sixty percent of these exchanged information as well as work between their members. Over half engaged in bulk purchasing, and one-third cooperated in marketing.[112]

Urban work groups are common in Latin America. In Lima, for example, street vendors are organized into self-defense organizations that settle disputes, organize street cleanups, and negotiate with local authorities. Groups of informal sector entrepreneurs promote and build markets once the right to sell is successfully defended. Informal transport operators have both informal work groups that organize the economic operation of routes and an interest association that negotiates with the authorities and organizes repair shops.[113]

Rotating credit associations have been identified in more than forty developing countries. In Korea they have existed for thousands of years and are called *kyes*. The *tandas* of Mexico, *tontines* of Zimbabwe and Cameroon, *chaer* of Thailand, and *bisi* of Pakistan are based on a monthly membership contribution with the entire amount distributed to a different member at the end of the month. Although the contributions earn no interest, rotating credit associations regularize savings, involve no expense, and minimize the problem of collection. Some African associations have over 400 members. In Egypt, where *jam'iyyat* are widespread, they avoid the Islamic prohibition on usury. Rotating credit associations are evolving into savings and credit societies in Cameroon and into processing and marketing cooperatives in South Asia. In Kenya they are investing in corn mills for their members. Rotating credit associations also evolve into more-general women's groups, without outside assistance. African peasant groups are also expanding a system in which the owner of a cow or sheep donates the first calf or kid to another group member and then keeps the second. The rotation system continues with the second group member.[114]

Although borrower's groups sometimes emerge from rotating credit associations, they are more often organized in response to the availability of outside credit or grants provided by INGOs or GRSOs. Some borrower's groups include compulsory savings as well as access to outside credit. Among the best known examples are the hundreds of thousands of groups organized by the Grameen Bank of Bangladesh. In Peru, the Institute for the Development of the Informal Sector (IDESI) had granted 38,000 loans through solidarity groups of five people as of 1989.[115]

Women seem to be particularly active in organizing pre-cooperative businesses either through borrower's groups or on their own. The Trickle Up Program estimates that of the 10,334 small group businesses they have promoted with one-time grants of $100, 56 percent are led by women.[116] An inventory of women's enterprises in Costa Rica concluded that there were at least 470 women's small group or pre-cooperative enterprises in the country, most of which had received outside help from Trickle Up, UNICEF, the Peace Corps, or the Costa Rican Federation of Voluntary Associations. Nonetheless, the enterprises were all self-directed and comprised mainly low-income women.[117]

Cooperatives. Pre-cooperatives are increasingly linked to the banking system by formally chartered credit unions. In 1987, according to Dichter and Zesch (1989:4), there were over 12,000 credit unions in Africa with almost 3 million members. In some countries, however, they are not sufficiently connected with each other or with the market. An indigenous credit union in Cameroon became the country's sixth bank in 1975. Four years later the government appointed a new director, the bank failed, and the members reverted to rotating credit societies.[118]

The macroeconomic impact of credit unions can be considerable. Dichter and Zesch (1989) found that African credit union members had deposited $500 million in their accounts by 1987. The credit union movement launched in Zimbabwe and Cameroon in 1983 included 200 organizations, a membership of over 50,000, and savings of over $15 million by the end of its first year of operations. In Kenya, credit unions have over 800,000 members with deposits of over $128 million in 1986 dollars. In one Kenyan credit union assisted by Technoserve, 72 percent of all loans went for development (as opposed to consumption) purposes, and 80 percent of these were spent in rural areas.[119] Asian credit unions have been forming umbrella organizations or federations for some years, as we shall see in Chapter 3. The Sri Lanka National Artisans and Craftsmen's Association, with 400 member organizations, emerged from a 700-year-old association.[120]

In Latin America credit unions have been extensively promoted and technically supported by the National Credit Union Association of the U.S. and by the Pan American Development Foundation. The 170 Mexican *Cajas Populares*, some organized as long as forty years ago, are particularly important in a country where the state has enormous powers of co-option. They charge lower interest rates than banks and provide scholarships for members' children.[121]

Formal cooperatives (including credit unions) are widespread in the Third World, although one estimate of 800,000 with 300 million members seems unrealistic, especially when compared with an estimate of 20 million members in Latin America.[122] For legal reasons, cooperatives are more likely than other GROs to have registered officially at some time. Paradoxically, however, they are more likely than other organizations to exist only on paper.

Cooperatives are often short lived and fail as economic enterprises. Only 5 of the 204 cooperatives registered in the Le Kef region of Tunisia in 1984 were successful.[123] The problems plaguing the Le Kef cooperatives—poor maintenance of equipment, poor accounting procedures, inadequate technical assistance, and access to credit—are typical of a majority of agricultural cooperatives all over the world.

Another reason for the frequent failure of cooperatives is that they are more likely than other GROs to have been promoted by foreign donors or governments. As products of the special historical circumstances of nineteenth century Europe, they were imported into the Third World during the 1950s and 1960s, when there was more confidence that Western know-how could somehow solve the problems of Third World poverty. Uphoff (1986:130) traces corruption in the Kenyan cooperatives to the way foreign structures were imposed.

Rigid standardized procedures, often mandated by governments, have also contributed to a high rate of cooperative mortality. In fact, Uphoff (1986:129) considers that many cooperatives in developing countries are essentially public sector organizations since the organizations are often created from above and respond mainly to government interests. The Sri Lankan Cooperative Credit Societies encouraged by a 1911 law functioned well until 1957, when the government replaced them with heavily funded Multi-Purpose Cooperative Societies that attracted corrupt leaders.[124] The coastal production cooperatives created after the Peruvian agrarian reform in 1969 were operated as state enterprises for a number of years, with more than half of the profits skimmed off by the state. This damaged incentives and led peasants to believe that they had merely exchanged one large landowner for another.[125]

Heavy-handed governments also tend to promote full production cooperatives based on collective land ownership. Yet outside assistance for the more modest goals of service cooperatives (bulk purchases, secure group credit) may be more cost-effective. The locally organized labor and service cooperative in al-Qarya, Tunisia, functioned well with some government aid but failed when it was absorbed and formalized as a full cooperative by the government.[126] Cooperatives trying to achieve a number of purposes can also become so complex that internal conflicts increase. Tendler (1987) notes that better-performing cooperatives concentrate on a few activities. It may be that co-ops should start with a limited number of service functions and take more on as clear needs develop and managerial abilities improve.

Outside assistance during this evolutionary process can help create successful, multifunctional enterprises based on either individual or collective land ownership. Technoserve's experience with multifunctional agrarian reform cooperatives in Peru and El Salvador demonstrates that they can become successful agricultural enterprises and can also provide basic social services for their members. Because of support provided by the Inter-American Foundation and a Uruguayan GRSO (the Instituto de Promocion Economico-Social), many Uruguayan cooperatives were close to financial independence by 1989.[127]

Whether agricultural cooperatives succeed or fail as enterprises, they frequently exclude poor or landless farmers and even women who own land. In Bangladesh, Karim (1985) found that wealthier farmers inevitably dominate cooperatives if allowed to join. In Egypt, cooperatives are mainly a government vehicle for distributing jobs to a few local secondary school graduates. Poorer peasants deliberately placed on the cooperative board are manipulated by richer peasants on whom they are economically dependent.[128] In Syria, after twenty years of top-down mobilization by the official Baa'th Party, only 20 percent of eligible peasants were cooperative members. Most Syrian cooperatives do not function well, and local landlords continue to derail government efforts.[129]

Even less-successful organizations can sometimes produce broader social and educational benefits, however. There are also cooperatives aimed specifically at helping the poor. Among these are a leather workers cooperative for the harijan (formerly untouchable) caste in Barpali, India, cooperatives among the Tiv in Central Nigeria, and Indian cooperatives in the highlands of Ecuador.[130]

The legitimacy and viability of cooperatives can also be enhanced by linkages with pre-cooperatives and other GROs. The successful and very large AMUL dairy cooperative in India depends on a network of farmer committees.[131] Syaffi Anshari, an Ashoka fellow in Indonesia, helped create marketing cooperatives of palm, sugar, and tobacco farmers as well as new cooperative construction industry materials by building on linkages between the Islamic *pesantrens*. A participatory evaluation of the effectiveness of rural cooperatives in Honduras concluded that cooperatives worked better in communities with many GROs than in communities with few organizations, even without formal linkages.[132] Large successful autonomous cooperatives may come to resemble GRSOs in their relationships with smaller groups. Manos de Uruguay, for example, provides jobs for 1,200 rural women and is the country's leading textile exporter.[133]

Craft cooperative membership generally includes a wider range of socioeconomic levels than agricultural cooperatives. Asia, with the most cooperatives in all categories, has a clear lead in industrial and crafts cooperatives (about 70 percent of the total). India alone had 14,250 registered hand weavers cooperatives by 1980, with many members from the poorest classes. Craft cooperatives are also numerous in Latin America but are less common in Africa, the Caribbean, and the Pacific. A regional survey of craft services and production in rural Ivory Coast showed less than 5 percent of craftsmen in six regions belonged to craft cooperatives. Although there were 400 craft co-ops in French speaking Africa, two-thirds of their 30,000 members are in Morocco and Tunisia.[134]

The cooperative model may be particularly ill-suited to seasonal economic activities such as fishing. A regional fisheries officer of the UN Food and Agriculture Organization (FAO) in Latin America wrote that cooperatives had failed so often that skepticism about joining them was widespread among fishermen. Indian fishermen have complained that cooperatives, unlike middlemen, will not loan them money, and in Ghana fishermen have found it difficult to meet loan payments during the season when herring are scarce. Credit schemes based on regular monthly payments do not respond to the seasonality of fishing, and fixed schedules and meeting places are difficult for fishermen.[135]

In addition to cooperatives, there are other types of community-based enterprises located on the conceptual border between the private sector and the independent sector:

- In Olinda, Brazil, the community has organized a waste management enterprise run by and employing residents, including composting, recycling, and aquaculture, with effluents fertilizing nearby fields. The enterprise is a significant local employer and provider of goods for local sales.[136]
- The failure of the Colombian agrarian reform in the 1970s coupled with high prices led *campesinos* to set up a number of community stores tied to the church or to regional peasant organizations. The stores have tried to achieve a number of community purposes as well as keep prices low, objectives which are often in conflict. Profits are, in effect, distributed to the community, if they exist at all. However, one store broke even by trucking produce into the city and returning with goods to sell.[137]

CONCLUSIONS AND LESSONS LEARNED

This chapter has dealt with a wide variety of GROs. It is important, however, that classification not get in the way of understanding the real functions of local groups. When viewed from the perspective of a local village, classification can be misleading, according to Bratton (1983:5), who describes how a farmer in Wedza, Zimbabwe, corrected him when he asked if his group was an extension worker group. "Does he [the extension worker] come here to join our group when there are fields to be planted or weeded?"

What is most impressive in terms of the future of sustainable development is that GROs are emerging almost everywhere in the Third World. Many of them have the advantage of building on traditional practices and forms of organizations. They are, in this sense, organic. Yet in enlarging their original functions to include an interest in development, environmental deterioration, gender relationships, or education they are merging with newer

GROs that have developed in response to urgent needs. Even if foreign assistance were to end tomorrow, the demand side behind the creation of GROs would continue to propel people to organize collectively for goals that individuals acting alone cannot achieve. With the exception of environmental deterioration and the loss of basic resources, the liberation of women's energy may be the single most important force fueling this grassroots explosion. It may even have a second generation effect on institutional sustainability. In Mexico, children who have been raised by activist mothers are already becoming politically active themselves.[138]

An intensive look at GROs raises a number of questions related to popular participation in development. Does self-help give unresponsive governments an excuse to do nothing? What about the opportunity cost of participation time for the poor? Is time wasted in grassroots competition for outside services? Does self-help inevitably decline as members become frustrated with the limits of their own power and with the "free rider" problem originally defined by Mancur Olson (1965)?

Self-help is at least as likely to drag governments into contacts with communities as to allow them to ignore their responsibilities, as we shall see in Volume 2. Few GROs are intent on creating truly self sufficient communities, and it would be impossible for some types of GROs, such as village health committees, to be independent of outside assistance. In the Latin American squatter settlements most *juntas de vecinos* engage in self-help, but squatters are hardly letting local or even national governments off the hook. Even where GROs are intent on greater self-sufficiency they often recognize the need for outside knowledge or training rather than financial support. According to Pradervand (1988:12), "One of the richest moments of our trip occurred in the small village of Badumbe, in Mali. After an entire day's discussion with forty peasants . . . [they] told us 'Don't give us money, give us ideas.' because ideas would permit them to forge their own means of fighting hunger."

What is the opportunity cost of participation and self-help, given that development is a "discretionary activity" after basic survival is assured? Far from being beholden to policy or forced to participate, members of GROs have generally decided in rational cost-weighing terms how much and what kind of participation makes sense. Some GROs advance their own interests by working with more than one outside agency.

Is time wasted competing for outside assistance? GROs do compete with each other. A Harambee group member in Kenya remarked that "we must pull while the others pause and run when the others walk."[139] During the 1970s squatter neighborhood organizations frequently competed for city services, and those that protested most loudly got a better response than those that did not. But the macroeconomic and social consequences of competition were beneficial if not always equitable. The competitive pressures in many Latin American cities have more recently produced a counter movement towards more politically powerful junta federations that eschew benefits for one neighborhood in favor of changes in government policy benefiting squatters as a whole.

Is self-help activity sustainable over time? Much of the grassroots activity is so recent and so fueled by the dimensions of the population/resource crisis that people will probably not give up once these organizations accomplish some modest gains. Earlier studies of Latin American squatter settlements, politically active for several decades, have shown that local activity does decline over time but is often reactivated when necessary.[140] The survival crisis has become so permanent in most of the Third World that the process of decline and reactivation may be a luxury that GROs can no longer afford. Uphoff's long-term participation in the Gal Oya irrigation project has lead him to question whether the selfish behavior of "free riders" or those who degrade the commons for their own benefit generally replace collectively rational acts. Although conflict over water was inevitably tied to an inadequate supply, there were also "incentives to increase that supply, if possible, thereby reducing conflict and enhancing productivity, coverting a zero-sum situation to a positive sum one by collective action."[141]

Because their survival is at stake, people at the grassroots level may learn more quickly from the failure of development projects than can outsiders who do not suffer the direct consequences of their own mistakes. The success of cooperatives promoted by the Comilla Project in Bangladesh depended on the farmers' knowledge gained from past cooperative failures. The farmers working with the failed Chilalo project in Ethiopia, in contrast, had no past cooperative experience.[142]

"Failure," as measured by outsiders, may also be coupled to increasing self-reliance, in reaction to outside direction. Export-oriented market gardening, introduced to Burkina Faso by INGOs during the early 1970s, failed because of rising fuel prices. What peasants had learned, however, became an organizing tool for promoting subsistence farming during the drought of 1973.[143]

Hirschman's (1984) concept of the preservation and conservation of social energy seems, therefore, particularly applicable to GROs. In Bafut Village, Cameroon, the Taiwanese promoted agricultural cooperatives in the early 1960s. The cooperatives failed soon after the Chinese left, but with help from the traditional chief the villagers decided to set up communities of 800 villagers organized into a general assembly and an executive committee that lists priorities and manages outside assistance. By 1986, six schools, five health posts, two water supply projects, and a cultural center had been established, with an average local contribution in cash and kind of 30 percent. Rice yields had increased, and a rice husking plant had been built along with village coffee, cocoa, and livestock plantations. The communities were cooperating with reforestation and new forage crops for cattle. They also joined an agricultural credit program sponsored by FONADER, the national rural development fund.[144]

Still at issue, however, is whether GROs will be able to become economically sustainable without outside assistance. A recent study of OEPs in Chile divides them up into those with no capacity to produce surpluses that are gradually using up their capital, those replacing their capital and adding new members but without plans for savings and new investments, and those with surpluses and increasing capitalization. Klenner and Vega (1989) found that the third type has been increasing in the late 1980s as socioeconomic heterogeneity increased among members. As of 1984, two-thirds of the estimated 120,000 participants in OEPs were low-income women. With worsening economic conditions more young people, more men, and more well-educated members of the middle class began to join. Not only did the number of OEPs continued to grow, but an increasing number were independent from their original support institutions. What appears to be happening is a kind of merger of the underground part of the private sector with the independent sector impelled by the failure of the political and macroeconomic system to provide for the needs of the vast majority of Chileans.[145]

According to Pradervand (1990:135) African peasant groups are increasingly realizing the value of savings and finding innovative ways to increase them. Among the systems of forced savings that are developing is a requirement that members provide an interest free loan to their regional federation, which then puts the money in a bank for six months and uses the interest to negotiate a much larger loan.

To sustain their activities over the long run, LDAs and IAs as well as cooperatives will need to build financial autonomy while continuing to seek outside assistance that bolsters their independence (see Chapter 7). LDAs may evolve into local governments with powers of taxation. Interest associations may increasingly undertake for-profit activities, and cooperatives will need to educate their members and improve profitability. To continue supporting GROs, GRSOs will need to develop for-profit activities as well, both because of weak Third World philanthropic traditions and because of the unreliability of donor assistance. Even if existing organizations are able to count on continuing foreign assistance, continued dependence will weaken donor ability to support promising new organizations.

This convergence between NGOs and the informal economic sector offers some promise for building a different model of society than that found in the developed countries. What is emerging is a renewed independent sector based on broad ownership, with profits invested in public as well as private goods and services. Although this sector includes both nonprofit and for-profit organizations, it will not replace either the governmental or the traditional business sectors.

The effectiveness of GRSOs, horizontal networks of GROs and GRSOs, and their ultimate impact on governments and other outsiders depends on the groups at the bottom of the organizational pyramid. This chapter has dealt with some of the failures and frustrations of GROs. But there is an immense body of evidence that GROs are not only the strongest and broadest part of the pyramid, they are also the *sine qua non* of effective and sustainable development. The yields for rain-fed farmers in Kenya who belonged to GROs were significantly higher than for those who did not belong, even though GRO members had lower ratios of extension agents per farmer than did nonmembers. And in Zimbabwe, the positive impact of membership in GROs became more powerful as rainfall and soil conditions worsened.[146]

The potential implications of the growth of GROs to institutional development do not only relate to their economic achievements. Equally crucial is the political role that the newly empowered will play, in conjunction with GRO networks, GRSOs, and even GRSO networks. Although the political role of GROs will be more fully explored in Volume 2, their relationships with other NGOs are explored more fully in the chapters that follow.

NOTES

1. A grassroots leader, quoted in Rahman, 1981, p. 44.
2. Interview, September 1991.
3. I owe this insight to Estelle James.
4. Fishel, 1979.
5. Etling, 1975, pp. 96–97.
6. See Gamer, 1982, p. 107, for example.
7. Smith, 1987a, p.6. Wisely, Oxfam withdrew funding.
8. The phrase is from Lutheran World Relief's publications.
9. Ergas, 1986, p. 323.
10. Pradervand visited 100 villages in Senegal, Mali, Burkina Faso, Zimbabwe, and Kenya during 1987. See Pradervand, 1990.
11. Bratton, 1983.
12. See Annis, 1987, and Fisher, 1984.
13. Vetter, 1986, p. 3.
14. See Smith, 1990, p. 261 and Koldewyn, 1986, p. 46.
15. Eldridge, 1984–85, p. 44; De los Reyes, 1986; Njonkou, 1986, p. 82.
16. They are supported by organizations in 3,176 villages, 399 unions, 65 upazillas, 22 districts, and 49 training centers (Khan, 1991; Crossette, 1991).
17. Crossette, 1988:A3.
18. Meeting with Middle East Division, Save the Children, 1989.
19. Van Nieuwenhuijze et al., 1985. See also Ralston, Anderson, and Colson (1983:90–91).
20. Annis, 1987, p. 21.
21. Pradervand, 1988, p. 8.
22. Bletzer, 1977, p. 5.

23. Wells and Wells, 1953.

24. John Useem's study is included in a volume edited by Margaret Mead (1955:144).

25. Anacleti, 1986.

26. Hyden, 1983, p. 9. Tribal councils like the *Jamaas* in North Africa respond to outside threats, and religious brotherhoods in Libya resisted Italian rule. Larson, 1984.

27. Taal, 1989, pp. 20-21.

28. The ayllu, for example, is a complicated but flexible Aymara lineage system that allocates the distribution of resources and labor. See Cusicanqui, 1990.

29. See Fishel, 1979, pp. 54–55.

30. See Ralston, Anderson, and Colson, 1983, p. 80.

31. Somjee, 1979, p. 39. See also Moore, 1966, p. 338.

32. Anheier, 1987, p. 426.

33. Dhungel, 1986; on Nepal see Dhungel, 1986; on Thailand see Calavan, 1986.

34. Samarasinghe, 1992, pp. 2–6.

35. Lopezllera Mendez, 1990.

36. Roth, 1987, p. 36. The post-independence Harambee movement grew out of these traditions.

37. Alliband, 1983, pp. 33–35.

38. The International Institute for Rural Reconstruction remains active today and has autonomous affiliates in many countries.

39. See Alliband, 1983, pp. 29–33. Other less successful interventions included a more expensive project in Sriniketan initiated in 1922 by activists with few technical skills.

40. Opposition from large landowners nearby made the participatory approach more difficult to implement in these years. Development projects that were initiated after the Peruvian agrarian reform of the 1970s did not face the same local political obstacles.

41. Okoli, 1982, p. 71.

42. LeComte, 1986, and Pradervand, 1988, p. 9.

43. Pradervand, 1988, p. 7.

44. Ergas (1986:323) estimates that there are thousands of urban as well as rural GROs in Africa also.

45. See Fisher, 1984, and Matos Azocar, 1986.

46. Harazim, 1990, p.25.

47. Thompson, 1990, p. 394.

48. An example is the Coordinating Council for Human Rights in Bangladesh; see Gain, 1991.

49. Jatoba, 1987; Max Neef, 1985, and Klenner and Vega, 1989.

50. Durning, 1989, p.12.

51. Peter Sollis (from Oxfam UK), panel on Conflict Resolution and Development, International Development Conference, January 24, 1991, Washington, D.C.

52. OECD, 1990, p. 248. There is no breakdown dividing these funds between INGO field offices and support for indigenous NGOs. For more details, see Volume 2.

53. See Fisher, 1986, 1989.

54. Vetter, 1986, p.3.

55. Telephone conversation with Chris Martin, December 16, 1992. This represents a significant increase over 1990, when David Beckmann, in an interview, estimated that 5 percent of projects involved NGOs.

56. See Fowler, 1990.

57. Cotter, 1988.

58. Abate and Kiros, 1983; Belamide, 1986. Tunisian political parties are also sponsoring GROs.

59. Ali, 1986; Esman and Uphoff, 1984, p. 191.

60. Terrant and Poerbo, 1986, and MacDougall, 1986, p. 108.

61. See OECD, 1988, p. 108, and Fowler, 1990, p. 31.

62. An International Fund for Agricultural Development mission called it "one of the best models of participatory rural development in South Asia." (Dhungel, 1986: 223). See also Ghai and Rahman, 1981, and Felsenthal, 1985–86.

63. Hirschman (1984) calls this the "conservation and preservation of social energy."

64. Edel, 1969, p. 49.

65. Terrant and Poerbo, 1986.

66. Thiele, 1986, p. 544.

67. Merschrod, 1980. Training can lead to more organizational spin-offs when it extends beyond obvious leaders. See Charlick, 1984, and Fisher, 1986.

68. Lecomte, 1986, p. 115.

69. OECD, 1988, pp. 32–33; Secretariat ONG/Zaire, 1988, p. 8.

70. Alan Fowler, in an August 14, 1989 letter to the author, notes that "profit may need to be redefined in so far as this is a *surplus* accruing to the beneficiaries as members who own the GRO rather than (say) a capitalist shareholder."

71. Fisher, 1977. The Harambee movement in Kenya was originally tied to the politics of the independence movement, but is locally accountable. The Federacion Campesina de Venezuela, created by cadres from the Accion Democratica party, has become relatively independent of partisan politics.

72. Uphoff, 1986, p. 276.

73. Healy, 1987, p. 3.

74. Aruna Kumari, "From Income to Empowerment: Field Lessons from India," Panel Workshop #3, Association for Women in Development, November 17–19, 1989, Washington, D.C.

75. IFDA, 1989d, p. 69. Many of these are linked to a GRSO called the India Institute for Integrated Rural Development.

76. Sheldon Annis (1987) lists nominally different groups in Latin America as church groups, labor organizations, political action committees, potable water associations, communal labor arrangements, cooperatives, youth groups, squatter associations, worker-owned businesses, ethnic burial societies, transportation collectives, peasant leagues, Catholic reflection groups, tribal federations, and microentrepreneur group credit associations. Except for local organizations that are not GROs, most are LDAs, IAs, pre-cooperatives, or cooperatives. An African listing includes elders councils, worker groups, age groups, neighborhood organizations, tribal structures, water unions, and rotating credit groups. (Rouille D'Orfeuille, 1984).

77. Fisher, 1984, p. 64.

78. Herrera and Lobo-Guerrero, 1988, p. 32.

79. In Indonesia, however, the village headman operates more as an arm of local administration (Uphoff, 1986:117).

80. See Ba, 1990.

81. Schneider, 1985, p. 33.

82. See Fisher, 1984, and De Soto, 1989, p. 26.

83. Fisher, 1984; De Soto, 1989, pp. 18, 26–27.

84. The Marcos regime utilized the *barangays* as an extension of centralized control, and the *Rukun Wilayahs* in Jakarta were appointed by municipal governments. In Singapore, municipal block committees were controlled from above and dominated by the well-to-do (Aldrich, 1980).

85. Yudelman, 1987.

86. Uphoff, 1986, p. 126.

87. My father, David Hawkins, remembers that in La Luz, New Mexico, where he grew up, there was an elected "water boss."

88. Bagadion and Korten, 1985, p. 73.

89. A World Bank assessment (Schuh, 1987:12) rated the project a success, although some associations are "fragile."

90. Deshpande et al., 1986.

91. See Dyson-Hudson, 1985. Peasant leagues, common in Latin America, tend to be regional networks. See Chapter 3.

92. Fisher, 1977. The "bench schools" of Colombia, in contrast, are often organized on a for-profit basis by individual entrepreneurs (Acuna Gomez et al., 1979:14).

93. See Uphoff, 1986, p. 300. On Thailand see Coombs, 1980.

94. Uphoff, 1986, p. 276; Messerschmidt, 1987, p. 381, and Khan, 1991.

95. Landim, 1992.

96. Postel and Heise, 1988, p. 39.

97. Telephone interview with Vicky Semmler of the IWTC, December 17, 1992. This figure included both GROs, GRSOs, and networks.

98. Guyer, 1986, pp. 411, 399.

99. Wanyande, 1987, p. 96, recent newspaper accounts.

100. Fisher, 1986.

101. Jahan, 1987.

102. The women's movement in India was intertwined with the Nationalist movement, beginning in the 1920s. Organized by educated, upper-class women, it was based on the idea of improving the position of women as wives and mothers (Caplan, 1985).

103. Conversation with Karen McGuinness of the Ford Foundation.

104. Visit to the Villa Hermosa Cooperative by the author when employed by Technoserve in January 1989.

105. Talk given by Brian Smith, Yale University, 1987.

106. Moreira Alves, 1984, p. 83. Base communities helped organize the Partido Trabalhador (Worker's Party), which won one-fifth of the vote in recent São Paulo elections. (Friedmann, 1989:13).

107. See, for example, Durning, 1989, p. 21; Belamide, 1986; Ashoka, 1988, p. 84; Mulwa, 1987, p. 111; and Pradervand, 1990.

108. See Eldridge, 1984–85; Ashoka, 1985. Buddhist monks in Thailand and Sri Lanka have helped organize many communities. See Chapter 4.

109. See Hirabayashi, 1986. For earlier citations, see Fisher, 1977, pp. 61–62.

110. Sawadogo, 1990, p. 60.

111. For discussions of work groups see Cernea, 1982, p. 124; Taal, 1989, p. 20; Bunch, 1982, p. 220, and Massoni, 1985, p. 39.

112. Bratton, 1983, p. 314.

113. De Soto, 1989, p. 86.

114. Despite their cross-national similarity Seibel and Massing (1974) identified sixteen different types of rotating credit associations in Liberia. For more on rotating credit associations see Cernea, 1982, p. 128; Chira, 1987; Chimedza, 1986, p. 75; Lecomte, 1986, p. 121; Ludwig and Chima, 1987, p. 195; Ralston, Anderson and Colson, 1983, pp. 108–111; and Van der Akker, 1987, pp. 145–147; Pradervand (1990:135) describes the livestock rotation system.

115. Diaz Albertini, 1989, p. 88.

116. Leet and Leet, 1989.

117. Centro de Orientacion Familiar, 1985. Some of the larger businesses had evolved into cooperatives.

118. Hyden, 1983, p. 126. Credit unions composed of employees of businesses or governments are not theoretically part of the independent sector.

119. Dichter and Zesch, 1989, pp. 2–3.

120. IRED, 1986a.

121. Jatoba, 1987; Gaytan, 1991–92, p. 7.

122. World Council of Credit Unions, 1988; Annis, 1987. In 1976 there were over 4,000 Argentine cooperatives, and favorable legislation has since increased their numbers. (Thompson, 1990: 394) There are over 400 agricultural cooperatives in Costa Rica with 200,000 members, or 25 percent of the economically active population (Carroll, 1992:211). There are 5,000 cooperatives in Colombia, with a membership of 2 million (Ritchey-Vance, 1991:33). According to Anheier (1987: 421), cooperatives in Africa are "very numerous" and have enjoyed "impressive and almost uninterupted growth since the colonial period."

123. Larson, 1984, p. 199.

124. Samarasinghe, 1992, pp. 12–13.

125. Fisher, 1989.

126. Larson, 1984, p. 199.

127. Fisher, 1989; Bendahmane, 1989, p.33. Ninety percent of Uruguayan dairy exports were from cooperatives in 1989.

128. Adams, 1986.

129. Hinnebusch, 1984, p. 117.

130. See Hirschman, 1984; Tendler, 1983; Hinnebusch, 1984, p. 117; and Esman and Uphoff, 1984, p. 63.

131. AMUL processing of butter and cheese assists the small farmers to cope with seasonal fluctuations in milk production. See Uphoff, 1986, p. 142.

132. Merschrod, 1980, p. 21.

133. Bendahmane, 1989, p. 34.

134. Ndjonkou, 1986.

135. Pollnac, 1985, pp. 189–223. Regional and national networks of fisherfolk seem to be flourishing in Asia, however. See Chapter 3, p. 60.

136. Bartone, 1986, p. 39.

137. Flora and Flora, 1988.

138. Logan, 1990. In Colombia in 1986, I found that teenage daughters of the founders of one women's club sponsored by Save the Children near Guadalupe had started their own literacy project.

139. Hyden, 1983, p. 19.

140. Fisher, 1984, pp. 67, 76.

141. Uphoff, 1992, p. 327–333. He also notes that the farmer groups were willing to tolerate some free riding "if the benefits from collective action to those who were prepared to join in outweighed their own cost of contribution" (p.353).

142. Karim, 1985–86, p. 33.

143. Lecomte, 1987.

144. Pavard, 1986.

145. It is not yet clear what has happened to OEPs since the Christian Democrats returned to power. However, the new government is strongly supportive of NGOs of all types.

146. Oxby, 1983, p. 84.

3

GRO Networks

[Networks reach] back...before simple human relationships became obscured by hierarchy and bureaucracy. In other respects, networks... leap forward...with globe-encompassing capability that subsumes the enduring aspects of authority and bureaucracy.

Lipnack and Stamps, 1984:294–296

What's interesting is that this [network] was something created out of our own heads, all of us together. We discovered that this struggle was ...the only alternative that we had in order to resist.

Chico Mendes

After a women's group in a village in Burkina Faso received a small cereal mill from UNICEF, they decided to pay a small amount each time they used it. The woman in charge of the mill explained that good fortune should be shared with even poorer people. "The mill that UNICEF has given us is a father-mill: he must make a son to take his place when he is old and weary, and a daughter to give to the neighboring village. Set the price of milling so that these children can be raised."[1] These words not only convey an understanding of sustainability and scaling out, they also illustrate the impressive mixture of idealism and pragmatism fueling the creation of GRO networks.

There are three general types of horizontal networks at the grassroots level in the Third World today: regional networks of individual GROs, informal economic networks, and more amorphous grassroots movements that extend beyond one locality but may not be based on GROs. Regional GRO networks and informal economic networks may be organized locally or by outsiders, whereas amorphous protest movements are more consistently founded at the local level.

Although some networks are rooted in traditional lineage systems, GRO networks, like their members, have proliferated rapidly in Asia, Latin America, and parts of Africa in recent years.[2] An NGO directory lists 10 in Mexico alone.[3] Although amorphous protest movements have historical antecedents (the Spartacus rebellion in ancient Rome, Nat Turner's slave revolt in the United States, and the Russian peasant movements coalescing around czarist pretenders), they have become more common in Asia and Latin America since the early 1970s. In addition to these three regional networking patterns, there are national networks of GROs in some countries.

GRO FEDERATIONS

Local Development Association Networks

Typical of LDA federations organized by outsiders are the *Maison Familles Rural* groups organized by French agricultural schools in seventeen countries. French NGOs have also promoted networking in Africa. In Senegal they are linked to hundreds of regionally federated LDAs and Senegalese GRSOs. One Senegalese GRSO called SOE (The Eucumenical Mutual Help Service) uses federated groups of GROs to promote credit programs, village wells, and medical clinics.[4]

Governments frequently sponsor or legally recognize networks of LDAs, even if they are organized without government assistance. The Togolese and Senegalese governments pay the salaries of LDA federation organizers, for example.[5] In Yemen, the 130 member Coordinating Council for Local Development Associations obtains government backing for school construction and teacher pay.[6]

Government support for individual LDAs may or may not limit networking. In Cameroon the Village Development Committees have 50 percent representation on the boards of regional (government) corporations yet have very little power and are not allowed to federate independently. In Colombia, however, government organized neighborhood councils began spontaneously federating themselves in the 1960s. By 1969, federations were active in 5 to 10 percent of the municipalities in the country, including several major cities and some isolated rural areas.[7]

Squatter neighborhood associations in Latin America were among the first indigenous LDAs to federate without government support. In the 1960s and early 1970s *juntas de vecinos* often tried to federate but failed to form citywide organizations because of official reprisal and competition for city services. New squatter federations continued to be formed, however, and some, particularly in Brazil and Venezuela, have since become grudgingly accepted entrants into the political arena. By 1984 there were three major federations in Rio de Janeiro coordinating 257 neighborhood associations.[8]

Instead of remaining strictly autonomous or seeking government support, many LDAs establish ties with existing GRSOs or create their own GRSO. Bina Swadaya, the largest GRO network in Indonesia, was created by the Usaha Bersama LDAs to provide technical assistance. In the Puttalam district of Sri Lanka there is a network of forty-two LDAs called "Vinivida—NGO Coalition for Eradicating Poverty Through Knowledge and Communication." Vinivida has created a clearing house for exchange of information and access to development services and outside assistance.[9] Village committees organized in Zimbabwe during the struggle for independence have village-level productive units and markets as well as district-level associations with regional markets and workshops for making tools. At the national level this Organization for Rural Associations for Progress (ORAP), made up of village representatives, has many international ties as well.[10]

Sometimes the professionals who organized a GRO network depart, and the beneficiaries take over. When the Bolivian anthropologists who had founded the Associacion de Parcialidades Indigenas in 1975 left the organization, the Indian representatives who remained were hired by the United Nations to do a tribal census. Although earlier projects run by the professionals had not been very successful, the restructured organization negotiated successfully for land for the Ava Chiripa Indians and defended exploited Indian workers in the Chaco Central.[11]

LDAs, as noted in Chapter 2, often fill political vacuums created by government weakness. LDA federations sometimes play an even wider political role. Neighborhood federations in Venezuela have become an alternative to political parties, according to Zambrano (1989:27). The Federacion de Asociaciones de Comunidades Urbanas (FACUR), founded in 1974, mobilizes people around neighborhood problems rather than elections and thus avoids being "occupied" by the political parties.

Interest Association Networks

Functional Interest Associations. Networking among local peasant organizations is common in some rural areas of Latin America. In Paraguay, where 80 percent of all agricultural land is owned by 1 percent of the population, peasant unions formed an assembly to demand land for the landless, forcing the Stroessner regime to legalize thirty-one peasant invasions in 1985.[12] The Mexican National Union of Autonomous Regional Peasant Organizations has been involved in land battles since the late 1970s. The Movement of Landless Rural Workers in Brazil had spread to sixteen states and organized forty-two encampments by 1989. In Santarem, Brazil, the Movement has gradually taken over peasant unions organized by the government during the early 1970s and has been able to organize diverse groups, including river fishermen and highland settlers displaced by the expansion of large estates.[13] In Honduras there are parallel peasant unions for men and women.[14]

A large number of regional peasant organizations have emerged in Mexico. In Chiapas there are three independent regional peasant networks not tied to the official PRI party operating in twenty-two regions of the state. One of these joined with teachers, settlers, transport workers, and students as an opposition coalition, which has been violently repressed by the police. Another regional peasant organization holds a week of political and cultural events in each locality each year including popular theater that exposes corruption and denounces repression.[15]

Peasant networks have also been organized in Asia and Africa. Philippine peasants, first organized during the 1930s, later organized regional associations that fought the Marcos government for land titles and lower interest rates.[16] The Committee to Fight for the End of Hunger in Senegal (COLUFIFA), was founded by a small group of farmers with help from the Associacion Jeunesse Agricole de Casamance, a GRSO, to promote food crops rather than exports and to discourage deforestation. Groups have their own trainers and promote better storage, fruit tree nurseries, tourism, literacy, and health centers. COLUFIFA has 20,000 individual members, regional organizations, and village committees in the Gambia and Guinea-Bissau.[17]

Other horizontal networks based on occupation include household workers' organizations in Latin America and fishermen's organizations in Asia.[18] PAMALAKAYA-Pilipinas, for example, is a national alliance of fishermen's organizations in thirty-one regions, provinces, and districts. With an individual membership of 50,000, PAMALAKAYA lobbies the Philippine government, provides training for its members, sequesters government fish ponds for collective use, and carries out exchanges with fishermen's organizations in other countries.[19]

Some interest association networks are based on single development sectors. A community health worker for a hospital in Maharashtra helped leaders from ten villages organize a regional Community Health Council. An evaluation of the village health committees in Panama concluded that the main reason they remained effective after government support declined was that they themselves created an active federation of health committees.[20] In Buenos Aires, 300 GROs representing 10,000 families have created a citywide housing network. With help from GRSOs they have formulated a citywide plan and are obtaining loans based on city ownership of 30 percent of the new buildings for commercial leasing.[21] Other networks focus on education. (See Exhibit 3.1.)

A horizontally organized sectoral approach may have as broad an impact on development as LDA networks that assume grassroots support functions. The Aguaruna and Huabisa Mechanical Services Network in Peru, controlled by forest Indian groups, has set up boat repair shops on five tribu-

---

Exhibit 3.1
A Peasant Encyclopedia

A network in Cajamarca, Peru, founded in 1987 links rural libraries into the Peasant Encyclopedia Project. "We are a working group of the Association for Rural Development of Cajamarca. We study, distribute, train, publish books in our own words, record songs, drawings, and photos. We are 1.2 million rural, 35% illiterate, and the poorest department of Peru. We know who we are and who we want to be." (IFDA, 1991:99)

---

taries of the Maranon River with an Oxfam grant for repair equipment. The tribes consider river transport to be the key to improved health, food production, marketing, and land rights.[22]

Although environmental issues such as deforestation are central to the work of many GRO networks and ethnic movements, sectoral networks focusing on forestry are becoming more common, particularly in Asia and Latin America. In Bangladesh, Proshika is organizing forestry networks. In Mexico, where 70 percent of total forest lands are securely held by indigenous communities or *ejidos*, sustainable forestry is used to increase community income on a regional level.[23] A Costa Rican GRSO, the Associacion de Nuevas Alquimistas (ANAI) organized a network of twenty-four forestry organizations in Talamanca within a year and a half.[24]

Categorical Interest Associations. When women's groups organize horizontally in Latin America, they combine the attributes of functional and categorical associations by concentrating on a single issue such as education or nutrition. An example is *Madres Educadores*, a network of community day care centers located in poor urban neighborhoods throughout Colombia. Community kitchens in Lima and Santiago cooperate with each other in obtaining outside assistance.[25]

Women's groups also formed the backbone of GRO networking during crises such as famine in Africa or the 1985 earthquake in Mexico City. The 19th of September Garment Workers Union, led by women, and the women's sector of the National Coordinating Committee of the Popular Urban Movement (CONAMUP) were instrumental in successfully pressuring the Mexican government to involve neighborhood organizations in reconstruction.[26]

GROs defined by ethnicity are increasingly united by environmental goals. Tribal networks in Latin America are uniting with each other regionally, nationally, and internationally to protect tribal land. In the Philippines, Manobo tribal activist Edtami Mansayagan, organized seventeen different ethnolinguistic groups in a joint protest of 2,000 people against outside exploitation of Mount Apo. Because Mount Apo is sacred to all of the different Luad peoples, they signed a *dyandi*, or blood pact agreeing to defend the land at all costs.[27]

Cooperative and Pre-Cooperative Federations

In contrast to LDA and IA federations, cooperative federations in the Third World have been formally established for some time. For example, in the 1950s the Mexican Catholic Church established the Secretariado Social Mexicano to organize credit unions and unite them with each other. Hand weavers cooperatives in India are grouped into state federations, and one national federation.[28]

It is, however, difficult to determine whether cooperatives and credit unions have contacts with each other or are merely tied to the same central federation, functioning as a GRSO. Established federations may also be little more than paper organizations, unable to assist their members with the problems typically besetting cooperatives. Most of the original Mexican *ejido* federations, for example, have either withered away or become government bureaucracies.[29]

Cooperative federations, like their member organizations, are somewhat more likely than other GRO federations to be dominated by elites. Carroll's (1992) study of seven GRO networks and twenty-three GRSOs concluded that GRO networks were less participatory and more prone to cronyism than GRSOs. Interestingly, four of the seven GROs were cooperative federations and two were regional service centers promoted by the Costa Rican government with some cooperative members. The exception to this generalization was SADECSA, a Chilean network of four small farmer societies that elects male and female representatives to its board and has helped member organizations become active enterprises.[30]

Unlike LDA and interest federations, which frequently organize themselves for limited purposes and then seek additional outside assistance, cooperative federations have to deal with the whole range of economic and management issues faced by their member organizations from the moment they are founded. Effective outside technical assistance in management can therefore provide the key margin needed for success.

Technoserve and the Inter-American Foundation have demonstrated that this is possible. Technoserve Kenya, a counterpart GRSO, worked successfully with the Kenyan Union of Savings and Credit Cooperatives and helped them develop a standard accounting manual for member organizations. TNS also helped with staff reorganization, employee evaluation and promotion, and management systems for improved financial control and work flow to aid members. The Inter-American Foundation has assisted cooperative federations in Latin America with financial and technical assistance for many years, with positive long-term results. The Central Llanera Uruguaya, founded in 1967 as a federation of wool cooperatives, now has 3,000 members, handles 10 percent of Uruguay's wool harvest, and has become the country's largest wool exporter. The El Ceibo federation of thirty-five cocoa cooperatives in Bolivia operates a small chocolate factory with a staff of 100, grosses $1.5 million per year, and controls more than half of the national harvest.[31]

Yet outside assistance alone does not fully account for the success of some cooperative federations. Carroll (1992:59) attributes El Ceibo's success to a "highly participatory style" of rotating representation on the administrative council as well as to timely IAF assistance.

Other cooperative federations are proving to be more successful and innovative than their members. In Cameroon the Cooperative des Artisans de Nylon (COOPAN), groups forty-eight member enterprises, assists them in marketing and handicraft promotion, and has, like some LDA federations, become a kind of GRSO. In Saint Lucia an agricultural cooperative federation with a staff of thirty-six promotes quality control, processing, and marketing.[32] Because cooperatives were weak in the Cartago province of Costa Rica, the Union Regional de Cooperativas (URCOOPAPA) serves both cooperatives and their individual members. URCOOPAPA has built storage areas for vegetables and helped improve marketing, output, and quality.[33] In the Piura valley of Peru, some of the most loyal customers for agricultural supplies sold through a cooperative federation are nonaffiliated agrarian reform cooperatives from other valleys that survived the dissolution of their own federations.[34]

Cooperatives may even be replaced by regional organizations. Cooperatives failed near Tres Postes, Ecuador, but beginning in 1980 their former members spontaneously organized areawide development committees that initiated small-scale education, health, and training programs. In part because women were instrumental in the initial movement, there were twenty-seven area committees established within a few years. These have remained active, although attempts to resurrect the cooperatives have failed.[35]

Even a combination of outside assistance and participatory management may be insufficient where politics is violent and polarized, and federations may not stick to assisting their members. In El Salvador there were several rival federations trying to federate rural cooperatives during the civil war. The Federation for Agrarian Reform Cooperatives (FESACORA), with twenty-three members, received support from AID and assistance from Technoserve. Other reform sector cooperatives joined an independent federation called COACES, which was more openly critical of the government and military. Oxfam provided assistance to FEDECOOPADES, a federation of eighty-one nonagrarian reform cooperatives.[36]

Pre-cooperatives face special problems in trying to create regional groups. Borrower's groups organized by GRSOs and INGOs are, like some cooperatives, tied to their donor but not to each other. Because they are small, pre-cooperatives, even if organized by outsiders, are based on strong member

Exhibit 3.2
Lima Squatter Settlement

Villa El Salvador totals nearly 350,000 people. Block after block of neat, self-constructed housing stretches over 8,000 hectares of desert. Nearly 200 nursery, primary and secondary schools—mostly built by community volunteers—enroll nearly 90,000 students. Virtually everyone knows how, or is learning, to read and write. Taking advantage of piped water, residents farm nearly 1,000 hectares that have been set aside for agriculture; once-barren sands yields tons of oranges, vegetables, sweet potatoes, papayas, and corn. What most impresses visitors is organization. Every block and every activity is intensely organized through crisscrossing neighborhood associations, women's groups, youth groups, artisan associations, and production cooperatives. An estimated 2,000 organizations are nestled within federations of larger federations, and these confederations largely control the democratically elected local government. In 1983, the city became an independent municipality. Its mayor, in turn, represents Villa El Salvador to the city of Lima and to the National government. (Annis and Franks, 1989:17)[37]

loyalty and cohesiveness. Expansion, particularly when initiated by outsiders, may "force the pace" of development just as small groups are beginning to benefit from new sources of credit or technical assistance. On the other hand, if promoted carefully, small federations can enhance the effectiveness of pre-cooperatives. The federations of women's clubs assisted by Save the Children in Colombia have only six to ten member organizations each and have become the agency that approves group or individual loan applications.[38]

Mixed Networks

There are also GRO federations that group different types of GROs. In the Philippines, local People's Councils coordinate cooperatives, LDAs, and peasant organizations around human rights and land tenure issues. The Society for Social Transformation in India invited hundreds of GROs that are members of the Movement for People Oriented Development to meet at Bhopal in 1990, followed by regional and state meetings. Discussion focused on the causes behind the many "bad" development projects in India and the possibilities for alternative approaches.[39]

Informal ties between different types of GROs can have a major impact at the local level, as the description from a large Peruvian squatter settlement in Exhibit 3.2 reveals.

INFORMAL ECONOMIC NETWORKS

Informal economic networks often emerge from traditional economic ties rather than from a desire to create a formal federation. In Zimbabwe there are traditional work-based exchanges of seeds and skills between communities.[40] The Center for Indigenous Peoples in Eastern Bolivia (CIDOB), grew out of the strong intercommunity economic traditions of the Chiriguano tribe and is managed by the Indian LDAs or *Capitanias*.[41] Yet economic interdependency may also emerge after a federation of LDAs, IAs, or cooperatives is organized. In Togo the Association of Village Enterprises requires that its members produce not only enough for themselves but a surplus to share with other villages.[42]

Economic networks often consciously sidestep or downplay committed participation in the money economy in favor of barter. Yet their awareness of the pitfalls of the money economy does not seem to preclude their entrance at a later stage, when they have acquired enough economic knowledge and muscle to avoid exploitation. A Bolivian barter and storage network called Ayni Ruway links a number of villages to a campesino-owned handicraft store in Cochabamba.[43] Green Zones, a regional economic movement organized by women in the midst of the civil war in Mozambique, grows and markets food near provincial capitals. Individual Green Zones throughout the country are members of the National Association of Agricultural Producers and work with government, traders, transport systems, and other farmers.[44]

Some economic networks are able to become self-supporting and create their own GRSOs. CIDOB in eastern Bolivia was organized by anthropologists from APCOB (Ayuda para el Campesino del Oriente Boliviano), but they were hired by the Chiriguano tribe for this purpose. Jatun Pukara in Potosi, Bolivia, unites seventeen communities producing quinua, wool, and wheat, and trains peasant community leaders. They use the profits from excess village crops to reinforce and consolidate new organizations. The Committee for Development Action, a regional training center in the Bamba-Thaialene area of Senegal, links three different ethnic groups and sixteen villages and is funded by a percentage of the profits from a communal field.[45]

Korten (1990) points out that economic linkages extending beyond one village do not necessarily lead to "economic transformation" even if they have well-defined plans and budgets. Yet once informal economic networks are established, there does seem to be a kind of built-in economic incentive promoting sustainability that may not be present either in formal GRO networks or in amorphous protest movements. With sensitive outside assistance (including GRSOs created from below) this process can be strengthened and accelerated. After an Ashoka organizer in Mexico City helped a barter network achieve economies of scale, group enterprises such as a carpentry group began to proliferate.[46] The Institute for Liberty and Democracy in Lima has assisted networks of informal enterprises and has challenged political and legal barriers to their growth. An international peasant barter network linked directly to lower priced produce for city dwellers in West Africa is being promoted by Agriculteurs Francais Developpement International and the Six S Association (an INGO founded by a Burkinabe sociologist) through trade stimulation groups. AFD and Six S are also facilitating international rural exchanges such as sheep for coconuts between women's groups in northern Burkina Faso and the Ivory Coast.[47]

In the Philippines there is a remarkable attempt to scale up the concept of assisting alternative economic networks. The Foundation for Community Organization and Management Technology headed by Sixto Roxas seeks to legitimate informal structures through policy change. The Foundation first defines a potential economic unit of approximately 22,000 households, based on geography. Regional household clusters have been organized that provide governing structure for local incorporated management units to serve households. Results are evaluated on the basis of increased household income above a defined poverty line. Vertically integrated processing and marketing is carried out through a sophisticated management information system that highlights idle land.[48]

AMORPHOUS PROTEST MOVEMENTS

Amorphous grassroots movements not based on GROs began to proliferate in Asia and Latin America during the 1970s.[49] Amorphous movements have continued to emerge since that time, even though many of them are short lived or gradually become less amorphous as they attract GROs into their orbits. Rural protest movements are usually based on land rights or environmental decline, but urban movements such as those that emerged in the Philippines and Burma during the late 1980s.

Grassroots protest movements have a particularly long history in Latin America. Peasant rebellions in Juchitan, Mexico, for example, date back to the seventeenth century, and spread more widely during the late eighteenth century with the breakup of the Bourbon regime of Maximilian and Carlotta. More recently, another protest movement in Juchitan evolved into a mass based political party. (See Exhibit 3.3.)

In Colombia during the 1970s, peasant, small farmer, and student movements outside normal political structures tried to redress the grievances of the poor through the promotion of protest demonstrations and civic strikes that sometimes led to seizures of public facilities at the local level. One hundred twenty-eight such demonstrations occurred between 1971 and 1980 in communities representing 18 percent of the national population.[50]

The defining characteristic of the rural protest movements that have emerged in recent years in the Third World is the access of the poor to natural resources. Bhoomi Sena and Shramik Sanghatana in Maharashtra

---

Exhibit 3.3
A Mexican Protest Movement

A regional movement called the Coalition of Workers, Peasants and Students
(COCEI) won a special municipal election in 1980 in Juchitán after fraud was
officially acknowledged. COCEI worked with local groups to staff health
clinics, pave streets, and establish a public library. They also negotiated with
state and federal authorities to secure credit for farmers, bypassing the local
PRI party. Middle-class reaction to COCEI's targeting of special interests gave
the federal government the ammunition it needed to occupy the city and call
for new elections. Mass COCEI protests blocking the Pan American Highway
led to new municipal elections, won by a PRI reformer who built a coalition
with COCEI. By creating a mass opposition movement and by being willing
to negotiate COCEI obtained political concessions. "Grassroots activists
throughout Mexico have understood these possibilities, and . . . leftist unions,
peasant federations, neighborhood organizations and regional political movements have . . . grown during the past 15 years." (Rubin, 1987:4)

---

and Shramjivi Samaj in Gujarat were founded by landless, tribal people
during the 1970s. However, since that time, the line between economic and
environmental protest has almost disappeared. Indeed, the poor of the Third
World were dealing with catastrophic resource constraints and expressing
their need for "sustainable development" years before the Brundtland Commission brought the term to international attention. A Mexican women's
movement organized because of chronic water shortages in Guadalajara
dramatized the issue by washing their children in a fountain in front of city
hall.[51]

Nowhere has this process been more dramatic than in Brazil. Brazilian
rural peasant unions sprang up all over Acre in the Amazon region in the
1970s in response to the ravaging of land with bulldozers and fires and
expulsion of the peasants by large landowners. When the government failed
to respond, violence grew and many peasants fled the area. Networking
between Acre organizations, those of other Amazon states and a national
organization representing indigenous communities appealed directly to the
World Bank to stop funding the Trans–Amazon Highway. There are also
movements of people displaced by dams, and many landless movements.
The Brazilian rubber tapper movements, brought to the forefront of international attention by the murder of Chico Mendes in 1988, had formed a
national association by 1985, with some organizers traveling for two weeks
to reach Brasilia and lobby against the destruction of the Amazon. The
fifteen rubber tappers' movements formed between 1975 and 1988 were
able to preserve 1.2 million hectares of forests, in alliance with indigenous
tribal peoples.[52]

Tribal groups in the Caribbean and in Chile, Colombia, Bolivia, and Peru are also forming protest networks, supported by Cultural Survival and other outside donors. The Regional Indian Council of Cauca (Colombia) has over fifty affiliated communities and a broad program of grassroots development.[53]

Although environmental movements like Chipko in India often include intellectuals and scientists, they are also the result of a strong grassroots reaction against environmentally destructive development. Environmental taboos, important to maintenance of resource balance, may account for the easy spread of grassroots environmentalism in Asia. Chipko's tactic of hugging trees to save them from bulldozers is not new. In seventeenth-century Rajasthan, hundreds of Bishnoi people were slaughtered while clasping trees that were being confiscated by their Maharaja.[54]

Environmental movements have also emerged in other vulnerable mountain areas in India such as the Western Ghats. There the Appiko movement, inspired by Chipko's success, mobilized in response to fungal disease devastation of monocrop eucalyptus planted by the pulp industry after it clearcut native forests.[55] Environmental movements are also strong in the Aravallis and Vindhya mountains and in all of India's tribal belts. In Kerala, there are grassroots protests supported by Catholic clergy against mechanized fishing. In the Doon Valley, at the base of the Himalayas, the Dehradun movement is directed against limestone quarrying, since limestone in fractured form provides the best and largest aquifer for sustaining water resources. Resistance also occurs wherever large dams threaten forest and agricultural land.

Environmental movements are also active in other parts of Asia. In Malaysia, the Sarawaks use massive human barricades to block logging roads, arguing that the timber industry threatens the forest they depend on for food, water, medicine, shelter, and clothing.[56]

Other organized protests share the characteristics of amorphous movements and GRO federations. In the mountainous region of Northern Luzon the Cordillera People's Alliance (CPA) includes an amazing variety of cause oriented tribal movements and GROs. The movement began with twenty-seven Ingorot groups in 1984 and now links more than 120 clans, tribes, and indigenous organizations called *atos*, *dap-ays*, and *ilis* as well as sectoral organizations of farmers, workers, peace pact holders, village elders, the urban poor, women, small-scale miners, youth and student groups, neighborhood captains, and even government employees. All are protesting the adverse impact of hydroelectric dams as well as military and human rights abuses. The CPA is also developing small-scale economic projects, educational programs, relief efforts, and medical clinics. It has ties to other human rights activists and to the Catholic Church.[57]

Movements that are short lived frequently spawn other movements or

---

Exhibit 3.4
Swadhyaya

Swadhyaya is active in hundreds of villages in Majarashtra and Gujarat.
Although the first groups were founded in the 1950s, few outsiders knew
about it until the Centre for Study of Developing Societies in Delhi was invited
to attend an Allahabad gathering of 400,000 grassroots participants from all
over India. Swadhyaya means study of self in Sanskrit, yet has become a kind
of "freemasonry" that encourages villagers to join political parties but not be
used by them. One outside donor waited four years before being given per-
mission to contribute. "What is extraordinary, and somewhat paradoxical, is
that the spiritual overtones in the incentives inspiring the ordinary Swadhyayee
have led to a much greater economic prosperity of the Swadhyayee villages."[58]
Stores have been set up to sell and barter village surpluses and small farms
are staffed by volunteer devotees with profits going to the village as a whole
to buy agricultural implements, for example. Environmental and spiritual
needs are united though trees that become places of worship. Tree-planting
rituals build on the Vedic tradition that trees are a living testament to the
presence of God.

---

formal federations more directly involved in sustainable development.[59] The
tribal movements in India have promoted "impressive economic gains,"
although they face severe marketing problems because of monopolistic practices.[60] Swadhyaya, a regional social movement in India, has become an
informal economic network as well. (See Exhibit 3.4.)

Some Latin American protest networks have also begun to evolve into a
more formal federated pattern, with the need for increased coordination
and representation to the larger society. CIDOB in Bolivia emerged from
tribal protests against outside exploitation for oil, sugar, and cocaine and
became a representative body with delegates. AIDESEP (the Inter-Ethnic
Association for the Development of the Peruvian Jungle), organized as a
protest movement in 1980, unites GROs representing two-thirds of the
300,000 Indians in the Peruvian Amazon.

Because of their origins, the simultaneous need to maintain egalitarian
values while creating more formal organizations appears to be almost taken
for granted by grassroots organizers. AIDESEP, which describes itself as an
arena where groups can share resources and experiences, lobbies for land
titles but refuses capital for development because it says this would create
a potential source of power over local communities. Outside contributions
are instead channeled directly to GROs. AIDESEP has provided training for
the Achuar, a remote tribe, to undertake survey work in preparation for
filing a land claim with the government.[61]

NATIONAL NETWORKS

Many of the GRO networks and movements described thus far have organized themselves into national federations from the bottom up. Regional grassroots networks in Bolivia such as Jatun Pukara and the Association of Wheat Producers (APT) from Cochabamba are exchanging visits and sharing information. In Senegal, a federation in the Kaolack region trades millet and salt for palm oil, dried fish, and honey produced by several federations in the southern part of the country.[62] The National Peasant Movement in the Philippines, founded in 1985, is a coalition of regional peasant networks working on agrarian reform with an estimated individual membership of 1.3 million. It has organized the occupation of 70,000 acres of idle or foreclosed land, and with the passage of land reform legislation has begun to shift to organizing cooperatives.

Other GRO networks were first organized at the national level. The Federation of NGOs of Senegal is a national federation of farmer's associations, not GRSOs. The Kenya National Farmer's Union, with 30,000 individual and 700 GRO members, encourages planting of indigenous tree species and the installation of solar energy and bio-gas on farms. National networks may be particularly vulnerable to political repression, however. Membership in the Chilean National Confederation of Peasant Cooperatives (CAMPOCOOP) declined from 80,000 to 7,000 during the Pinochet era, even though it survived and reorganized itself regionally.[63]

Outside assistance sometimes promotes national organizing. In Ecuador, seventeen regional peasant federations held a national meeting in 1986, with support from the Inter-American Foundation, the Ecuadorean Volunteer Service, and the Department of Compensatory and Out-of-School Education.[64] In Mexico the IAF is supporting the Comision Forestal of the Union de Organizaciones Regionales Campesinas Autonomas (UNORCA) in its efforts to create a national coordinating body of regional and local efforts in marketing, technical assistance, and sustainable forest management. Outside support for international exchanges of GRO networks has also increased (see Volume 2).

SUSTAINABLE DEVELOPMENT: LESSONS LEARNED

1. GRO networks, by providing a built-in mechanism for scaling out, offer a great deal of promise for communicating what actually works, internationally as well as nationally. In addition, participatory evaluations in conjunction with neighboring groups can be a vast improvement over a single GRO evaluating itself, even if it has support from a GRSO.

2. The use of barter by informal economic networks widens local markets and gives the poor their own vested interest in cooperation between communities. Barter also bypasses some of the exploitative aspects of the

money economy and buys time for village industries to grow stronger before they need to compete on an equal footing with the outside world. In Bamba-Tialene, Senegal, the regional committee was founded to dissipate ethnic rivalries between three groups as well as to promote savings and development.[65]

3. Both informal and more-formal economic networks, such as cooperative federations, need outside assistance, yet they must also become strong and autonomous if they are to become institutionally sustainable. Fortunately, "outsiders" are no longer limited to governments or INGOs. GRO networks (both LDA federations and economic networks) are also establishing linkages with existing GRSOs or even setting up their own grassroots support organizations. Even initial government sponsorship can be compatible with increasing autonomy.

4. There is, in addition, evidence that networking per se enhances institutional sustainability. For this reason, GRSOs, international donors, and governments should do more to enhance ties *among* borrower groups rather than focusing exclusively on their own ties with each group. Even donors that assist cooperative federations frequently help them to assist individual member organizations rather than strengthening ties between them. Facilitating contacts among informal economic networks, cooperative federations, and pre-cooperative federations would strengthen this goal.

5. Although IA and LDA federations also need to plan for economic sustainability, their major impact on sustainable development may be through political organizing on issues such as land reform (see Volume 2).

6. IAs focusing on a single development issue can broaden the development agenda. Health and microenterprise development can be combined, for example. Women's organizations and health groups both offer a source of untapped potential for outside assistance on family planning and family health. Networks that increase educational and economic opportunities for women can also have an impact on fertility.

7. Women's networks and even networks that include but are not limited to women can have a major impact on women's empowerment. The Amicale regional federation in Burkina Faso established a modest upper limit on dowries and fines any member who violates the limit.[66]

8. Environmental movements also communicate politically, based on their massive scale and deep commitment. Their understanding of resource deprivation is like a red flag for the rest of the planet. At a time in history when ethnicity is becoming increasingly violent and intolerant, their positive use of ethnic and interethnic bonds is an important strength.

9. Networking also has its costs. Unforeseen side effects can occur, such as a large increase in the demand for water due to increased numbers of vegetable gardens. Products may be produced without sufficient knowledge of the regional or national market, and actions in one village may undermine what happens in another, despite communication between villages. Net-

---

Exhibit 3.5
A Brazilian Neighborhood Movement

The Nova Iguacu neighborhood movement in Brazil represented 120 neighborhood associations by 1985. Yet the 6,000 people who attended meetings
represented only 3 percent of the population of the neighborhoods, and the
government did not respond to the movement's demands. The exhausting
nature of daily survival makes it difficult for people to get to meetings, even
if they can afford the bus fare."...The changes which have occurred are
generally subtle and fragile. In this sense, many analyses of grassroots movements have erred on the side of exaggerating the novelty, strength, and autonomy of grassroots popular movements."[67]

---

working can also take up valuable time and resources. Very rapid growth
can lead to feuding and mistrust. This happened in Senegal between 1976
and 1984, as some small federations acquired as many as 300 member
GROs within a few years.[68]

10. The process of federation should be gradual enough for members to
be able to learn from each other as well as from outsiders. Also important
is the need to train a second generation of leaders. Without this training,
there is a danger that the creative, committed process now occurring in the
Third World will lose momentum.

The terrible conditions, economic constraints, and sheer fatigue under
which most people live have fueled grassroots networking, but they can also
weigh it down, as a study of a Brazilian neighborhood federation summa-
rized in Exhibit 3.5 shows.

Although there is an enormous amount of development activity and institution building bubbling up from below, the right mix and quality of
outside technical assistance and self-reliance is not easy to determine. And
even self-reliance may degenerate into self-serving behavior. One large Senegalese peasant federation is already "generating bureaucrats" according to
Pradervand (1990:171). The content of what should be expanded remains
a serious question, as yet only partially answered. What is undeniable,
however, is that there is now sufficiently varied and innovative evidence
that GRO networks are a cohesive and powerful mechanism for scaling out.
They are in the forefront of understanding the connections between poverty
and environmental degradation if not yet the population issue.

NOTES

1. Lecomte, 1986, p. 21.
2. Segmentary lineage systems may account for the ease with which a farmer's
network among the Tiv in Nigeria has spread.

3. Lopezllera Mendez, 1988a.

4. Rouille D'Orfeuille, 1984.

5. Ibid. In Senegal this support included 51 of 500 villages by 1985.

6. Lutz, 1983; Tutwiler, 1984.

7. Lecomte, 1986; Edel, 1969.

8. See Fisher, 1984; Zambrano, 1989; and Moreira Alves, 1984. Some Brazilian federations combine middle- and lower-class neighborhood groups but do not include *favela* residents, while others are made up solely of *favela* organizations (Mainwaring, 1986:7).

9. IRED, 1987, p. 15; IRED, 1988, p. 6.

10. IRED, 1987a, p. 8; Nyoni, 1987, p. 51; and Jamela, 1990, pp. 21–23.

11. See Smith, Rehnfeldt, and Barbieri, 1988, p. 64.

12. Williams, 1987, p. 27.

13. Grzybowski, 1990.

14. Regional women's peasant groups are active in Mali, Niger, and Burkina Faso as well (IRED, 1988:3).

15. Harvey, 1990, p. 183.

16. Oxfam, 1986b, p. 2; Lara and Morales, 1990.

17. At first COLUFIFA received no foreign funding, but it now obtains help from French and German NGOs. See Pradervand, 1990a, p. 51.

18. Household workers' organizations are organized internationally by the Latin American and Caribbean Household Workers Organizations, founded in 1988. Maria Garcia Castro, Roundtable #40, Association for Women in Development, Washington, D.C., November 17–19, 1989.

19. See IFDA 1987b, p. 68; IFDA 1988, p. 67; Toledo, 1988, p. 69. Fishermen's networks are also active in Malagasay and Reunion. The Asian Cultural Forum on Development has sponsored exchanges between them (IRED, 1988:8).

20. Alliband, 1983; La Forgia, 1985. Carroll (1992:63) notes that health networks of GROs are uncommon in Latin America.

21. Interview with Guillermo Voss of the PADELAI housing organization, Buenos Aires, September 1991.

22. Oxfam, 1984, p. 5.

23. Bray, 1991, pp. 16–17.

24. Carroll, 1992, p. 215.

25. Goff, 1990, p. 21, and Friedmann, 1989, p. 12.

26. Fowraker, 1990, p. 7. In a pan-urban movement such as CONAMUP, there was plenty of room for men to enter later and relegate women organizers to less-responsible roles (Logan, 1990).

27. Discussion with Edtami Mansayagan at the Asia Society, Spring 1991. Mansayagan is the leader of the Filipino Center for Development.

28. Njonkou, 1986; Lopezllera Mendez, 1988, p. 1.

29. Fox and Hernandez, 1989. *Ejidos* are agricultural cooperatives, originally established during the 1930s by President Lázaro Cardenas.

30. Carroll, 1992, p. 26. Carroll calls GRO networks MSOs or member support organizations.

31. Dichter and Zesch, 1989; Ferrin, 1987; Healy, 1987, p. 3; Carroll, 1992, p. 59.

32. Cordoba, Novion, and Sachs, 1987, p. 2; La Gra et al., 1989, p. xiii.

33. Carroll, 1992, p. 235.

34. Carroll, 1992, p. 194. See also Fisher, 1989, on parcelization.

35. Vozza, 1987.

36. Pettit, 1987.

37. Since this passage was written, the Shining Path guerrillas took over and terrorized Villa El Salvador. The habits of cooperation re-emerged, however, after Anibal Guzman, head of the Shining Path, was arrested in 1992.

38. Fisher, 1986.

39. Conversation with S. R. Hiremath, Society for Social Transformation, Asia Society, April 1991.

40. Sawadogo, 1990, p. 66.

41. Reed, 1987. Carroll (1992:89) calls these "Indian governments," but they fit the quasi-governmental/quasi-voluntary character of other LDAs.

42. IRED, 1986a, p. 26.

43. Uphoff, 1986, p. 323.

44. Ahsah Ayisi, 1990, p. 45.

45. IRED, 1988, p. 12; OECD, 1988, p. 43; Pradervand, 1990.

46. Ashoka, 1988, pp. 52–53.

47. Pradervand, 1990b, pp. 38–39.

48. Korten, 1990, p. 85.

49. Sometimes protest movements emerge from GROs, however. During the early 1980s, Rio had a grassroots citywide "Movement against the High Cost of Living," which coordinated activists from neighborhood associations to mobilize people to advocate a price freeze.

50. Santana, 1983; Ritchey Vance, 1991, p. 29.

51. Logan, 1990, p. 155.

52. Horrigan, 1986, p. 14; Aeppel, 1987; and Grzybowski, 1990.

53. Macdonald, 1987.

54. Rush, 1991, p. 55.

55. Shiva, 1986.

56. IRED, 1988, p. 15.

57. IFDA, 1987a, pp. 64–65.

58. Rahnema, 1990, p. 26.

59. An earlier example was the Social Christian Campesino Movement, founded in Honduras in 1963, which led to the development of more recent campesino movements (Inter-Hemispephic Education Resource Center, Honduras, 1988:5). See also Hirschman (1984) on the preservation and conservation of social energy.

60. Eldridge, 1984–85, p. 415.

61. Reed, 1987.

62. IRED, 1988, p. 12; Pradervand, 1990, p. 140.

63. Carroll, 1992, p. 239.

64. Burstein, 1986, p. 49.

65. Pradervand, 1990, p. 85.

66. Ibid., 1990, p. 119. In many countries the high price of dowries effectively binds young brides to their husband's families even if they are abused or exploited.

67. Mainwaring, 1985, pp. 12, 29.

68. Lecomte, 1986, p. 89.

4

Grassroots Support Organizations (GRSOs)

Forgive me! It is first necessary to modify the term NGO. ADRI [Action for Integrated Rural Development] and other similar Rwandan organizations prefer the term OAIB (organization to support base initiatives). It sounds more positive. It better explains what we do, what we are and what we would like to be. It avoids the aberration of having to define ourselves by what we are not.

                                                                Simeon Musengimana

In country after country, the evaluators met people...who were undoubtedly among the best and the brightest that their country, or any country, had to offer—people whose reputations and abilities grew with their years of service.[1]

NGOs work harder than governments, are less menacing than parties, and possess human and financial resources that are scarce among the common people.

                                                                Rubem Cesar Fernandes[2]

Grassroots support organizations work with GROs in communities other than their own and are usually staffed by paid professionals, although they may also use middle-class volunteers.[3] Some GRSOs are membership organizations, but a majority are not. GRSOs generally work with existing GROs or help create new ones. Unlike GROs, which may make profits, GRSOs are nonprofit organizations, although some are developing for-profit fund-raising activities. In contrast to GROs, which grew from traditional organizational roots, GRSOs began to emerge in the 1960s.[4] Despite these distinctions, there is often a fine line between GROs and small, locally based GRSOs.

This chapter begins with a discussion of the causes of GRSO proliferation and proceeds with a rough estimate of their numbers and locations in the Third World and an assessment of the likelihood that this growth will continue. This is followed by a discussion of their numerical impact on beneficiaries. The chapter concludes with an assessment of the role of GRSOs in the broader independent sector as a way of classifying them. The role of GRSOs in the poverty-population-environment crisis will be the subject of Chapter 5.

THE GRSO EXPLOSION: A MACRO VIEW

GRSOs were first organized during the late 1960s and early 1970s.[5] Since then there has been a steady and sometimes explosive growth in their numbers throughout the Third World due to an ample supply of international funding, unemployment among professionals, and the demand for shelter from political repression.

The Role of International Funding

The most obvious reason for the explosive growth in GRSOs is the increased availability of international funding. In India, for example, half of the estimated annual investment in voluntary action (excluding GROs) comes from foreign agencies.[6] Only 5 percent of Rwandan organizations are wholly dependent on internal funding. Zimbabwean organizations raise an average of only 5 percent of their money within the country. There were few GRSOs in Mali until the mid 1980s, when funding led to the creation of "ever-larger numbers" of organizations and the "meteoric rise" in GRSOs "almost totally attributable to AID," with European human rights organizations in distant second place.[7] Smith (1990:238) found that twenty-four of forty-five International NGOs surveyed in Europe, Canada, and the United States supported development in Colombia. All but five funded GRSOs rather than their own field workers.

Because INGOs sometimes create their own counterparts and sometimes fund existing GRSOs, the line between indigenous and foreign organizations is not always clear. A continuum representing increasing autonomy would begin with field offices of INGOs staffed by expatriates and end with the few GRSOs with no foreign support. In between would be counterpart GRSOs primarily linked to one INGO with national staff, the more autonomous GRSOs founded locally who acquire one major donor, and others with several sources of foreign and domestic support. Autonomous GRSOs, in contrast to both INGOs and their counterparts, concentrate their headquarters and field operations in one country.[8] Counterparts should be considered GRSOs, however, because they are part of a general trend towards increased autonomy.

High Unemployment Among Professionals

Unemployment among professionals, which may or may not be combined with political dissent, is a second factor contributing to the emergence of GRSOs in many countries. Hundreds of Indian students, confronted with meager prospects within the governmental, university, and industrial "gerontocracies," dropped out of school or left professional jobs in the 1970s to work on the grassroots level. When the Peruvian military regime laid off 3,000 professionals in 1976–77, a large number of new GRSOs were created. The prior reformist military regime had promoted GROs, providing government professionals with development experience. Laid-off civil servants in Mali and Zaire also created GRSOs.[9]

Political Shade and Political Space

Foreign assistance can also support a third motivating force behind the creation of GRSOs, namely the need for "shade" for political dissidents. The Peace Corps and other North American organizers arriving in Latin America in the mid-1960s brought protection from political oppression with them, although in extreme situations, such as Argentina in the late 1970s, official terrorism inhibited GRSO formation.[10]

This worldwide baby boomer phenomenon has been stronger in Latin America and Asia than Africa, but its remarkable consistency and appropriateness to the challenges of poverty and the failure of politics as usual further fueled its spread.[11] As young intellectuals occupied the political space left open by ineffective or repressive government and weak civil societies, they began to create a new nonpartisan politics, committed to learning from and with people at the grassroots rather than perpetuating past ideologies.

Indonesian GRSOs, for example, were formed by ex-student activists as an alternative to Marxism. Frustrated at the failure of attempts to overthrow the government in 1974 and 1978, many activists decided they needed support from peasants and urban workers. Indian activism emerged from a long tradition of charitable and Gandhian voluntary action but challenged its welfare delivery approach. Brazilian GRSOs were founded by secular and Catholic leftists who challenged "the authoritarian traditions of relations with popular sectors typical not only of the dominant social sectors but also of the traditional left."[12] A Mexican GRSO activist describes the nongovernmental movement as participatory rather than representative, multicentric rather than centralized, local and global rather than national, informal and spontaneous rather than based on blueprints, and committed to simplicity and spirituality rather than unnecessary consumption.[13]

GRSO organizing often accelerates with the overthrow of dictators. One of the earliest examples of this occurred in 1961 in the Dominican Republic. The death of Trujillo led to an "outpouring of civic and social action that eventually led to the establishment of many different kinds of NGOs and community groups."[14] Fifty percent of the ninety-two GRSOs listed in a Uruguayan directory were organized between 1984 and 1986, after the end of the dictatorship, even though there had been an initial organizing surge in the late 1970s.[15] In the Philippines, militant students who had gone underground in the 1970s emerged and began to form GRSOs with the end of the Marcos regime. Returning Brazilian exiles organized hundreds of GRSOs during the 1970s.[16]

Although GRSOs emerged both before and during periods of dictatorship in Asia and Latin America, they have not emerged as consistently under authoritarian regimes in Africa. Under African regimes that range from relatively democratic (Senegal, Mauritius, Botswana, and Zimbabwe) to relatively repressive (Burkina Faso, Rwanda, and Togo) GROs and GRSOs have increased in numbers.[17] Because most African governments have limited abilities to deliver services, GRSOs have filled the gap "by default as much as by design."[18] GRSOs do not generally proliferate under dictatorial regimes with strong service delivery capability and/or control of rural areas such as China, Ethiopia, Vietnam, and Cuba.

Despite the generally similar conditions underlying the growth of GRSOs in the Third World, there is enormous variety in the ways in which they are initially organized. The next section explores their origins.

THE GRSO EXPLOSION: A MICRO VIEW

GRSOs are usually founded by groups of well-educated young intellectuals who often have specific technical experience. Whatever the political and economic mix of individual motivation, a kind of nonideological commitment to becoming deprofessionalized has emerged in Asia, Latin America, and, to some degree, in Africa, that undermines past class, caste, and gender hierarchies.[19] Interactions between professionals and the poor produce enhanced professionalism but also ensure its continuing differentiation from the old professionalism. According to Padron (1986a), Peruvian GRSOs have low staff turnover despite low salaries because of a "commitment to the poor" as well as limited professional opportunities elsewhere.

GRSO founders come from many different professional backgrounds. Vandana Shiva, organizer of the Chipko environmental women's movement in India, was trained as a physicist. Priests founded Aqua Viva in Mali and Populorum Progreso in Ecuador. Archbishop Alvaro Perolla founded a GRSO in Colombia. A hydraulic engineer founded GARY (Groupement Cooperacion D'Artisan Ruraux) in Burkina Faso, and a naval architect founded BRAC in Bangladesh.[20]

Some second-generation organizations break off from parent GRSOs, because of new approaches or interests. Proterra in Peru focuses on environmental legal challenges while its spin-off organization concentrates on agricultural extension.[21] GRSOs may also emerge from professional rebellions within established rural development programs. The Deccan Development Society in India is an outgrowth of a rural development program started by a major industry in Hyderabad. Professionals hired for the project saw the constraints of their institutional framework and wanted to establish a more responsive organization that could incorporate irrigation and social forestry. PROCESS in the Philippines and Solidarite Paysanne in Zaire were originally tied to government agencies. When Solidarite Paysanne achieved autonomy it shifted from assisting officially registered cooperatives to supporting twenty-six village units with regional commissions on water, literacy, and agriculture.[22]

Although some GRSOs are government spin-offs, most GRSOs sponsored by government (sometimes called GONGOs) are not autonomous. Egyptian GRSOs, financially dependent upon the Ministry of Social Affairs, are often staffed by ex-ministry employees. Some Kenyan organizations get more than half of their funding from the government, and in Mali there is a plethora of government sponsored organizations.[23] Autonomy can, nevertheless, be enhanced by government employee membership organizations. In Chiapas, Mexico, a professional membership organization of doctors employed by the government is sponsoring community pharmacies, researching indigenous medicine, and planting "medical gardens" with assistance from UNICEF.[24]

Only a tiny minority of GRSOs are organized by political parties, but party activists often use their experience to found autonomous organizations.[25] Jaya Arunachalam, a founder of the Working Women's Forum in Madras, was a Congress Party organizer who became disillusioned with her party's inability to alter the plight of poor women.[26] Peruvian GRSOs, according to Barrig (1990:382), are "hewn from three quarries; the universities, the political parties of the left and the Catholic militants."

Some INGOs create indigenous counterparts that evolve toward increasing autonomy. A U.S. PVO, Opportunity International, for example, promotes enterprise development organizations with a five-year autonomy plan. Other GRSOs owe their origins to chance meetings between individuals from the Third World and interested Europeans. ASSEFA in Tamil Nadu was founded by a Sri Lankan and an Italian. A Burkinabe sociologist, Bernard Leda Ouedrago, and Bernard Lecomte from Belgium founded the Six S Association in Burkina Faso, with fund-raising located in Geneva.[27]

Not all GRSO organizers come from the educated middle class. The growth of the women's movement, in particular, has led to the employment of social organizers from a wide background. At a workshop for thirty-three women working for ten Pakistani GRSOs in 1985, "One participant was illiterate, some had a few years of schooling, while others had post-graduate degrees ... Almost half of them were the main economic providers for their families and almost all of them ... [were] carrying on their work against tremendous odds, often defying societal norms."[28]

GRSOs, like GROs, are also founded by villagers who leave, obtain an education, and return to provide financial and sometimes technical assistance for village councils. These are particularly common in Africa but also occur in Asia and Latin America. In Tamil Nadu, six young *harijan* (untouchable) women college graduates returned to their village and created a GRSO that has built clinics, trained widows as paraprofessional health workers, and organized a landless association of thousands in five districts. After a landowner raped an eleven-year-old girl, the association's mass protests led to his arrest.[29]

COUNTING GRSOs

In the mid-1980s Van der Heijden (1985:3) estimated that there were between 15,000 and 20,000 GRSOs in Asia, Africa, and Latin America. This figure included 2,500 GRSOs in Latin America. It was also based on 12,000 projects, including INGOs and GRSOs, in Africa, and 30,000 projects in Asia.

All such figures are, of course, extraordinarily speculative. The "birth rates" of organizations are scarce and their "death rates" unavailable. The somewhat more recent figures presented below were not all collected in the same years, and definitions of what constitutes a GRSO or "development NGO" can vary. Whether or not foundations are included may depend on what the term means in each country. In Latin America, GRSOs are often called foundations, whereas in Asia, many foundations are strictly grant-making in their approach and do not get directly involved in grassroots development.

Some estimates and directories include inactive organizations. Strictly charitable associations are not GRSOs, yet there are certainly grey areas in trying to assess the role of a particular organization, and some researchers may have included them. Finally, some estimates include INGOs, and others fail to indicate what the acronym *NGO* includes.

On the other hand, no directories claim to include all organizations in a country. Many organizations providing support to GROs are not as obvious as the typical GRSO. Some of these emerging GRSOs begin as GRO federations and others evolve from other types of organizations. Isolated regional organizations often attract less international publicity and funding.[30] This may shorten their life spans but may also cause them to be overlooked. Regional GRSOs are probably numerous in many countries, according to the directories that take account of them.[31] In areas of Bangladesh neglected by the large GRSOs, the Water Decade Forum uses UNICEF and WHO backing to support a network of regional GRSOs in advancing community

---

Exhibit 4.1
GRSOs in Peru

According to Padron (1988b:14, 27), approximately one-third of 1,000 social benefit organizations are GRSOs. GRSOs exploded in numbers between 1979 and 1982, with a majority being founded by Catholic activists and unemployed technicians who had been part of the reformist military regime of Velasco Alvarado. Then a process of survival of the fittest began, dependent on technical skills and ties to GRO networks and total numbers declined. During 1989 and 1990, numbers again increased, probably due to the continued availability of foreign assistance. (Barrig, 1990)

---

water supply and sanitation.[32] In addition, some large GRSOs have split up and become federations of regionally based organizations, while other national federations have been created from regional GRSOs. Bharat in India was established as a national federation of twelve regional Self-Employed Women's Associations.[33] Finally, the dramatic growth of environmental organizations is only partially reflected in those statistics that are five or more years old. It may be that overestimates and underestimates balance each other out to some degree.

Although the following tables include a range of directories and other estimates and probably give a very rough idea of the general order of magnitude of GRSOs in many countries, they should be used only as a starting point for more careful country-specific research. (See Exhibit 4.1.) In some cases numbers of other types of intermediary nonprofits (mostly charities) are included to provide a sense of the larger independent sector, and of the comparative numbers of GRSOs and other nonprofits in one listing or directory.

Latin America

Tables 4.1 and 4.2 list estimates from Latin America and the Caribbean. By adding the totals (using the average figures—where there is some disagreement within one year) the total number of GRSOs in these countries is probably over 5,500. Since many of these figures are now five years old, it is difficult to estimate how accurate they are, to say nothing of the varying definitions used. I have found no figures on Surinam, Guyana, Cuba, or the remaining Caribbean island nations, but it seems likely that they have several hundred more, and 6,000 may be a good estimate.

Africa

Table 4.3 presents the figures for Africa. The figures available for Africa should be viewed with particular caution. The UNDP directory, unlike most

Table 4.1
Intermediary Nonprofit Organizations: South America

Country	Publication/ Reference Dates	Source	Total # Orgs.	GRSOs	INGOs	Other Nonprofit Organizations	Notes
Argentina	1989	GADIS	115				Sources exclude 1,200 foundations, many of which are involved in grassroots support (Thompson, 1990, 1992).
	1992	World Bank	161	153	5	3	
Bolivia	1985	Schneider	227				
	1990	Bebbington		385			
Brazil	1988	Landim		1,208			Landim estimates that there are at least twenty percent more GRSOs than are listed.
Chile	1983	Vio Grossi	100+				Thompson lists 500 GRSOs, 75 "church NGOs," 69 "research centers," and 102 "environmental NGOs."
	1992	Thompson		700+			
Colombia	1985	Schneider	200				The CIDESAL directory lists over 5,000 nonprofit organizations, including charities, chambers of commerce, GROs, GRSOs, etc. Roughly one in six is a GRSO. Ritchey-Vance, of the IAF, estimates that the correct figure is considerably higher. *
	1990	CIDESAL (est)		1,000+			
Ecuador	1985	Schneider	300				
Paraguay	1990	CIRD (est)		78			The directory lists 300 nonprofits of all types.
Peru	1988b	Padron		350			See box in text.
	1990	Diaz Albertini		400			
Uruguay	1990	Barreiro & Cruz	92	72	5	15	
Venezuela	1992		107				Interview with Christopher Hennin, World Bank.

* Interview with Marion Ritchey Vance, August 12, 1991.

Table 4.2
Intermediary Nonprofit Organizations: Central America, Mexico and the Caribbean

Country	Publication/ Reference Dates	Source	Total # Orgs.	GRSOs	INGOs	Other Nonprofit Organizations	Notes
Belize	1989	CNIRD	11				
Costa Rica	1986	CINDE		50 (est)			
	1992	World Bank	130	105	25		
Dominica	1989-90	CNIRD & OAS (est)		12			
Dominican Republic	1986-88	CEDOIS	119	70			This is only a partial listing of Dominican GRSOs.
El Salvador	1988-92	Est. from: Interhemispheric Resource Directory, El Salvador; Partners of the Americas; World Bank		26			
Grenada	1989	CNIRD		12			
Guatemala	1988	Ganuza		200+			There has been a burst of GRSO development since 1985, when the military dictatorship ended. FUNDESA estimates the total to be 400, including some GROs.
Haiti	1990	IAF	74				Members of the Haitian Association of Voluntary Associations only.
Honduras	1988	Est. from: Interhemispheric Resource Directory, Partners of the Americas.		58			
	1992	World Bank	95	70	22	3	

Table 4.2 *(continued)*

Country	Publication/ Reference Dates	Source	Total # Orgs.	GRSOs	INGOs	Other Nonprofit Organizations	Notes
Jamaica	1987-89	Est. from: Council of Voluntary Services, Partners of the Americas, CNIRD		21			The CVS directory lists 168 mostly charitable organizations. This established charitable sector may have partially precluded the rise of GRSOs.
Mexico	1988-90	Est. from: Lopezllera Mendez, CMIF		460+		400+	
Nicaragua	1988	Lopezllera Mendez	12				
Panama	1992		31				Interview with Christopher Hennin, World Bank. Eleven of eighteen environmental organizations are also GRSOs (Partners of the Americas, 1988).
St. Lucia	1989	CNIRD	8				
	1990	IAF	17				
St. Vincent & The Grenadines	1989	CNIRD	13				
Trinidad & Tobago	1990-92	Est. from: CNIRD & World Bank	19				

84

Table 4.3
Intermediary Nonprofit Organizations: Africa

Country	Publication/ Reference Dates	Source	Total # Orgs.	GRSOs	INGOs	Other Nonprofit Organizations	Notes
Angola	1992	UNDP	31	9	8	14	
Benin	1992	UNDP	113	78	16	19	
Burkina Faso	1992/1985	Atang	87				
	1992	UNDP	131	41	76	14	
Burundi	1992	UNDP	18	3	13	2	
Cameroon	1985	Schneider	12				
	1992/1989	Atang	52				
	1992	UNDP	45	27	15	3	
Cape Verde	1992	UNDP	30	10	1	19	
Central African Republic	1992/1988	Atang	25				
	1992	UNDP	34	16	12	6	
Congo	1992	UNDP	44	37	2	5	
Ethiopia	1992/1988	Atang	60				
	1992	UNDP	68	12	53	3	
Gabon	1992	UNDP	5	2	2	1	
Gambia	1992	UNDP	38	19	18	1	

Table 4.3 *(continued)*

Country	Publication/ Reference Dates	Source	Total # Orgs.	GRSOs	INGOs	Other Nonprofit Organizations	Notes
Ghana	1988	UN	50				
	1992	UNDP	111	88	14	9	
Guinea	1992	UNDP	69	31	30	8	
Guinea Bissau	1991	Handem		6			Handem (1991;11) writes that "many others are in formative stages".
	1992	UNDP	37	1	33	3	
Ivory Coast	1992	UNDP	48	34	11	3	
Kenya	1985	Schneider	370				
	1988	UN	430				
	1992/1987	Atang	400				
	1992	UNDP	208	85/115	80	15/45	
	1992/1990	UNDP		130			
Lesotho	1992/1988	Atang	121				
	1992	UNDP	64	20/30	10		
Liberia	1992	UNDP	41	15/33	5	3/18	
Malawi	1992	UNDP	23	5	9	7	
Mali	1992	UNDP	120	46	67	7	

Madagascar, Comoros, Mauritius, Reunion & Seychelles	1989c	IFDA	114			This figure is the number of members in an informal network that includes some individuals.
Mauritius	1992	UNDP	48	30		18 Mauritius is also included in above data.
Mauritania	1992	UNDP	9	4	5	
Mozambique	1991	Clark	120			
	1992	UNDP	27	6	6	13
Namibia	1992	UNDP	144	58/93	40	9/44
Niger	1992	UNDP	64	22	37	5
Nigeria	1985	Schneider	650			
	1991/1992	Atang	229			
	1992	UNDP	233	167	7	59
Rwanda	1985	UNICEF	133	90/100	30/40	
	1992/1985	Atang	133			
	1988	UN	150			
	1992	UNDP	64	38	20	6
Sao Tome & Principe	1992	UNDP	14	4	7	3

Table 4.3 (continued)

Country	Publication/ Reference Dates	Source	Total # Orgs.	GRSOs	INGOs	Other Nonprofit Organizations	Notes
Senegal	1985	Dieng	50				
	1992/1988	Atang	133				
	1992	UNDP	72	41	26	5	
Sierra Leone	1992	UNDP	35	19	6	10	
Swaziland	1992	UNDP	55	32	10	13	
Tanzania	1992	UNDP	56	34	14	8	
Togo	1985	Schneider	23				
	1992	UNDP	85	50	28	7	
Uganda	1992/1987	Atang	94				
	1992	UNDP	47	17/22	28	7/12	
Zaire	1992/1988	Atang	275				
	1992	UNDP	93	83	7	3	
Zambia	1992	UNDP	49	17	9	23	
Zimbabwe	1992/1987	Atang	80				
	1992	UNDP	121	41	31	49	

other sources, makes it possible to differentiate between GRSOs, INGOs, and charities (defined as purely humanitarian, with no long-term developmental impact) with some accuracy in most countries and with less accuracy in others (Liberia, Kenya, Uganda) where it provides little information beyond the organization's name and address. However, in the case of the larger countries, the UNDP (United Nations Development Program) directory lists far fewer organizations than do other sources. It tends to exclude, for example, many of the organizations listed in a United Nations (1987) environmental directory that are engaged in grassroots support.

The problem with the other estimates, which are probably more accurate than the UNDP totals, is that not all explicitly say whether or not INGOs are included. Atang's (1992) estimate for the ten countries he studied was 1,609, including an estimated 200 INGOs. The UNDP directory, which appears to do a more thorough job listing INGOs than GRSOs, lists approximately 350 INGOs for the ten countries studied by Atang, a figure not too far removed from his.

Atang's (1992) estimate of 4,500–5,000 GRSOs and INGOs in the forty-five countries south of the Sahara seems reasonable. Even the incomplete and inconsistent data in our table add up to over 3,000 NGOs. By extrapolation, we could subtract approximately 20 percent for INGOs and the small number of charities in his estimate, leaving a probable figure of 3,500–4,000 GRSOs south of the Sahara.

GRSO activity seems to be increasing in much of Africa. Consortia of GRSOs have been organized in Gambia, Djibouti, and Somalia, and a small group of organizations works with the World Bank in Burundi. Hospitals and churches are engaged in grassroots support in Malawi, and there is a Malawian version of the Grameen Bank. FAVDO (Forum on Voluntary Development Organizations) for Africa is helping organizations in Zambia set up a consortium. Botswana, Lesotho, and Namibia have active independent sectors, including environmental organizations engaged in grassroots support.[34] Malian GRSOs, spurred by increased foreign funding, have increased in numbers since the mid 1980s. Although most South African NGOs have focused on the political struggle at the community level, their mandate is beginning to broaden to include development. They are also beginning to network with GRSOs from other African countries.[35] On the other hand, some large countries have few GRSOs. Most Ethiopian NGOs are international, and only five of the thirty-two NGOs working in Eastern Sudan were national.[36]

Asia

Available data for Asia are presented in Table 4.4. Even with eleven Asian countries not included, and even assuming there are only 5,000–10,000 GRSOs in the Philippines, there are at least 20,00–25,000 organizations

Table 4.4

Intermediary Nonprofit Organizations: Asia

Country	Publication/ Reference Dates	Source	Total # Orgs.	GRSOs	INGOs	Other Nonprofit Organizations	Notes
Bangladesh	1985	Rahnema		500-600			Rural GRSOs only.
	1989	Durning		1,200			
India	1985	Rahnema		6,000			McCarthy's estimate includes local charities, and can be compared to 20,000 "voluntary service organizations" estimated in 1981. (IIRR, 1981). Durning's figure may have been accurate by the late 1980's.
	1985	Schneider	7,000				
	1989	Durning		12,000			
	1989	McCarthy	100,000				
Indonesia	1985	Schneider	277				McCarthy's estimate is limited to "social activist NGOs."
	1989	McCarthy		1,000			
Nepal	1989	PACT		140			
Philippines	1992	Ledesma & Desena	21,000				Includes charities, environmental organizations and NGO networks, but excludes civic clubs, commercial organizations, and political organizations.
Sri Lanka	1987	AIRD News		100+			Rural GRSOs only.
	1991	IFDA #80	555				Probably includes INGOs, but not charities
Thailand	1985	Tongsawate & Tipps	113				The first two estimates include GRSOs & INGOs.
	1988	CIDA	300				
	1989	PACT		200			

included in the seven countries listed above. GRSOs have proliferated almost as rapidly in Indonesia as in the Philippines, and include environmental, women's, and human rights groups. All three are oriented toward strengthening community groups and are committed to popular participation in decision making. "There is a real NGO community across these boundaries."[37]

It is unlikely that GRSOs in most of the remaining Asian countries would add much to this total. There are few GRSOs in Vietnam, Laos, Papua New Guinea, Hong Kong, Bhutan, or Burma. In Singapore the Community Chest tends to squeeze out other voluntary efforts. Thirty-one Korean foundations sponsor scholarships and academic research, but their social development expenditures are dwarfed by the government.[38] The many citizens' movements organized in Taiwan since the early 1980s have middle-class members and resemble voluntary organizations in developed countries.[39] In China there are few if any GRSOs, but a semiautonomous independent sector is emerging from 75 foundations and social service agencies, 270 scientific associations, and 280,000 informal groups (similar to GROs) that receive government funds. Advocacy groups are rare, except for women's organizations, and a few overseas charities that solicited contributions for African famine victims in 1985. One interesting exception is the China Association for Science and Technology, which has held over 1,000 conferences in ten years and organized dozens of its members to sponsor the Haiana Province Symposium on Large Scale Agricultural Construction and Ecology.[40] Another autonomous research program, The Research Center for Social Development of Contemporary China, is housed at Peking University.[41]

However, there are larger numbers of GRSOs in Pakistan and Malaysia, and 20,000 is a conservative estimate for Asia. If we add this to the estimated total of 6,000 for Latin America and 3,500–4,000 for sub-Saharan Africa, the 15,000–20,000 total estimated by Van der Heidjen in 1985 could safely be increased to 30,000–35,000 as of 1990. If the Philippine figures exclude GROs, then the total figure could be 10,000 more.[42]

Other Countries and Regions with Few GRSOs

As with GROs, the factors propelling the growth of GRSOs do not seem to be operating with much force in the Middle East, partly because opposition or even alternatives to state power tend to be expressed as Islamic fundamentalism. A directory of GRSOs specializing in "Urban Self Reliance," for example, listed twenty-four organizations in Asia, forty-five in Latin America, seven in Africa and only three in the Middle East.[43] Except for International NGOs, assistance at the village level in the Middle East is often religiously oriented and charitable rather than developmental, even where Islam does not dominate. One Lebanese community was ethnically divided between Maronite Christian sponsors of a school and social center, Greek orthodox sponsors of a clinic, and Roman Catholic sponsors of other charitable activities—all for their own members.[44]

This general picture masks considerable variations between countries, however. Christian and Jewish minorities in some countries are active in health, rural development, and education. In Egypt, the largest GRSO is a former Coptic charity and other organizations, although tied to the Ministry of Social Affairs, are active in grassroots support. Some Moslem brotherhood groups provide assistance for their villages of origin and there are some charismatic GRSO leaders who have organized clinics, teacher training institutes, and village water project with the help of urban volunteers.[45] In fact, there are probably hundreds of organizations in Egypt that actually function as GRSOs.[46] Because registration is complicated, some nonprofit organizations are registered as for-profit corporations and are not counted. Nonetheless, the Egyptian government says that 1 million Egyptians are dues-paying members of registered organizations, and 300 of them have memberships of 100 or more.[47]

Jordan has several thousand voluntary organizations that constitute almost a national pastime.[48] Although most of these are traditional charities, younger activists are pushing them in new directions and there are an estimated 400 Jordanian GRSOs.[49] In Lebanon during the 1970s a number of so called "social democratic NGOs" were founded. Some survived the civil war, took care of the homeless, and secured food supplies. "The society was almost run by NGOs," according to El-Baz (1992). Some family planning groups are active, and organizations such as the Najdeh Association work with women in the refugee camps.[50]

The Palestinian independent sector has also grown rapidly in the absence of a Palestinian government. By 1967, there were sixty-eight local charities active in the territories, Gaza town, Jerusalem, Hebron, Ramallah, and Nablus. Today there are hundreds of charitable societies and GRSOs composed of engineers, doctors, and lawyers in Gaza alone, including both membership associations and foundations. Palestinians are disproportionately represented in numbers and in wealth in the total number of foundations in the Arab world established during the last twenty years, according to Ibrahim (1990), and many are taking a leadership role in development. The Palestinian Agricultural Relief Committee, for example, promotes and supports agricultural cooperatives. And in West Jerusalem, there are some nonprofit joint associations of Israelis and Palestinians such as the Alternative Information Center. Jewish voluntary groups also support the Galilee Society for Health and Research organized by a group of Israeli Arab doctors.[51]

By the late 1980s, development was becoming a more central issue in the Middle East, and nongovernmental research centers were publishing position papers on illiteracy, unemployment, democracy and human rights. According to El-Baz (1992:4), charities were moving beyond disaster relief to grassroots support. However, he notes that emerging GRSOs in the Middle East tend to be more subordinate to governments and less internally democratic than GRSOs in other areas. Obviously, this trend was either non-existent or imperceptible under strongly repressive regimes such as those in Syria or Iraq.

In addition to countries left out of GRSO proliferation, there are dramatic regional contrasts within some countries. India has huge numbers of GRSOs, but they are relatively scarce in the northern states of the Punjab, Haryana, and Himachel Pradesh, and no GRSOs worked in the fifty most backward *talukas* of Gujarat as of 1989. Few Indonesian GRSOs are active in northern Sumatra, and few Mexican organizations work in the state of Chihuahua.[52]

CONTINUING PROLIFERATION

Despite regional variations, GRSO proliferation is impressive. The big question is whether GRSO numbers are still increasing, are leveling off, or are actually beginning to decline. There is little evidence to indicate that either the demands creating GRSOs or the supply of foreign assistance are being dramatically curtailed. Determining whether the growth rate is leveling off or continuing to increase is particularly complex, since it clearly varies with national circumstances.

What has happened since 1985? A low-growth scenario would be that the enormous growth in GRSOs that began in the 1970s has leveled off, with birth and death rates beginning to equal each other. A high growth scenario would be that the birth rate of new organizations is continuing to exceed the rate at which organizations fail or become inactive. The evidence available is insufficient to estimate which of these alternatives is most probable, although there is some evidence to support Cernea's (1988:3) contention that "The NGO curve is still rising."

- According to a PACT (1989:30) report "Bangladesh NGOs seem to be proliferating and the number of those receiving foreign funds is also growing" due to a better official climate than in the early 1980s, increased donor funding, rising popular demand, growing unemployment, and a demonstration effect.
- From 1985 to 1990 the number of Indonesian "social associations" registered with the Ministry of Home Affairs increased from 112 to 449.[53]
- According to Ledesma and Decena (1992), 5,000 Philippine NGOs were created in the first three years of Aquino's government.
- Though government positions opened up with the return to democracy in Latin America, GRSOs continued to increase during the 1980s.[54] In Argentina and Brazil hyperinflation reduced the scope of state action, providing additional space for both GRSOs and GROs. The number of GRSOs in Rio de Janeiro increased from thirty-two to sixty-four between 1987 and 1991.[55]

- The stronger Latin American states such as Costa Rica and Mexico are providing greater bargaining incentives for the poor and those working with them, according to Annis (1989:213). Yet in many other countries governmental incapacity and the continued depletion of productive and natural resources by power elites fueled the growth of GRSOs, particularly those interested in the environment.

- According to Atang (1992:8), the upward trend continues in Africa.

Evidence from the Dominican Republic suggests that two related factors have been crucial in assisting GRSOs to expand and create offshoots. The first is a focus on economic development and the provision of credit to low-income groups. The second is an emphasis on human resources and productive skills. Moreover, in the Dominican Republic, "there is a common interest in experimenting with new ideas, a bounty of organizations among the rural and urban poor to test them, and a willingness to share information about what does and does not work."[56]

According to Vetter (1986), three key institutions created after the death of Trujillo were responsible for the vitality and continued expansion of NGOs of all types in the Dominican Republic. In 1979 the Pan American Development Foundation established the Dominican Fund to provide credit and technical assistance to small entrepreneurs. The Fund expanded when the Inter-American Foundation began underwriting commercial banks to increase credit access. Simultaneously, the Dominican Federation of Cooperatives, representing 165 local affiliates and 70,000 people, used $1 million from IAF to set up the Financiera para el Desarrollo y la Cooperacion (FICOOP). Although FICOOP is only one of fifteen such institutions to operate on a nonprofit basis, its status is similar to a commercial bank and it has direct access to the Central Bank and discounted loans as well as to international funds. It weathered a recession both because of these ties and because of its ability to use its national cooperative network to channel credit to small farmers. Finally, the Inter-Institutional Housing Council was formed after the 1979 hurricanes to create new ways of building low-cost housing. Through its activism, two Dominican Foundations, with financial help from the IAF, were able to develop guidelines for managing high levels of trained voluntary labor and to find locally available, sturdy, inexpensive construction materials. These three organizations had a "centrifugal" impact by promoting spinoffs such as a federation of thirty-two tricycle vendor organizations and a "centripetal" impact as Dominican GRSOs increased ties with each other through organizations such as the Centro Dominicano de Organizaciones de Interes Social (CEDOIS). The rapid growth of Dominican NGOs over several decades altered the structures and dialogue of development as networking between GRSOs and with GROs increased institutional sustainability.

THE IMPACT OF GRSOs

The question of how many people benefit from all this activity is perhaps even more arbitrary than the question of how many GRSOs there are in the Third World. Schneider (1985:300) estimates that at least 100 million people benefit from NGOs of all types, 25 million in Latin America, 60 million in Asia, and 12 million in Africa. This estimate is based on the assumption that 10,000 can benefit from one project in Latin America, thousands in Africa, and hundreds of thousands in Asia, because of different population densities.[57]

At first glance it seems unlikely that the *average* number of beneficiaries for 2,500 Latin American GRSOs, for example, is in the tens of thousands, even if the meaning of *beneficiary* is stretched and even if all of the activities of affiliated and unaffiliated GROs are included. However, more-recent evidence supports Schneider's contention. A study of 261 (out of an estimated 400) GRSOs in Guatemala found that although nine of twenty-two provinces had no GRSO headquarters, many of those located in Guatemala City had regional programs covering more than one department and there were over 1,200 programs in the country, well distributed among different regions. Ninety-four GRSOs collectively estimated that they benefited 3.1 million people, *discounting the beneficiaries reached by promoting development and public health over the radio*. Although the smallest organizations claimed as few as 200 beneficiaries, the average number was 38,000. The study therefore estimates that the 400 GRSOs provide services to over 5 million people.[58] Extrapolating the Guatemalan evidence from 400 GRSOs to 30,000 in the Third World, a figure of 375 million is obtained. Since Guatemala's population density is higher than most of Africa and Latin America, if not Asia, *this estimate could be cut by two-thirds*, and it would still support Schneider's estimate.

The massive numbers of people reached by some GRSOs is further confirmation of their overall impact, even if claims are discounted by half.

- The Six S Association in Burkina Faso, Mali, Senegal, and Mauritania is reaching 5 million peasants and their families through 3,000 GROs.

- GRO networks evolving into GRSOs are building large popular bases. The Committee to Fight for the End of Hunger in Senegal (COLUFIFA) has more than 20,000 members.

- In Zimbabwe, ORAP (The Organization of Rural Associations for Progress) builds on GRO organizing to reach 60,000 people.

- A survey of only thirty GRSOs in Bangladesh showed that they employed over 7,000 workers and serve over 10 percent of the rural population. Ten of those surveyed assisted over 50,000 people each. BRAC, the largest Bangladesh GRSO, with a staff of 3,600, is working with 4,356 GROs in 2,225 villages and has provided oral rehydration training for 11 million households.[59]

- As of 1990, the Grameen Bank had 763 branches, disbursed $7 million per month, and had 830,406 shareholders or members from 18,887 villages. Repayment rates are 98 percent.
- Seva Sangh Samiti, founded in 1966 in Calcutta, has developed a vast irrigation plan, sponsors twelve schools, wells, health posts, and estimates that 100,000 people benefit in Amta, Jikhira, Bankhurau, and Barakpore.
- Working Women's Forum has become a chain reaching from the grassroots into a national movement-union of over 100,000 workers in three southern states of India.
- The Mexican Foundation for Rural Development provides loans to over 13,000 peasants per year through 300 professionals located in 36 development centers.[60]

Of course, with the world's population projected to double by the year 2050, all such estimates are becoming relatively less important. While beneficiaries per GRSO may increase with increasing population density, the benefits received will be increasingly diluted as the poor are forced to consume the environment. Bangladesh today, with a dense population of 106 million, provides a preview of the enormous stakes involved. GRSOs that provide credit, including 400 (of the 763) branches of the Grameen Bank, have made Herculean efforts to reach an estimated 6 percent of the population below the poverty line.[61] Health and family planning GRSOs already work in 13,000 of 80,000 officially recognized villages, yet unless government, GRSOs, and INGOs vastly extend their reach, educate women, and promote family planning, other development efforts will fail to impact poverty and protect the environment and will only delay the inevitable catastrophe.

The urgent need for governments and INGOs to focus on this "problem of problems" is matched by an unparalleled opportunity to build on the remarkably consistent proliferation of GRSOs throughout the Third World. The next section explores some equally consistent ways of classifying them. Yet GRSOs also vary in functions and membership, and some carry out member-serving activities as well as grassroots support. The final section of this chapter explores this variety within an overall look at the independent sector. Chapter 5 focuses on the role of GRSOs in meeting the poverty-environment-population crisis in the Third World.

CLASSIFYING GRSOs: BY ORIGIN AND PURPOSE

GRSOs can be divided into two groups—those founded by outsiders who enter a community to support GROs and their networks and those that grow out of local communities through migrants returning to their villages or GRO federations creating their own GRSOs. There is only a fine evolutionary line between horizontal networking and assisting oneself by hiring outsiders. Yet the original culture of an organization often defines its purposes, whether it emerged from a GRO network, was created by dissident university students, or was founded by refugees from a government bureaucracy.

GRSOs can also be classified as those that mainly provide services (clinics, agricultural extension) and those organizing the poor and promoting social change. Except for cooperative federations, GRSOs created from below are less likely than those with top-down origins to concentrate exclusively on service provision. However, the converse does not hold true, for many GRSOs created from above promote empowerment or organize against injustice and inequality.

Organizations that provide credit while empowering people to bypass moneylenders or protect small farmers from large landholders while helping them increase production are promoting both development and social change. Proterra in Peru has "completely changed agricultural production in the Lurin Valley" but also works on land tenure laws at the national level.[62] Jopage in Zaire is self-financing, owns a mill, and sells agricultural products while battling price speculation by the customary chiefs. Empowerment, or what Carroll (1992) calls "capacity building," ties development services to social change. Related to these dual roles is the pride that GRSOs often take in providing a third alternative to either capitalism or socialism. Adi Sasono in Jakarta is building a national cooperative network for street vendors, scavengers, and prostitutes into a profitable economic movement.[63]

Not all GRSOs are what they appear to be, of course. Some, are headed by outright charlatans who exploit the availability of foreign funding. In Zaire, a fictitious village group was promoted by a former minister for his own gain. Victor Hugo Cardenas, of the Confederation of Peasant Farmers in Bolivia argues that "Bolivian NGOs...reproduce the behavior of the conquistadors vis à vis the peasant associations."[64] There are also less blatant attempts to promote the fortunes of favored groups. Patron-client ties diluted the effectiveness of a GRSO federation in Senegal and its member organizations.[65] "Planter NGOs" in the Philippine island of Negros help preserve an inequitable land tenure system while extending social welfare measures.[66] In Latin America, "there is a long and unhappy history...of national NGOs taking over or diverting for other purposes funds allocated to women's projects.[67] Most Arab NGOs, according to El Baz (1992:10), are not internally democratic, and a study of twelve Indian GRSOs found only one that was serious about participation.[68]

Other GRSOs are honest service providers who sell their technical services to foreign donors or governments in the absence of strong grassroots linkages. Korten (1990:102) distinguishes between "voluntary organizations" (GRSOs) and "public service contractors" in terms of their choice between social mission and market share and notes that there is "pressure on VOs to become PSCs." Yet if grassroots organizing and a clear sense of purpose *precede* donor or government contacts, then hybrids between the two categories can retain their autonomy and commitment to empowerment. (See Volume 2, Chapter 3.)

In fact, most observers believe that GRSOs committed to empowerment vastly outnumber corrupt organizations, if not service contractors.[69] Moen's intensive (1991:96) study of GRSOs in Tamil Nadu concludes that challenging local power structures is difficult, that GRSOs are often hierarchically organized, but that corruption is not widespread. Corruption was "extremely rare" in the nineteen-country Club of Rome study, and according to Schneider (1985:188–197) "We found attention to the poor almost everywhere." Latin American GRSOs were characterized by Twose (1988:24) as "extremely effective" in reaching the poor and in "helping communities to rediscover ancient collective work practices." Carroll (1992:85, 141) emphasizes their strong code of ethics, their "pervading sense of mission" and their emphasis on "transparencia" or open communication. A sample survey of Thai organizations found that 62 percent gave priority to the least developed area where they were working. Most Indian GRSOs also focus on neglected areas and socioeconomic groups.[70] Moreover, "to focus on the performance and scale of individual VOs (GRSOs) is to risk losing sight of the aggregate phenomena that they represent."[71]

There have also been attempts to classify GRSOs in terms of religion, autonomy, or structure, but formal types evolve over time and are not always tied to functional roles.[72] During the early 1980's Indonesian charities evolved into GRSOs and Indian GRSOs were evolving from service provision to an increased emphasis on empowerment.[73] Although many Colombian GRSOs avoid confronting local power brokers, applied research institutes run by social scientists have educational programs for workers or campesinos and act as policy advocates for these groups.[74] Grassroots support as a functional role can be better illuminated by looking at the independent sector as a whole.

CLASSIFYING GRSOs: WITHIN THE INDEPENDENT SECTOR

A broader look at the independent sector in a typical country can clarify the wide range of organizations potentially involved in sustainable development through support to GROs. Table 2.3 on GROs described only local actors interested in development and covered the governmental and private business sectors as well. Table 4.5 describes only nonprofit organizations, although cooperative or credit union federations have local for-profit member organizations. The table excludes local GROs but includes their regional federations, since these typically support GROs. GRSOs of all types are indicated with a star. The types of nonprofit organizations that may or may not act as grassroots support organizations are indicated by a star in parentheses.

Table 4.5
The Independent Sector in the Third World: Actors at the National and Regional
Levels

| | MEMBERSHIP ORGANIZATIONS | | NONMEMBERSHIP |
	Individual	Umbrella	ORGANIZATIONS
DEVELOPMENT ONLY	Women's GRSOs*	Federations of Women's Organizations*	Research Organizations (*)
		GRO Networks (*)	Foundations (*)
		GRSO Networks(*)	Other GRSOs*
		Development Theatre Networks*	Development Theatres*
DEVELOPMENT AND OTHER ACTIVITIES	Women's Organizations(*)	Federations of Women's Organizations(*)	Foundations(*)
	Human Rights Organizations(*)	National Labor Federations(*)	Charities(*)
	National Professional Organizations(*)	Financial Federations(*)	Hospitals(*)
	Religious Instititutions(*)	Religious Federations(*)	Universities(*)
OTHER ACTIVITIES ONLY			Research Organizations
	Women's Organizations	Federation of Women's Organizations	Foundations
	Human Rights Organizations	National Labor Federations	Charities
	National Professional Organizations	Financial Federations	Hospitals
	Religious Institutions	Religious Federations	Universities
			Arts Organizations

* GRSOs
(*) May or may not be engaged in grassroots support activities.

The vertical axis is divided into organizations that work only on sustainable development (this could include family planning or environmental organizations), those that are involved in development that also carry out other functions, and those that are part of the independent sector but have little or nothing to do with development. Notice that some types of organizations are in more than one box. Some charities, for example, are developing grassroots support activities and others are not. Federations of women's organizations may be more or less focused on development. When they are also carrying out other functions, they may or may not carry out grassroots support activities.

Although GRSOs play a unique role in strengthening democratic decision-making at the grassroots level, the overall institutionalization of the independent sector also promotes democratization. And some groups not engaged in grassroots support may, like GRSOs, have a targeted impact on the process.[75] The Brazilian Bar Association and Brazilian Press Association, linked to portions of the upper and middle class, played a major role in the liberalization of the military regime.[76] In Argentina a middle class women's organization called Conciencia works on "selling democracy" through public debates and meetings.[77]

What is particularly striking, however, is the spread of the idea and practices of grassroots support among vastly different types of organizations. While the small group of professionals that obtains foreign support and then begins to work with one or more GROs is the most typical pattern, other organizations are adding grassroots support to their repertoire without necessarily giving up other functions.

In assessing this complex picture, we begin with individual membership organizations. The most dynamic and numerous of these are women's GRSOs, which, unlike other GRSOs, usually have individual members.

Membership Organizations: Women

The growth of GRSOs concerned with women in development has been the most dramatic component of their overall proliferation. In 1975, eighty NGOs (including INGOs) attended the Mexico City Conference on women. In 1985 in Nairobi, 9,000 participants representing several thousand organizations attended the nongovernmental forum.

The following is only a very partial listing of the dramatic growth of Latin American GRSOs focused on or directed by women:

• There are at least 31 GRSOs in women's programs in Antigua and Barbuda, the Bahamas, Barbados, Dominica, Saint Kitts, Saint Lucia, Saint Vincent, and Trinidad and Tobago.

• There are eleven national women's organizations listed in a Mexican directory, but many others are directed by women.

• In Lima as of 1986 there were seventy GRSOs working with women's GROs.

• 251 out of 1,141 GRSOs (and some charities) in a Brazilian directory focus on working with women. By 1989 there were 444.[78]

Women's GRSOs tend to view themselves as part of a broader grassroots movement with membership extending from local chapters or GROs rather than as a separate support institution. In the Philippines, for example, Katipunan ng Bagong Pilipina has 28,000 rural members for whom it provides educational materials for training and organizing. PILIPINA, another national membership organization of women, provides alternative educational services for grassroots women and promotes legislation that supports women. Samahan ng Kababbailhang Nagkakaisa (SAMAKANA) works with women in urban areas through city chapters.[79]

With few exceptions, such as parts of the Caribbean where charitable approaches still predominate, a majority of women's organizations throughout the Third World are promoting the message that sustainable development will fail without the full involvement of women.[80] The initial shift from "women's projects" involving housekeeping skills or handicrafts to microenterprise development is now being replaced by the broader conviction, based on overwhelming evidence, that declines in infant mortality, increased acceptance of family planning, environmental preservation, and income generation all depend on educating and involving women.

The transition from organizing women to organizing women for development is described by an organizer for The Society for Rural Education and Development of Tamil Nadu:

Women were interested in solving village as well as women's issues...[and] organized to meet the thasildar (a government official) to request a road be built from their village to the drinking well. In the past only men went to...government officials...I was surprised at the way the women questioned the Thasildar and I believe the men too were surprised...when a revenue inspector visited the village to mark the route for a new link road, the men agreed to his proposed sketch. But the women did not agree and wanted it to be redrawn to fit the peoples' needs.

This shift to a central development role for women is strengthened by changes in gender roles that enhance the productive and human potential of men. (See Exhibit 4.2.) The Society for Rural Education and Development began organizing women separately but then shifted to holding both separate and combined meetings to which men were invited.[81] Organizations founded by men are beginning to recognize this. As Andre Eugene Ilboudo, founder of Vive le Paysan in Burkina Faso argues, "Women are very important to our methodology. We have simple ways of communicating this. Development without women is like having ten fingers and only working with five."

Women who direct other kinds of GRSOs also bring this point of view to their work. The Kenya Water for Health Organization (KWAHO) led by Margaret Mwangole, had developed over 100 water related projects for women by 1987. KWAHO is using clinics that include a source of clean water as the initiating point for other development approaches.[82]

GRSOs of all types are directing more programs toward women. In Tamil Nadu, Moen (1991:57–58) found none that focused solely on men. Moen notes, however, that it is as if male development workers are saying India

---

Exhibit 4.2
CIMCA

CIMCA (Capacitacion Integral de la Mujer Campesina) in Bolivia uses pictures
to comfortably allow women to discuss their own lives. They first used older
women as trainers, when men were not allowing their wives to attend. The
"rotofolios" were directed not against men, but against rigid gender roles. As
a result of the training, men are sharing responsibility for gathering firewood.
In Quererani, each office of the local Associacion Familiar Campesina is jointly
filled by husband and wife teams, in harmony with the traditional dualism of
Andean culture. The European Economic Community has asked CIMCA to
train the campesinas in its projects and CARITAS is asking for assistance in
redesigning its own approach. Twenty trainees have been elected to leadership
councils in various provinces of Oruru, where CIMCA has been working.
Four *campesinas* have been elected to offices on the Executive Committee of
the departmental federation representing several hundred thousand small
farmers. (Healy, 1991:26)

---

will be saved by women "in their spare time." Male development workers
have trouble relating to women as professionals, and women professionals
are usually dependent and not assertive. Women's GRSOs such as Unity
for Social Action in Bangladesh are, therefore, training other GRSO staff
in gender relationships.[83]

A strong commitment to research places women's GRSOs on the cutting
edge of change in other respects as well. The Korean Women's Development
Institute, a policy-oriented research organization, does participatory research on such topics as the health status of rural women. The Women's
Development Association of Nepal carries out pilot projects through fourteen branches in sixty-six local communities on income generation, hand-
icapped services, literacy, health, and legal advice.[84]

Women's organizations are also in the forefront of the environmental
movement. In 1986, Lingkog Tao Kalikasan, a "small but feisty" Philippine
GRSO led by Sister Aida Velasquez, set up a Secretariat for an Ecologically
Sound Philippines to address environmental problems affecting women,
farmers, youth, and minorities.[85] The Sudan branch of SOS Sahel International helps women run a nursery program out of their homes, and in some
villages over 90 percent of the women are participating and selling seeds
back to the project. The National Council of Kenyan Women organized the
Greenbelt Movement to assist women in solving environmental problems
and to teach them to distinguish between problems like desertification and
symptoms like famine.[86] Greenbelt has involved more than 80,000 women
and a half-million school children in establishing over a thousand local tree
nurseries and planting more than 10 million trees, with a survival rate of

70–80 percent. Seedlings are provided to groups that prepare land as prescribed. Extensive follow-up is provided through Greenbelt rangers (often physically disabled) who check progress and offer advice.[87]

In addition, the distinction between feminist and women's organizations is beginning to blur in some countries, as middle- and lower-class women define their common interests. The Association of Nicaraguan Women lobbies for legislation to make men financially responsible for their children and provides legal aid for women. In Mauritius, a women's center supported by the Women's Liberation Movement and the Domestic Employees Union holds seminars on women's rights and family planning. The Brazilian women's movement has had a major impact on legislation and on the role of local police departments in protecting women against domestic violence. COFEMINA in Costa Rica specializes in dealing with violence against women, provides direct assistance to victims through peer support groups, and lobbies the government on women's rights.[88] The Awareness Center of New India, an Oxfam partner in Bihar, organized a marriage forum that combats the dowry system, supports intercaste and interfaith marriages, and encourages widows, if they wish, to remarry, despite Hindu taboos.

Yet because some GROs initially reject feminist demands, middle-class women have been pushed to take account of the survival needs of the poor. The Second Latin American Feminist Encounter held in Peru in 1982 prodded Peruvian feminists to establishing ties to poor urban women initially by setting up community kitchens and milk distribution networks. Peru Mujer, one of the organizations that grew out of this movement, promotes urban gardens and training in weaving and marketing as well as legal changes benefitting women in general.[89] Unidad Feminina in Colombia brought upper- and middle-class women's organizations together to discuss the country's pressing socioeconomic problems. The result was the creation of the Associacion Colombiana de Promocion Artesanal, which has developed a comprehensive strategy for reviving crafts in low-income areas.[90]

Membership Organizations: Professionals

Professional membership organizations that combine grassroots support with member services have a more targeted impact on grassroots empowerment than other middle-class voluntary organizations.[91] The Colombian Association of Medical Faculties was an early lobbyist and supporter of family planning clinics. In Togo, an interprofessional membership organization of 500 craftsmen called GIPATO has organized a vocational and appropriate technology training program with help from the International Labor Organization. In Rosario, Argentina, a group of architects has helped organize housing cooperatives and tree planting.

Doctors have tended to work from within their official positions in hospitals to establish outreach and preventive health care clinics without organizing professional membership GRSOs. Medical students, however, sometimes create GRSOs. Lingap Para Sa Kalusugan Ng Sambayanan (LI-KAS) in the Philippines, founded by a group of young medical students in 1976, has become a leading GRSO on rural health and nutrition in nineteen very poor villages. Lawyers more often work on grassroots support in their spare time. For example:

• In Bangladesh a national association of women lawyers organized a project that traveled to 68,000 villages to teach millions of women (and men) their basic legal rights. They later organized a women's health coalition patterned on an international family planning program and coordinated their efforts with other development agencies.

• The Socio-Legal Aid Research and Training Center organizes women in Northeast India and monitors abuses against the poor.

• There is also an activist association of women lawyers in Uganda.

• In Madaripur, India a group of young lawyers started concentrating on the rights of abandoned women in the late 1970s.

• In Rajasthan lawyers established TALAEC, the Tribal Areas Legal Aid and Entitlement Center.

• A Costa Rican association of attorneys and law students (CEDARENA, Environment and Natural Resources Center) has established a research center on environmental law, and is analyzing legislation for advocacy purposes.

• Other GRSOs concentrate on providing legal assistance to GROs. Servicios Tecnicos Legales Y Economicos (SETELEC) in Honduras, for example, helps GROs become legally registered and provides them with economic and technical assistance.[92]

Not all professional membership organizations are composed of people with advanced degrees: ABACED in Senegal (Association des Bacheliers pour l'Emploi et le Developpement) researches employment for its members and carries out development projects relating to empowerment such as rural credit and literacy projects. Young secondary graduates are chosen as members after an exhaustive interview and probationary period of two to six months, and a one-year field apprenticeship with a GRSO or INGO. Agricultural graduates, for example, are given community development skill training. ABACED views itself as a field university and holds biannual membership retreats, publishes a newsletter, has a reference library, and publishes monographs on development. Members are encouraged to document their experience. The average age of the members is thirty, and thirty members have been placed with other organizations (ABACED, n.d.).

Membership Organizations: Human Rights

The return to democracy in Latin America has redirected social energy formerly invested in human rights into concern about sustainable development. Accion Popular Ecumenica in Argentina, for example, formerly concentrated on human rights but now works with small farmers in the Andean area on self-built housing and health centers. In Brazil, the influence of environmental activists on the women's rights movement has led to increasing concern with providing women with family planning services.[93]

Re-democratization has also democratized the human rights movement itself as protecting the human rights of millions of the poor begins to outweigh earlier concerns about repression against dissident intellectuals. The Centro de Cultura Luiz Freire in Brazil, a network for GRSOs and other public interest groups, supports legal aid for the poor, alternative education programs, and a network of human rights organizations in northeast Brazil to combat landlord exploitation. In India, human rights groups have been moving away from support for opposition political parties and toward support for grassroots movements for some time.[94]

The other side of the coin is that environmental activists in Asia are increasingly concerned about human rights and are committed to the notion that Asia's environment cannot be sustained without sustaining its human communities. This, in turn, requires land tenure reform since Asian environmentalists contend that people are better guardians of natural resources than are governments or large landowners. The Coordinating Council for Human Rights (CCHR) in Bangladesh, organized as a network of human rights, GRSOs, and environmental organizations in 1986, has set up machinery for providing legal aid to environmentally threatened local communities. The Council holds seminars for journalists, and its regional chapters circulate *Human Rights News*. Over 2,000 of its members observed the 1991 parliamentary elections, and it has successfully intervened in land grabs, deforestation, and tribal conflicts as well as police cases involving corruption and eviction from slums.[95]

This broadening and merging of the human rights movement with concern about sustainable development has, if anything, strengthened the international human rights movement. There are now an estimated 4,000–5,000 indigenous human rights organizations, broadly defined to include both human rights and other concerns such as sustainable development. The African human rights movement has grown particularly fast. African human rights organizations have thousands of members, and human rights are preached in schools, pamphlets, and on the radio.[96]

GRO and GRSO Networks

Chapter 3 focused on how GRO networks, organized to enhance horizontal communication, begin to assume some of the functions of GRSOs. Nonprofit organizations at the intermediate level (including GRSOs), also organize consortia or federations in the Third World. These may undertake grassroots support, development but not grassroots support, or other issues.

Exhibit 4.3
Theater in the South Pacific

The Solomon Islands Development Trust calls itself a "learning group" made up of thirty-five mobile teams that conduct village level theater workshops. The Trust also works with environmentalists. "No longer does development focus on economics alone.... Rural people ... enjoy being reminded that it is they who are the nation's major wealth makers through their gardening, fishing, home-making, child-rearing, house making and many of the other normal and natural village works." (IFDA, 1990c:107)

Most GRSO consortia, to be discussed in Chapter 6, are involved only indirectly in grassroots support through their organizational members. However, some consortia also carry out their own grassroots support activities. Labor and financial federations that are involved in development, may or may not be involved in grassroots support. For example, a labor union federation that provides housing loans for its members is involved in development but not necessarily in grassroots support activities.

The most intriguing example of a cross between grassroots support and another issue are development theaters that integrate an artistic pursuit with grassroots training. They are usually composed of volunteer actors and are often grouped into horizontal networks. They have been reported in Zambia, the Philippines, Bolivia, Jamaica, India, Botswana, and the Solomon Islands. (See Exhibit 4.3.) In Kerala during the 1950s an organization called Kerala Sastra Sahitya Parishad began using theater to bring scientific information to villages. By the mid-1980s its annual science for agriculture competition involved 300,000 people.[97] In Botswana the annual theater festival focuses on community development issues. The University of Sierra Leone sponsored a regional workshop on Community Theatre for Integrated Rural Development.[98]

Nonmembership Organizations

Development research organizations often evolve into activist GRSOs through community level contacts. Among these are the Asian Development Forum, INADES in the Ivory Coast, and the Centro de Estudios Rurales Andinos in Peru. DESAL, founded in Chile in the early 1960s, was able to obtain European support after it began supporting educational institutes and service centers for GROs. The Brazilian Center of Alternative Technology of Vicos, created by an Ashoka fellow, links rural unions, agricultural colleges, and students to help save and spread traditional but productive agricultural practices. In Argentina, constant military intervention in the universities in the 1970s led to the development of many private research centers with activist programs. An Ashoka fellow in India has organized The House of Science as an intermediary between scientists and grassroots communities.[99]

The commitment to "participatory research" enriched by activism and based on planning and evaluation with potential beneficiaries also leads universities towards grassroots support. Mayan graduates of the western branch of the University of San Carlos in Guatemala organized a network of development organizations and a Mayan research organization called CISMA (Centro de Investigaciones Socioculturales Mayas) that unites local organizations with sophisticated research and computer capabilities. A recent study focused on the development implications of traditional elder's councils.[100]

Although most research organizations are autonomous, there is some tradition of university involvement in grassroots organizing, and even GRSOs attached to public universities seem to be fairly autonomous. Long-established university programs in Asia include the Graduate Volunteer Program in Thailand, the Pakistan Institute for Development, the Indonesian study service movement, and the Extension Service of Silliman University in the Philippines.[101] In Chile there were eighteen development-oriented university research programs as well as thirty independent development research centers as of 1990.[102] In the settlement of Ajusco near Mexico City residents have enlisted the help of university professionals and ecologists in fighting relocation, growing vegetables, planting 5,000 trees, and writing a proposal to the local authorities for a productive ecological settlement including mushroom cultivation, pest control, fish farming, rabbit rearing, and recycling.[103]

Two OECD Directories of Development Research and Training programs underline the importance of universities. In forty-six African countries approximately half of the 431 organizations listed in the directory were based at universities. In twenty-five Latin American countries 243 of 428 were based at universities.[104] (See Exibit 4.4.)

In other cases, a research component may be added by an organization already involved in grassroots development. The Centro de Educacion Tecnologia in Chile set up the Comision de Investigacion en Agricultura Alternativa (CIAL) in 1984 to improve its agricultural research capacity. As of 1987, CIAL was sponsoring 74 development research projects including soil management and crop protection and was heavily involved in networking with university agronomy schools.[105]

Foundations may or may not be involved with development, but those that are often have programs of grassroots support. In Latin America, the term *Fundacion* is often name for GRSOs, which may or may not have an endowed source of funds. Foundations in Latin America have frequently been involved in microenterprise development. In Venezuela, for example,

---

Exhibit 4.4
A University GRSO in Brazil

UNIJUI operates within the state sponsored Ijui University, Rio Grande do Sul and involves 5000 students and 200 professors from twenty disciplines. It receives support from FIDENE (Fundacao de Integracao, Desenvolvimento e Educacao do Noroeste do Estado), which is made up of professors, municipal authorities, churches, other voluntary groups, and labor unions. Local GROs have helped professionals redesign the curriculum as well as provide grassroots assistance. The university is known for the excellence of its rural extension training. Originally founded in 1957, UNIJUI continued throughout the dictatorial period, but with the political opening in 1981, GRSOs developed under its umbrella on topics as diverse as health, agrarian reform, and women. For example, the Department of Finance and Administration provides training for local governments, unions, and cooperatives, and the education department runs a model school for rural teachers. A spinoff is the Regional Development Movement involving cooperatives, governments, business, and unions in regional development planning. (Frantz, 1987; Carroll, 1992:83–84)

---

the Mendoza Foundation sells discounted construction materials and helps neighborhood associations provide housing loans.[106]

Religious Organizations

Religiously inspired GRSOs may be either membership or nonmembership organizations, and they may be single organizations or umbrellas. As of the early 1980s a majority of African GRSOs were tied to churches.[107] A number of dioceses in Kenya are particularly active in sustainable development activities. The Eglise du Christ in Zaire, with 12 million followers, is working in sixty-two communities on health promotion, primary schools, and tree planting. Churches have been active for some time in Niger, Nigeria, and Zimbabwe as well.

Ecumenical umbrella organizations of African churches have also assumed direct grassroots support roles. The United Christian Council of Sierra Leone founded a Commission on Churches in Development in 1979 that holds seminars, offers technical and financial assistance, and cooperates with other GRSOs and INGOs. For example, a fish farming project was carried out in partnership with Heifer International.[108] The Christian Service Committee of the churches in Malawi is active in tree planting, and the Federation of Protestant Women in Zaire focuses on women's nutrition through radio and television. Among the other active umbrellas that function as GRSOs are the Sudan Council of Churches and the Christian Relief and Development Association in Ethiopia.

As securalization proceeds, however, African church umbrellas are also promoting nonreligious GRSOs. The Tototo women's project in Kenya was organized by the National Council of Churches in Kenya in 1963. Despite periodic meeting and reports to NCCK, the director and social worker functioned autonomously, with support and oversight from a volunteer management committee. A Rwandan survey of 124 organizations concluded that although 71 percent had ties to churches, most were secular in orientation.[109]

Religion is also an important organizing force behind GRSOs in Latin America. As early as the 1960s, Vatican II, the inspiration of Pope John XXIII, and the Christian Democratic political movement lead to the creation of both development and human rights organizations. In many countries this organizing process promoted and was itself nourished by thousands of Christian base communities. Yet it also involved the Church hierarchy. In Mexico the hierarchy created the Centro de Estudios y Promocion Social (CEPS), which cooperated with the Fundacion Mexicana para el Desarrollo Rural in establishing thirty regional technical assistance and savings and loan centers.[110] Twenty-four Chilean bishops support church social action agencies, and there are ten to fifteen organizations tied to other churches in Chile. Over one-third of Brazilian and one-sixth of Chilean GRSOs are Catholic in origin.[111]

Since the 1970s, however, religious organizing has been supplemented if not supplanted by the rise of secular GRSOs in Latin America. Religious organizations, including Protestant ones, have increased ties to secular foreign donors. The Oficina de Pastoral Social of the Diocese of Azogues in Ecuador, for example, has ties to International Voluntary Services at U.S. PVO. FUNDCEDI (Fundacion par la Educacion y Desarrollo Integral) in Guatemala, organized by the Calvary Church Association, now has many international donors and no religious ties.[112] In Brazil, secularization proceeded in spite of the continued vitality of Christian base communities. Less than 3 percent of Brazilian organizations are still directly tied to the Catholic Church, although those that are, such as the Pastoral de Favelas, are important.[113]

Despite secularization, however, crises such as the Mexico City earthquake in 1985 have led to the creation of new religiously inspired networks. In Honduras, political killings in the early 1980s resurrected earlier religious organizing. Supporters of liberation theology organized GRSOs, unions, peasant organizations, and an umbrella organization called CONCORDE in the 1960s. With support from CARITAS, Catholic Relief Services, and the Social Communication Division of the Church, CONCORDE sponsored four radio stations and assisted the Federation of Savings and Credit Cooperatives and nine campesino training centers. By the early 1970s the Church began to withdraw support because of CONCORDE's growing ties to militant peasant unions. Ten years later, however, the killing of two

CARITAS workers and the arrival of refugees from El Salvador and Guatemala led to a resurrection by the Church's regional training center of the
leadership training models developed during the 1960–75 period.[114]

Religion is a less consistently important organizing force in Asia, although
religious organizations are active in some countries. In Tamil Nadu, over
half of a sample of thirty-three GRSOs were secular, Christians are active
in Gandhian organizations, and Hindus work for Christian ones.[115] One-
third of a sample of the largest "approved charities" in Sri Lanka in the
early 1980s were religious, and Christian churches began venturing into
social action during the 1960s, spurred by the leadership of the Centre for
Society and Religion (Protestant) and the Catholic Social and Economic
Development Center.[116] Buddhist monks in Sri Lanka "do more ecology
than praying," according to a GRSO activist.[117] And in Thailand, Buddhist
monks have been involved in rural development for some time and are
increasingly involved in tree planting and other environmental activities at
the village level. Indonesian GRSOs such as Lembaga Studi Pembangunan
work through the traditional Islamic Pesantrens. A large environmental
network in Malaysia (SAM) that helps victims of deforestation, over-fishing,
and industrial pollution has recently obtained the support of the Islamic
Youth Movement, a "critical advance," according to Rush (1991:73).

The recent emergence of grassroots support functions within Islamic charities in the Middle East is an addition to previous charitable activities, not
a symptom of secularization. In Egypt there is an extensive Islamic welfare
structure, for example.[118] Coptic Christian organizations in Egypt have also
moved beyond the social welfare orientation. The Zabaleen Association,
set up to assist the extremely poor garbage collectors of Cairo, was founded
by a Coptic priest with help from a local consulting firm, Environmental
Quality International. The garbage collectors have benefited from improved
donkey-cart design and loan programs to start waste recycling.[119]

Other GRSOs have nonreligious philosophies or ideologies, particularly
in Asia. Gandhian organizations in India concentrate on small-scale industries such as shoemaking, weaving, and soap making, although some are
moralistic and cling to antiquated business practices dependent on government subsidy, according to Alliband (1983). Although Christian and Gandhian groups predominated in India in the early 1980s, less-ideological
GRSOs have subsequently increased more rapidly.

Despite national variations and secular trends, the religious and philosophical roots of GRSO activity provide some important organizational
advantages, and religious ties are likely to remain important in every region
of the Third World. Religious organizations in Nepal are more able than
are secular organizations to remain autonomous from the government. In
Chile, COPACHI helped unemployed workers organize microenterprises
despite the political repression of the military junta. Its successor, the Vi-
cariate of Solidarity, decentralized development projects through commu-

nication between local dioceses. In Thailand, the presence of a Buddhist monk means that all labor done or donations of cash or materials can be interpreted as *tham bum* or "merit making."[120] "NGOs are struggling in their reforestation projects, yet the monks have transcended many problematic socio-cultural barriers. . . . The potential of the monks to affect change is enormous; they have the trust and respect of many, the necessary rapport at the village level, and a willingness to learn and immerse themselves in local activities."[121]

SUSTAINABLE DEVELOPMENT: LESSONS LEARNED

This discussion of the proliferation and variety of GRSOs holds some important lessons about their institutional sustainability and, therefore, their potential for implementing sustainable development.

1. The forces fueling the GRSO explosion in the Third World are still important, if altered in form. International funding, if anything, has become more institutionalized, as donors increasingly prefer partnerships with GRSOs to sending expensive expatriate experts to the field and setting up field offices. Unemployment among the highly educated continues, pushed by the expansion of educational opportunities in the Third World since the early 1970s. In spite of a trend toward democracy in many countries, the need for "political space" continues and, as in the past, GRSOs continue to be founded under varied political conditions and by a wide variety of people. In addition, recent statistics support the notion that the GRSO curve is still rising.

2. One of the conclusions of Chapter 2 was that outside donor support focused on grassroots training was a particularly powerful force behind the creation of GROs. The example from the Dominican Republic in this chapter suggests that training and institutional support for productive skills also strengthen GRSOs and leads to networking and organizational spin-offs. Support for sustainable income generation can have a feedback effect on institutional proliferation and sustainability.

3. The numerical impact of GRSOs as well as their total numbers in many countries imply that they are building a vested interest in their work among GRO members. Since vested interests usually sustain *inequitable* institutions for many years, creating vested interests among the poor may be equally sustainable. In addition, most of the organizations with the largest numerical impact on beneficiaries focus on income, the core of vested interests among any group.

4. Despite some exceptions, GRSOs have a generally positive reputation. At the very least they contribute to an overall growth of the independent sector and the strengthening of civil society. At best, they play a more specific role in strengthening democratic decision making at the grassroots level as well.[122]

5. Even more remarkable is the spread of the idea and practice of grassroots support beyond the standard GRSO, founded by a small group of idealistic professionals. GRSOs, in other words, turn up in unexpected places.

- Membership organizations such as ABACED in Senegal are integrating member services with grassroots support.

- Women's membership organizations seem to be particularly suited to integrating middle-class and low-income members. Women's professional organizations are mobilizing vast numbers of highly qualified professionals in some countries. And by liberating women and men from rigid gender roles, they help release human energy and creativity for sustainable development.

- Human rights organizations, building on democratization in some countries, are able to redirect their efforts toward the poor and towards the environmental catastrophes that confront the poor most directly.

- GRSOs are also housed in larger nonprofits such as universities, hospitals, or religious institutions. Religion seems to be lending an organizing power to new GRSOs in some countries, even as established ones become more secular.

- GRO networks are more likely to provide direct support to member GROs, whereas GRSO networks usually provide grassroots support indirectly, through their GRSO members. Where individual GRSOs are weak, however, as in some African countries, GRSO networks may need to provide direct grassroots support. Chapter 6, which focuses on GRSO networks, underlines the notion that networking, while requiring organizing time and effort, pays off in increased interaction, learning, and cooperation.

- In spite of the advantages of membership organizations, autonomous university programs and research institutes not based on membership bring high-level talent to the process of sustainable development, enriched by their contacts with GROs.

6. Still at issue in terms of the sustainability of GRSOs is whether the thousands of remarkable individuals who created them, beginning in the early 1970s, are training others to take their places. Although little research has been done on this question, the ability of a U.S. NGO called Ashoka to find mostly young "public sector entrepreneurs" in the Third World suggests the pool of potential talent is ample. Whether this potential is being sufficiently linked to the middle aged "baby boomers" who created GRSOs all over the world remains to be seen.

Although the major focus of this chapter has been institutional sustainability, GRSOs are placing an increasing emphasis on sustainable economic strategies at the grassroots level. The next chapter explores this focus in more detail and outlines the problems and opportunities in linking it to the environmental and population crises.

NOTES

1. USAID, 1989, p. 12. The section quoted is attributed to Louise White.

2. Translation of Fernandes, 1988, p. 11.

3. See Chapter 6. for a discussion of the use of volunteers.

4. The spread of GRSOs in India grew out of the traditions of humanism and liberalism resulting from the 1942 famine and 1947 partition, according to Sivaramakrishnan (1977:108).

5. For an excellent historical discussion of the forces behind this movement in Colombia beginning in the 1960s, see Ritchy Vance, 1991, pp. 18–23.

6. UNICEF, 1985.

7. De Graaf, 1987, p. 281; Twose, 1987, p. 9.

8. Bratton, 1989, p. 28.

9. Sheth, 1983, p. 14; Padron, 1987, p. 74; Twose, 1987, p. 9; and Kabarhuza, 1990, p. 33.

10. See Reilley, 1989, p. 17; Landim, 1987, p. 32.

11. The term *baby boomer* was used by Kathleen McCarthy (1989).

12. Landim, 1987, p. 34. The value systems of Brazilian GRSOs tied to unions or parties remain independent, according to Landim.

13. Lopezllera Mendez, 1988a, p. 60.

14. Yudelman, 1987, p. 180.

15. Barreiro and Cruz, 1990.

16. Landim (1988a:38) estimates that about 9 percent of GRSOs were created during the 1960s, 35 percent during the 1970s, and 55 percent between 1980 and 1985.

17. Gueneau, 1988.

18. Bratton, 1989, p. 2.

19. This term was first used in Mexico after the 1968 student revolt, when students began working in urban squatter settlements. See Esteva, 1987; Sheth, 1984.

20. Schneider, 1985, p. 183.

21. Carroll, 1992, p. 177.

22. Rouille d'Orfeuille, 1984, IFDA, 1986a, p. 77.

23. Schneider, 1985, and Clark, 1991, p. 81.

24. Lopezllera Mendez, 1988a, p. 132.

25. A Brazilian directory lists 7.7 percent (of over 1,000 GRSOs and charities) tied to political parties. Landim, 1988.

26. Garilao, 1987, p. 114.

27. Schneider, 1985, p. 184.

28. Said Khan, 1987, p. 12.

29. Fatima, 1984, p. 47.

30. In Indonesia, national GRSOs, called BINGOs (Big NGOs) are accused of garnering most of the donor support. (PACT, 1989:65–66).

31. PACT, 1989; Directorio de Instituciones de Chile, 1990:266–289; CINDE, 1986; Bebbington, 1991.

32. The project results contrast favorably with the high-cost tube well projects of the 1970s. (PACT, 1989:12).

33. Zeuli, 1991, p. 82.

34. United Nations, NGLS, 1987a. For a discussion of the activist role of Namibian GRSOs in refugee projects, human rights, and education, see Shaw, 1990, p. 17.

35. Williams, 1991, p. 11.

36. United Nations, NGLS, 1988, p. 39.

37. Prijono, 1990, p. 623. See also Eldridge, 1984 and 1988.

38. Jung, 1990, p. 681. There are some activist environmental organizations in Korea, however, such as the Citizen's Coalition for Economic Justice.

39. Hsiao, 1990, p. 683.

40. Ganmei, 1990, p. 592; Zhang, 1990; Whiting, 1989.

41. Unpublished notes from the World Bank data base, September 17, 1991.

42. Inqueries to Ledesma and Decena about what is included in their estimate have not been answered.

43. Cordoba-Novion and Sachs, 1987.

44. Joseph, 1984, p. 148.

45. Ibrahim, 1990, p. 353; Tendler, 1987.

46. See, for example, Hunt, 1985. EL Baz's (1992) estimate of all registered voluntary organizations in Egypt is 12,000, including charities and registered GROs such as cooperatives.

47. Ibrahim, 1990, p. 355.

48. Discussions with the Middle East Division of Save the Children, September, 1989. El Baz (1992:14) maintains that there are 627 "NGOs" in Jordan, probably including charities.

49. Williams, 1990, p. 31. It is not stated how many of these are charities, however.

50. IFDA, 1991, p. 102.

51. *New York Times*, November 12, 1989, p. 27.

52. Brown and Korten, 1989, p. 32; Gupta, 1990, p. 12; Clark, 1991, p. 47; and Lopezllera Mendez, 1988.

53. Cooperatives, some GRSOs, and organizations founded by governments were excluded. (Prijono, 1990:618). Included were GRSOs such as the Indonesian Family Planning Association and professional federations.

54. In Uruguay, the GRSO growth rate leveled off after increasing explosively when the military was overthrown (Barreiro and Cruz, 1990).

55. Landim, 1992, p. 9.

56. Vetter, 1986 (emphasis added).

57. These figures were based on the estimates on p. 80 and include INGO projects. Atang's (1992:7) calculation of the number of NGOs per million rural population in twelve African countries shows "NGO density" to range from 2.1 in Ethiopia to 93 in Lesotho. However, in a sparsely populated country such as Lesotho, GRSOs probably have far fewer beneficiaries.

58. FUNDESA, 1989, pp. 20–21.

59. Fasle Abed speech, Interaction Forum, May 1989.

60. IRED, 1987c, p. 4; Brundtland Bulletin, 1990a, p. 56; Pradervand, 1990, p. 51; Jamela, 1990, p. 20; Alauddin, n.d.; Khan and Bhasin, 1986, p. 15; Lewis, 1990, p. A25; Grameen Dialogue, 1990:16; Schneider, 1985, pp. 336ff; World Bank, unpublished data base, September 17, 1991.

61. Williams, 1990, p. 32. It is doubtful that including more recently established Grameen branches would increase this by more than 1 to 2 percent.

62. According to Carroll (1992:206), it has recently split into two cooperating organizations.

63. Crossette, 1988:A13.

64. Les Recontres de Cotonou, conference sponsored by the Fondation de France and reported in *Monday Developments*, February 18, 1991.

65. Anheier, 1987b, p. 25. Anheier in a 1992 discussion with the author noted that the more recent "professionalization" of Senegalese GRSOs had diluted their grassroots ties as well as the power of the Marabout patrons.

66. Goertzen, 1991. Josephine Atienzas of the International Institute for Rural Reconstruction notes that GRSOs have proliferated so rapidly in the Philippines since the mid 1980s that a much wider range of organizations is emerging. Interview, June 29, 1992.

67. Yudelman, 1987, p. 182.

68. Cited in Fowler, 1988.

69. Langer, 1985.

70. Tonsawate and Tipps, 1985, p. 54; Muttrega, 1990, p. 11; USAID, 1989, p. 12.

71. Brown and Korten, 1989, p. 21.

72. James, 1982; Smith, 1990; Sheth, 1983; Padron, 1986.

73. Eldridge, 1984–85, and Sheth, 1983, p. 19.

74. Smith, 1990, p. 243.

75. Political parties, generally considered to be part of the government (and opposition) sector, sometimes create GRSOs. See p. 79.

76. Fruhling, 1985, pp. 8, 45.

77. Christian, 1986.

78. OAS, 1990; Lopezllera Mendez, 1988; Barrig, 1990; Fausto, 1988; Landim, 1988, p. 11; and Landim, 1992.

79. Information obtained from a booklet prepared for the International Women and Health Meeting in the Philippines, November 1990, Quezon.

80. OAS, 1990; Council of Voluntary Social Services (Jamaica), 1987. Traditional charities were well developed in some of the former British and French territories. However, some of these charitable women's groups are beginning to address women's rights.

81. Fatima, 1984, p. 47.

82. United Nations, Non-governmental Liaison Service, 1987, p. 36.

83. Ashoka, 1989, p. 141.

84. IWRAW, 1987; PACT, 1989, p. 114.

85. Rush, 1991, p. 80.

86. Pezzullo, 1986, p. 8; Mathai, 1992, pp. 23–25.

87. Postel and Heise, 1988, p. 39.

88. IWRAW, 1987; Jacquette, 1986; Oberg, 1989, p. 33.

89. IFDA, 1987a, pp. 69–70.

90. Goff, 1990.

91. Yet membership organizations such as the Chilean affiliates of the Rotary and Lions clubs, local YMCAs, and YWCAs in some countries, and Scout and Guide organizations also support local communities. (Thompson, 1990:393)

92. Schneider, 1985, p. 178; IFDA, 1989:69–70; Brundtland Bulletin, 1991, p. 34.

93. Reilly, 1990, p. 43; IFDA, 1987a, p. 68.

94. Ashoka, 1986; Sheth, 1983.

95. Gain, 1991; interview with Philip Gain, April 1991.

96. Thoolen, 1990; Peterson, 1991a.

97. McCord and McCord, 1986, p. 64.

98. Malamah-Thomas, 1989, p. 710.

99. Ashoka, 1989, p. 54.

100. C. Smith, 1990: 80–81.

101. Weyers, 1980, p. 232.

102. Thompson, 1990, p. 393.

103. Schteingart, 1986.

104. OECD, 1984; OECD, 1986. GRSOs housed within the departments of public universities, however, should probably not be considered part of the independent sector.

105. FAO/FFHC, 1987, p. 7; CET, 1989.

106. Speech by Luisa Elena Mendoza de Pulido, Interaction Forum, May 8, 1989.

107. Aremo, 1983.

108. United Nations, 1988, p. 35.

109. Leach, McCormack, and Nelson, 1988, p. 3, and UNICEF, 1985.

110. Lopezllera Mendez, 1988a.

111. McCarthy, 1989, p. 25; Thompson, 1990, p. 393.

112. Inter-Hemispheric Education Resource Center, Guatemala, 1988, p. 40.

113. Landim, 1988. Over 5 percent have ties to Protestant churches, 7.7 percent to political parties, and 5.5 percent to universities.

114. Inter-Hemispheric Education Resource Center, Honduras, 1988, p. 5.

115. Moen, 1991.

116. James's (1982) typology of Sri Lankan nongovernmental organizations includes Christian, secular international, local (often Buddhist) such as Sarvodya, which receive foreign funding, and local organizations, such as the Prisoner's Welfare Association, that do not.

117. Interview with A. Lalith de Silva, Chairman of the Environmental Foundation of Sri Lanka, March 1990.

118. Investment companies, set up to handle deposits in accordance with Islamic law, contribute to an extensive welfare system of hospitals, day care centers, and schools. Similar charitable systems exist in Saudi Arabia, Kuwait, Qatar, and the United Arab Emirates. (Ibrahim, 1987:22).

119. Tendler, 1987.

120. Khan and Basin, 1986, p. 15; Fruhling, 1985, pp. 27, 36; Calavan, 1986, p. 96.

121. PACT, 1989, p. 165.

122. For more on democratic decision making, see Julie Fisher, "Is the Iron Law of Oligarchy Rusting Away in the Third World?," forthcoming.

5

Poverty, Environmental Degradation, and Population Growth: The Role of GRSOs

> The Poor will eat up the environment for the sake of survival: we cannot prevent them from doing so.
> Muhammad Yunus, founder of the Grameen Bank[1]

This chapter concentrates on how GRSOs are confronting the three horsemen of the current apocalypse in the Third World. Although increasing poverty, environmental degradation, and population growth are closely interrelated, the directions of causality are complex and multidimensional. Overpopulation leads to deforestation or soil exhaustion, which leads to increasing poverty. Increasing poverty leads to migration to more remote areas where the cycle begins again. Landlessness, an absence of opportunities for women, and a lack of hope that children will survive, on the other hand, provide little incentive for the success of birth control. And environmental destruction by outside interests can increase poverty even if the people and the environment have coexisted for generations.

Whatever their substantive focus and whether or not they specialize or promote integrated development, GRSOs almost always use nonformal adult education.[2] Although nonformal education may include literacy, it most often focuses on some combination of preventive health care, agriculture, and enterprise development. Until the late 1980s, however, training did not often deal with the connections between poverty and environmental deterioration. Although two-thirds of Schneider's (1985) worldwide sample of ninety-three GRSOs focused on food or water, only ten dealt with soil erosion and twenty-three with reforestation.

Since the mid-1980s, rising environmental concern has increasingly been tied to sustainable development, widely defined as ensuring that natural resources will continue to be available for future development efforts. Barraged by the many facets of the environmental crisis—soil erosion, deforestation, water pollution, and toxic waste—GRSOs have adapted and broadened their mission. A wide perusal of recent accounts of GRSO activity reveals a kind of branching out to every conceivable sector related to sustainable development. For example, EQUATIONS in India was established to explore the income producing potential of ecotourism. The Brazilian Association of Canoeing and Ecology (ABRACE) in Amazonia is using canoeing to dramatize the plight of the rainforest and provide preventive health care and medical assistance on its river trips.[3] CEFEMINA (the Feminist Information and Action Center in Costa Rica) promotes self-help housing built around shared courtyards where endangered plant species are grown.[4]

In contrast to the wide variety of information available about organizations focusing on poverty, the environment, or both, information about indigenous health and family planning organizations is scarce and difficult to uncover. My impression, partially confirmed through conversations with population specialists from several international organizations, is that GRSOs specializing in or incorporating family planning and health have not proliferated as rapidly as those active in other fields, even though INGOs such as the International Planned Parenthood Federation (IPPF) have affiliates in many countries. Integrating family planning and health into the broader and more robust general development of GRSOs is therefore crucial to the future of sustainable development.

Although the goal of sustainable development requires GRSO activity across a mind-numbing range of interrelated problems, initial interventions may need to be focused carefully if they are to arrest this downward spiral. Multisectoral strategies have often been too thinly spread, and the spin-off effects emerging from a successful initial intervention are more likely to be sustained than an attempt to do everything from the beginning.[5] Providing women with a cook stove that reduces the time they must spend gathering wood can give them the time to initiate small businesses. It can also have a positive impact on deforestation. Other spin-offs, such as the impact of a family planning program on natural resources, may be long term but are equally important to understand from the beginning.

This chapter begins with a discussion of those organizations that focus on the lack of jobs and income as the fundamental cause of poverty. Next explored is the expansion and potential impact of the environmental movement, and, finally, GRSOs that specialize in or include family planning in grassroots support are studied.

POVERTY: ENTERPRISE DEVELOPMENT

The most widespread form of enterprise development in the Third World is based on the concept of microenterprises, employing up to five people.

Although microenterprises have existed for generations, the provision of credit by outsiders has enabled many very low income people to start small businesses. Loans are guaranteed not by collateral but through a locally based credit or borrowers' group, often smaller in membership than most GROs. What has been called the "minimalist credit" approach to enterprise development is utilized by INGOs, but was really pioneered on a mass basis by such GRSOs as the Grameen Bank in Bangladesh and the Self-Employed Women's Association (SEWA) in Amedabad, India.

The Grameen Bank works with thousands of borrowers' groups through its own network of bankers on bicycles who start at 6:00 A.M. and cover fifteen miles per day. The first two loans go to the poorest members in a group, and no individual gets a loan if one member does not repay. Repayment rates average 98 percent. By December 1986, its 295 branches served 234,343 members, three-fourths of them women. More than 100 branches per year have been added since that time and, as of 1989, more than 400,000 loans averaging $60 each had been extended to purchase tools and livestock.[6] By 1990, as noted in Chapter 4, membership reached over 830,000 in 763 branches.

The Self-Employed Women's Association, founded in 1972, can either be described as a GRSO tied to vendor groups or a trade union for the informal sector. By 1987, it was working with sixty different rural and urban trades in three states with over 50,000 members. SEWA provides credit, has its own bank, and supports a system of cooperatives. It also provides day care and literacy classes for its members. Although SEWA was originally founded to fight the police harassment of street vendors, it has more recently extended its membership to trash collectors and farm laborers. By taking on one trade after another, SEWA was able to work as a broker with established banks before it created its own.[7]

The growth of women's GROs has been intertwined with the spread and success of the microenterprise development movement. SEWA in India, which has only women members, and the Grameen Bank, with a majority of women borrowers, would never have been able to spread their message so rapidly without the high participation and repayment rates of women borrowers. Annapurna Mahila Mandal, founded in Bombay in 1975, organized local groups who prepare the noonday meal for blue-collar workers. Annapurna provides these GROs with assistance on literacy and women's rights as well as access to small loans.[8] There are also many smaller GRSOs that focus on women and have a large impact even though they may not reach the poorest of the poor (see Chapter 7). The Organization for the Development of Women's Enterprise in Honduras, for example, is working in twenty-seven villages, providing women with small loans.[9]

Although the distinction between microenterprises (often based on the family) and small pre-cooperative enterprises of friends or neighbors is not always clear, there is an increasing interest in focusing on jobs and income in a number of countries. A study of ninety-eight GRSOs in Nepal, for example, found that twenty-four were engaged in microenterprise development. In Chile more than sixty GRSOs use this strategy.[10]

In contrast, most GRSOs organized before 1980 provided integrated rural services without much attention to income generation. A recent Latin American study concluded that social development organizations that later added income producing activities did better than GRSOs that had moved in the opposite direction.[11] Many multisectoral GRSOs now promote enterprise development as part of an integrated rural development strategy, and there seems to be a tendency for them to work with larger community based enterprises rather than microentrepreneurs. The Country Women's Association of Nigeria has organized integrated health services and a cooperative food store. But it also provides training in management, rural crafts, and cooperative organizing, and facilitates market links and transportation for member cooperatives. In Mexico, the Fondo Mixto para el Fomento Industrial de Michoacan (FOMICH) directs its research and outreach activities towards clean water, food crops, and the production of solar heaters made with local bricks.[12] It also assists village textile cooperatives, rehabilitating textile machinery, and tying local artisans to research centers at the University of Michoacan.

Fewer GRSOs work with middle-sized cooperatives or other community based enterprises than with microenterprises. Those that do generally provide more than credit and encourage the "scaling up" of economic activity.

• Indonesia: The Institute for Collective Enterprise (LPUB) had assisted 315 cooperative enterprises with both credit and training by 1980.

• Zimbabwe: A Cooperative Self-Finance Scheme leverages coop equity into far larger credit for member cooperatives. According to founder Andrew Nyanthi, an Ashoka Fellow, "If co-ops do not have children they will not survive.[13]

• Guatemala: FUNDAP specializes in highlands wool enterprises and helps select hybrid sheep stock, provides sheep veterinary care, helps develop wool processing and cleaning facilities and works with community members on wool product development and marketing for internal and external markets.[14]

• India: The Institute of Small Enterprises and Development provides consultancy services for the poor, trains entrepreneurs, and keeps a databank on rural industries, decentralization of power, appropriate technology, and agro-processing.

• Philippines: NORLU (Northern Luzon Cooperative Development Center Inc.) in Baguio trains cooperative leaders in finance and promotes trade between cooperatives. NORLU is also creating a databank on labor law, taxation, and cooperative statutes.

• Rwanda: The Center for Cooperative Training and Research provides specialized training for treasurers and assists pre-cooperatives to become cooperatives. During 1987 it assisted seven cooperatives as well as seventy-five pre-cooperatives.

PRADAN (Professional Assistance for Development Action) in India was founded in the early 1970s by a group of young graduates who began

---

Exhibit 5.1
Trickle Up

Trickle Up, a New York–based PVO, which specializes in providing one-time grants of $100 to get small businesses started in the Third World, reports that 646 out of a total of 2,010 of their "volunteer coordinators" were from "local nongovernmental organizations." Even more significant, while representing less than a third of volunteer coordinators, these 646 have promoted 5,522 out of the 10,709 businesses started with Trickle Up funding since 1979. These coordinators were linked to 201,842 out of 292,658 beneficiaries and the businesses they helped nurture had profits of approximately $4 million out of a total of $6 million in profits for the entire Trickle Up program. Trickle Up found that "businesses coordinated by local non-governmental organizations earned profits at least 50% higher on average than any other type" (including governmental volunteers and volunteers from INGOs).[15]

---

assisting other GRSOs in improving both management and technical assistance. Now, with a staff of more than fifty they assist large community-based enterprises in technology, management, and financial skills so that they can become profitable as well as provide jobs. Although PRADAN uses strategies very similar to Technoserve, an INGO, there were few contacts between the two organizations until the late 1980s. Vijay Mahajan, a founder of PRADAN, calls the similarities a case of "parallel evolution."[16]

Other innovative ways of reaching larger numbers of people through enterprise development began to develop in the late 1980s. (See Exhibit 5.1.) Among these were alternative economic networks linking GROs (see Chapter 4). The Cooperative Self-Finance Scheme in Zimbabwe, described above, assists cooperatives in building their own banks. This draws them into a "bracing system independent of government and characterized by rigorous planning and open accountability."[17] In Ecuador, the Corporacion de Estudios Regionales Guayaquil (CERG) believes that too much emphasis in enterprise development has been placed on helping individual producers and not enough on the economies of scale. CERG helps artisan chambers of commerce qualify for commercial bank loans, and promotes trade fairs, catalogs, and fashion shows for joint marketing. It also helps entrepreneurs patent technical advances and make them available to others as well as linking them to factory outlets for raw materials.[18] In Piaui, Brazil's poorest state, CERMO (Manuel Otavio Center for Popular Rural Education) has overcome the classic insularity of model farms by using its agricultural education center to promote grassroots networks that assist local groups with staff, technical, and market leverage.[19]

Development Alternatives in India combines an interest in appropriate technology with enterprise development. (See Exhibit 5.2.)

Exhibit 5.2
Development Alternatives

Development Alternatives (DA) promotes sustainable development through mass deployment of appropriate technologies, thus combining social purpose with the franchise approach of big business. DA generates and improves technologies that poor entrepreneurs can manufacture, package, promote, and sell on a mass scale. They also provide entrepreneurs with high-quality technical and managerial consulting services on scientific and other technically related activities selected to maximize impact on the poorest people, employment, self-reliance, participation, physical and social capital, institutionalization, resource use, and environmental quality. Examples of products include stabilized soil brick machines, paper and board making equipment, efficient cooking stoves, handlooms, solar devices, bio-gas generator kits, food storage bins, multipurpose hand presses, windmills, and integrated village energy systems. Their services are also available to international agencies, government and NGOs of all types for planning sustainable development strategies, environmental impact statements, and management plans and programs.[20]

Despite all this enterprise development activity, two different types of linkages between the formal private sector and the independent sector are still weak in most countries. Economic linkages and ties to the wider market are still tenuous. And philanthropic ties reflecting support for enterprise development are still rare.

Women may participate successfully in a village revolving loan fund and create a group enterprise yet still be unable to walk into a bank and obtain a larger business loan. For their part, GRSOs often fail to get involved in promoting wage employment through strategies that address markets. An analysis of microenterprise development projects in Zimbabwe concluded that both INGOs and GRSOs concentrate on their own small projects, and have a "naive optimism" about market forces in relation to microenterprises, with few ties to the private sector.[21] Innovations are needed, such as self-contracting by GROs to promote labor-intensive development or increased local opportunities for nonfarm employment.[22]

Some Latin American GRSOs with access to "critical aspects of the agribusiness system" are successfully promoting agricultural diversification, however. Uniao Nordestina de Asistencia Tecnica (UNO) in Brazil links rural and urban enterprises. UNIDAD in Ecuador supports communally owned bakeries to expand nonfarm employment.[23] CIDE in Chile is helping urban microentrepreneurs learn to approach and build linkages with major factories through simulation games.[24] Tendler (1987) also found that "better-performing" organizations such as SEWA, conscious of market forces, deliberately started with beneficiaries already producing a marketable product that was not subject to competition from large-scale capital intensive industries. Their supplies of inputs were insured, sales markets were in place, and their services were in scarce supply, with high social value. They often had support from powerful consumers and were involved in traditional collective tasks, requiring work of an on-going nature.

The business sector's relatively weak support of poverty-focused enterprise development in most countries may reflect weak philanthropic traditions or the fear that cooperatives could become potential competitors. Exceptions to this general pattern include the business-backed Carvajal Foundation of Colombia, a linchpin in microenterprise development. In India, liberal tax deductions introduced during the 1970s promoted the formation of business charities. The Tata industries have adopted over thirty villages in Poona and Jamshedpur and supported development projects including crafts production and agricultural development as well as social services.[25] Nigeria Shell Petroleum Development Company helped set up a GRSO in Imo state that became independent of the company. The Fundacion Mexicana para el Desarrollo Rural has corporate backing for its support of microenterprises and cooperatives.

Business leaders have also been extremely active in the Philippines. Philippine Business for Social Progress, the Bishops Businessmen's Conference, and the Association of Foundations are all active in grassroots support activities. An Asian Institute of Management Survey concluded that 60 percent of a random sample of businesses had community involvement programs, including social services such as housing, health, or education. Although contributions averaged less than 4 percent of net profits before taxes, they often leveraged foreign donor funds as well. Trends in assistance included more emphasis on long-term development, partnerships with other GRSOs and government, employee volunteer programs, and an increasing number of company foundations.[26]

ENVIRONMENTAL ORGANIZATIONS

Can ash into wood return?
Be careful, then
How much you burn.

John Conover

The status of NGOs has never been higher. NGO activity throughout the world continues to live up to this judgement, displaying remarkable growth and intensification as international interests surrounding ECO '92 grow sharper.[27]

At first we were like the Sierra Club, we sued the wildlife director to keep the boundaries of the reserve intact. We didn't understand the poverty issue that caused the poor to invade the wildlife reserves. Now

we litigate after we have developed concrete alternative proposals with
economic potential for the poor.

A. Lalith M. de Silva,
Environmental Foundation of Sri Lanka

   Although the environmental movement has been growing throughout the
Third World, environmentalists began organizing as early as the 1970s in
Asia. In Indonesia there are an estimated 600 organizations involved in
environmental protection. Most of those listed in a directory published by
WAHLI, an environmental network, are increasingly engaged in grassroots
support activities that attack poverty as well as environmental decline.[28]
There are 170 environmental organizations in Sri Lanka, and the National
NGO Council of Sri Lanka has eight groups of member organizations in
watchdog roles over coastal belt, rivers, inland waters, forests, soil, control
of herbicides and pesticides, urban environment, and waste management.[29]
Friends of the Rainforest for Tropical Wilderness Campaign in the Philippines has more than 10,000 members, including students, young professionals, farmers, and women working on everything from green manuring
to herbal pesticides to tree planting. Funds come from the sale of old newspapers, aluminum cans, bottles, and seedlings.[30] Proshika in Bangladesh is
encouraging the rediscovery of traditional crop rotations and intercropping
of rice, vegetables, and fruit trees while using popular theater to show people
why the forest is receding.
   In India, there were over 500 environmental organizations as of 1990,
many of which were GRSOs. They range in size from the Jamboji Silvicul-
tural League in Tamil Nadu that uses sixty volunteers to plant trees and
promote wildlife conservation to the World Wide Fund for Nature with
branches in every state and a big headquarters in New Delhi. Although
groups such as the popular science movement began organizing during the
late 1960s, 80 percent of Indian environmental organizations were founded
after 1970 and more than half after 1980. The Vikram Sarabhai Centre for
Development Interaction (VIKSAT) has trained many thousands of farmers
in Gujarat in tree planting and soil and water conservation and has promoted
the creation of 70 tree growing cooperatives. Samaj Parivartana Samudaya
(SDS) in Karnataka led villagers in a "pluck and plant" demonstration after
Karnataka Wood Pulp Ltd. seized common lands of the village. The villagers
plucked the company's eucalyptus saplings and planted fruit and fodder
trees.[31]
   There are fewer estimates of the numbers of environmental organizations
in Latin America, even though their numbers have also expanded. Two
directories that cover Latin America together list 57 environmental organizations in the Caribbean, 57 in Central America, 38 in Mexico, and 121
in South America, excluding university research programs. A high propor-

tion of these are engaged in grassroots support and sustainable development activities (30 in the Caribbean, 13 in Central America, 5 in Mexico, and 43 in South America).

These two directories give only a very partial picture, however, and tend to exclude hundreds of development organizations that have taken on environmental activities.[32] CENDA in Bolivia, for example, began with assistance to a Quechua and Spanish bilingual newspaper and radio station in an extremely poor, isolated area called Raqaypampa, and has expanded into many other activities, including reforestation.[33] A Peruvian environmental directory lists seventy-two organizations, almost all of which, with the exception of a few like the zoo, are involved in sustainable development and grassroots support.[34] RENACE, the National Ecological Action Network in Chile, had 110 members by 1992, most of whom were GRSOs. Chile also has a Non-governmental Environmental Education Network.[35] A Brazilian government survey concluded that there were over 500 environmental organizations in Brazil. However, because Brazilian environmental organizations are also involved with many issues such as electoral reform and the Annual Encounter of Alternative [Economic] Communities, the environmental movement is complex, growing, and difficult to assess. There are Green parties in some states and there is conflict among socialist, capitalist, and "realist" environmentalists.[36]

Latin American GRO networks are also merging their developmental and environmental concerns. AIDESEP in eastern Peru, for example, promotes traditional crops with raised-bed infiltration ditch production, interplanted with nitrogen-fixing trees to enrich soil, and aromatic flowers to repel insects. These are surrounded by a mixed-species tree plantation that provides leaf litter and crop yields during the dry season.[37]

Recent information on Africa is more difficult to obtain, but in 1987 the Environmental Liaison Center in Kenya was in "regular contact" with some 10,000 research organizations, technical institutes, universities, and other organizations, 1,700 of which were in Africa and 3,300 in other parts of the Third World.[38] These figures obviously include many government, international, and pure research organizations as well as GRSOs. However, there are signs that the nongovernmental environmental movement has grown since then. Mauritius, for example, has enough environmental organizations to have an environmental network.[39]

As in Asia and Latin America, the environmental movement in Africa increasingly encompasses GRSOs that formerly concentrated on development, more narrowly defined. In Senegal, with help from the Six S Association, the local Naams organizations in six villages have built a large dam and a number of caged rock check dams to trap drinking and irrigation water and slow soil erosion. The Naams also pile stones in long rows along contours to hold back rainwater runoff and increase yields.[40] The Islamic African Relief Agency in Sudan has planted the first Research and Investment

Forest of 17,000 seedlings to demonstrate that reforestation can be prof-itable.[41] In Zimbabwe, the Women's Institute is actively promoting forestry to raise the standard of living for their 1,000 local groups and the Asso-ciation of Women's Clubs, with 200 member organizations, has received funding to hire a full-time forester and program coordinator.[42]

GRSOs that focus on legal rights are increasingly involved in the envi-ronmental movement throughout the Third World. The Peruvian Society for Environmental Rights lobbies the Congress, undertakes research and legal action in defense of environmental legislation, and provides mediation services for environmental controversies involving local communities.[43] The Consumer's Association of Penang (CAP) in Malaysia works with rural communities, handles complaints, and has established grassroots consumer societies in fifty schools that are linked to its legal center by newsletter.[44] Kuala Juru, a fishing village, was nearly destroyed economically when nearby factories discharged poisonous effluents. CAP helped the villagers publicize and get official action against the problem after local youth col-lected water samples that were then analyzed by university scientists. CAP and an environmental organization, Sahabat Alam Malaysia (SAM), got the Ipoh High Court to award an interim injunction to the people of Bukit Merah to stop a factory from producing and storing thorium hydroxide, a radioactive substance.[45]

Although awareness of the need for sustainable development was boosted by the publicity surrounding the Brundtland Commission (1987) findings, many of the practical techniques leading to both development and environ-mental preservation were invented and promoted in the 1970s, when de-velopment specialists and journalists began to write about the need for "appropriate," "alternative," or "intermediate" technologies for the Third World.[46] By the early 1970s a reaction had already set in against the costly, environmentally damaging technologies often espoused by big development agencies. Although there is now more recognition that modern technologies are not necessarily damaging to the environment and that each case should be judged individually, the appropriate technology centers founded during the period as well as the international networks that link them are another important institutional resource for sustainable development.[47]

Most appropriate technology research centers belong to the independent sector, and many are GRSOs as well. Among these are the Appropriate Technology Development Association in Lucknow, India, the Technology Consulting Center in Ghana, CAMERTEC (Center for Agricultural Mech-anization and Rural Technology) in Tanzania, Dian Desa in Indonesia, and CEMAT in Guatemala, an affiliate of Appropriate Technology Interna-tional.[48] The African Center for Technology Studies, established in 1982 in Kenya, researches and experiments with technologies through different kinds of local institutions. It also identifies policy options and works closely with the government. In Nepal, the Centre for Rural Technology works on sustainable agriculture, renewable energy, ecology, and rural housing through participatory action research.[49] The Commission for Research into Alternative Agriculture in Chile is composed of academics who study the problems of the poor.[50]

The range of technologies developed by these centers is extremely broad. The Salvadoran Center for Appropriate Technology runs a school for bicycle mechanics and is promoting microenterprises to produce and repair bicycles. Ricardo Navarro, the director, has coauthored a book integrating bicycle development into development planning and on developing a bicycle industry in Latin America. In Zaire, CADIC (Le Collectif d'Actions pour le Developpement Communautaire et Industriel) is assisting cooperatives with appropriate technologies relating to water, energy, agriculture, animal health, rural education, and brick and tile production.[51] Other sustainable development innovations might be called new ideas rather than new technologies. Anisuzzaman Khan, a trained wildlife biologist and Ashoka Fellow, is working with the Nature Conservation Movement in Bangladesh to train an endangered species of otter to chase fish into fishing nets, thereby transforming a pest into an economic ally.[52] Other GRSOs have resurrected sustainable traditional technologies such as Asian rice-fish farming that combines insect control with an additional protein supply.

GRSOs that focus on environmentally appropriate technologies are particularly numerous and well established in Latin America:

- Ecuador: The Fundacion Ecuatoriana de Tecnologia Apropriada works on biogas, rural housing, and small hydraulic turbines. The Centro Andino de Accion Popular (CAAP) in Quito focuses on traditional medicine, rescuing traditional knowledge, and agricultural marketing. It also has a health program. CATER (Centro Andino de Tecnologia Rural) founded in 1980 at the National University at Loja, has developed an appropriate technology network that includes other countries. It also has a training program for peasants.

- Paraguay: BASE-ECTA (Education, Communications, and Alternative Technology) works on nonformal adult education and alternative technology. The Centro de Promocion Campesina de la Cordillera in Paraguay was organized by a peasant federation (CPCC) to promote the alternative development of agroforestry, apiculture, fodder production, and marketing.

- Bolivia: The Servicios Multiples de Tecnologias Apropiadas (SEMTA) researches appropriate highland technologies including organic potato production, biological pesticides, vegetable production in greenhouses, medicinal plants, and small-scale irrigation. This research not only supports grassroots efforts; it also grows out of the ethnobotanical knowledge of the Kallawaya Indians.

- Brazil: Projeto Tecnologias Alternativas in Rio de Janeiro is a network of farmers and research centers.

- Chile: CETAL (Center for Studies in Appropriate Technology for Latin America) in Chile is working on manure producing latrines for urban areas and energy-

---

Exhibit 5.3
Thailand: Charities, Health, and Family Planning

Charitable activities concerned with health have a long history in Thailand.
In the nineteenth century, elite women set up an organization to help injured
soldiers which later became the Red Cross. The National Council on Social
Welfare was founded in 1960 as an umbrella organization for charities. However, a stronger focus on development began with the founding of the Thai
branch of the Rural Reconstruction Movement in 1969. Between 1974 and
1978, twenty-one new voluntary organizations were established, including the
Community Based Family Planning Service (now the Population and Development Association), which focused on preventive health care for the whole
family through training of village-level workers. PDA was able to build on a
high literacy rate and the lack of religious opposition from Theraveda Bud-
dhism.[53]

---

saving cooking pots. There is also a Center for Experimentation in Appropriate
Technology in Chile.
- Colombia: The Centro de Tecnologia Campesina (CETEC) in Cali promotes in-
  tensive home gardens and low-input technologies for cassava growers and sug-
  arcane laborers. CETEC works with FUNDAEC (a rural university), The
  Foundation for Application and Teaching of Science and IMCA, the Instituto
  Mayor Campesino.
- Peru: CIED, the Centro de Investigacion Educacion y Desarrollo in Lima, works
  on crop diversification and soil and water conservation. The Centro Ideas in
  Cajamarca focuses on soil erosion and the disappearance of traditional crops.
  (Sources: IFDA, 1986:77; IFDA 1990a:101; Baquedano, 1989:122–123.)

HEALTH AND FAMILY PLANNING

The primary health care organizations of Asia were among the first to
integrate family health and family planning. (See Exhibit 5.3) This emphasis
on family health was based on training large numbers of village paraprofessionals and focused on preventive medicine, nutrition, and family planning.[54]
The Indonesian Planned Parenthood Association (PBKI), an affiliate of the
International Planned Parenthood Federation (IPPF), began village programs
in 1957 and is now one of the largest GRSOs in Indonesia. Other GRSOs
in Indonesia and South Korea used thousands of village-based mothers'
clubs to spread primary health care and family planning. The Community
Based Family Planning Service (CBFPS) of Thailand had worked in 113
districts and 12,000 villages making up 23 percent of the population of
Thailand by the end of 1977. Pregnancy rates declined 40 percent in sample
surveys in the CBFPS districts, and the cost was one-tenth of a comparable
government program.[55] In all of these countries GRSOs have created models
for more massive government programs.

Early foreign financial support in Asia led to a branching out of the indigenous population and family planning movement over several decades. In Bangladesh, there were seventy-two organizations primarily in the health sector as of 1984, and many of these included family planning.[56] Yayasan Indonesia Sejahtera (YIS), founded in the late 1960s as a network of clinics, works throughout the country, integrates health with community development, and is one of the thirteen largest GRSOs in Indonesia. With assistance from AID, it operates a training center for both the government and other GRSOs and serves as a conduit for AID financial assistance to other organizations. Indonesia also has many family planning programs in hospitals. And the Center for Population Studies at Gadyat Mada University in Yogyakarta is highly respected for research that contributes to the efforts of other family planning and population organizations.[57]

There has been less branching out in Latin America, although affiliates of the International Planned Parenthood Organization reach enormous numbers of people. Profamilia in Peru was founded in 1978 by the Peruvian Association of Pharmaceutical Companies and is now one of the largest GRSOs in the country. The Colombian Profamilia provides nearly every family access to its comprehensive national coverage.[58] BENFAM in Brazil was founded in 1965 by a group of gynecologists with funding from IPPF. What has become a massive national program gradually built up a network of general health clinics combined with health education in poor neighborhoods. Thanks to increased accessibility and growing demand for family planning, Brazilian fertility has begun to decline dramatically, at least in cities. According to BENFAM, two-thirds of married women now use contraception, and the population bomb has been deactivated although the government has done little.[59]

International family planning assistance has had a weaker impact on African NGOs than on NGOs in Asia or Latin America.[60] Despite rising interest in "Southern NGOs," donors interested in population were focusing heavily on African governments by the late 1980s, motivated by the severity of the African population crisis and the receptivity of most African governments to family planning assistance. U.S. donors had a third reason for shifting to African governments, since the strict prohibitions on using AID money for organizations that also perform abortions did not, paradoxically, apply to foreign governments.[61]

Whether or not this constrained the development of indigenous family planning NGOs in Africa and elsewhere, it represents a shift from funding patterns that promoted earlier institutional development in Asia and Latin America. In fact, four-fifths of GRSOs in the health sector in six Indian states obtained no foreign donor support.[62]

INGOs have managed to continue funding a wide variety of family planning and health organizations that may not always look like GRSOs. Family Health International has partnerships with a variety of governmental and nongovernmental organizations engaged in research in contraceptive technology and reproductive biology in a number of countries. Family Planning International Assistance (FPIA, a division of the Planned Parenthood Federation of America) has supported The Union of National Radio and Television Organizations of Africa, with headquarters in Kenya, in producing six radio programs on family planning distributed through its branch offices in Senegal, Burkina Faso, and Mali. In Burkina Faso, FPIA is funding a Midwives Association of 150 members, while in Kenya support is given to an independent clinic whose board includes a hotel owner, a representative of the Ministry of Health, and two local chiefs. In Nepal the Red Cross is involved in family planning. In Zaire and Indonesia FPIA supports large labor federations that carry out family planning projects. The Union Nationale des Travaileurs du Zaire operates 37 health facilities that include family planning services.[63]

Yet organizations specializing in population and family planning have not proliferated as rapidly as have other GRSOs. According to Schneider (1985:37) only twelve out of the ninety-three projects studied involved family planning, even though one out of four projects focused on health care. Although undocumented activity is difficult to uncover, my own more recent search fortifies this hypothesis, even in parts of Asia and Latin America.[64]

Clearly, restrictions on international assistance are only part of the explanation for this phenomenon. In many countries cultural, political, and religious barriers have inhibited the emergence of population organizations or even the incorporation of family planning into the programs of other GRSOs. Pakistan, for example, has lagged way behind Bangladesh and Indonesia in family planning because of religious fundamentalism. Women's GRSOs often lack the infrastructure to become heavily involved in health care, and other GRSOs are not yet convinced that rapid population growth is a major cause of poverty. They may also fear incurring the hostility of some GROs.

Yet there are countries that seem to contradict this overall pattern. A strong voluntary health sector, important to the emergence of family planning in Thailand, also facilitates extension into family planning in some parts of Africa, even though coverage is still small. The Association for Family Welfare in Guinea has seven branches and provides family planning as well as more-extensive general health care than the government system. The Private Health Association of Lesotho, an umbrella that provides 45 percent of all health services in the country, is part of the World Bank's Lesotho Population Project. In Tanzania, Kenya, and Ghana, nonprofit organizations provide more than half of all health services, including family planning.[65]

GRSOs in Ghana seems to be particularly active in recognizing the need for family planning. The Planned Parenthood Association, founded more than twenty-five years ago (1967), also organized the Union of NGOs for Family Planning with twenty member organizations.[66] PPA is also organizing a network of GROs called "Daddies' clubs." Among the other organizational spin-offs:

• The Ghana Federation of Business and Professional Women has built a maternal and child health clinic for the Ministry of Health.
• The Ghana YWCA has a training program in health, nutrition, and family planning advice and counseling.
• Eleven thousand individual volunteers from the Ghana Registered Nurses' Association, supported by its sixteen institutional members, volunteer their time on holidays to provide family planning.[67]
• The Presbyterian Church of Ghana trains local leaders in family planning assistance, the Methodist Church trains traditional birth attendants, and the Christian Council (a consortia of ten churches) runs a clinic that provides family planning services and offers training and public information.
• The Ghanaian Organization of Voluntary Agencies, a GRSO network, researches family health care needs, offers training to its member organizations, and sells and teaches about contraceptives at the village level.

Not surprisingly, family planning organizations are also active in Kenya, where the population growth rate still exceeds 3 percent per year. The Kokuit Based Family Health Association works with fifty women's GROs in villages and has even sent volunteers to the Sudan. The Chogoria hospital, with church support, has developed a family planning and health program in forty-two villages. Some traditional charities are using hundreds of volunteers, including traditional birth attendants, to promote family planning and are evolving into GRSOs. At the same time, existing GRSOs without many volunteers are having more difficulty expanding into family planning.[68]

In other African countries, resistance to family planning is still significant, and there are fewer voluntary organizations willing to take on family planning. In Uganda, few organizations other than AMREF (African Medical Research Foundation) and the Family Planning Association are active. Zimbabwe's colonial history reinforced "genocidal" notions of family planning, and long delays in official registration have discouraged new entrants to the field. Zimbabwe's IPPF affiliate is a parastatal organization, the Zimbabwe National Family Planning Council (ZNFPC), which has not encouraged competition from Population Services Zimbabwe, the only GRSO in Zimbabwe that provided family planning services as of 1988.[69]

There are three ways in which the relatively weak growth in GRSOs specializing in family planning and health in Africa and elsewhere could be strengthened. The first would be a concerted international effort to utilize the growing women's movement and to integrate concern about family planning into broader programs that educate women and provide them with income-earning opportunities. A considerable amount of research indicates that projects that both educate women and provide family planning and health assistance have a more dramatic impact on fertility than does the simple provision of contraceptives.

Moreover, spreading knowledge about family planning through existing women's organizations would probably be more effective than creating new organizations specializing in population. The Zimbabwean National Family Planning Council became so overburdened that it has trained 20,000 members of the Association of Women's Clubs in family planning, despite its governmental ties. Women organized several of the largest family health and family planning organizations in Mexico, including FEMAP in Juarez, Mexfam in Mexico City, the Red de Grupos para la Salud de la Mujer (Network of Women's Health Groups) and the Rural Health Promoters in Tabasco.[70] Women's GROs have been used to implement family planning in Indonesia, Korea, and Brazil. The Bangladesh Women's Health Coalition, founded in 1980, operated six clinics by 1988 that included prenatal care, maternal and child health, and reproductive counseling and services.[71]

However, women's GROs are generally unable to afford investment in health infrastructure and need to be linked to and supported by primary health care facilities. Hospitals or clinics initiating grassroots support activities would, in turn, benefit from established linkages between women's GRSOs and GROs. Some IPPF affiliates have already set up such linkages. The Planned Parenthood Foundation of Nigeria, for example, trains village promoters in family planning and parenthood skills in cooperation with the Country Women's Association, which focuses mainly on enterprise development.[72] The networking activities of Family Care International demonstrate that even a small INGO can facilitate such linkages. (See Exhibit 5.4.)

A second strategy would be to use GRSO networks or umbrella organizations to spread specialized knowledge among a greater number of member organizations. The potential impact of GRSOs that assist other GRSOs in family planning is considerable, whether they create their own network or carve out this role for themselves within an already established network. The Negeri Sembilan Family Planning Association in Malaysia, founded in 1962, assists other GRSOs in family planning, youth, family life, and welfare through its affiliation with the Federation of Family Planning Associations Malaysia. In Nepal and the Philippines GRSO consortia are training their members to provide family planning services. The Zimbabwe Christian Council, a church umbrella, has undertaken an education program to overcome resistance to family planning.[73] A Bangladesh network of organizations specializing in the urban poor is developing neighborhood dispensaries for health and family planning.[74] Other GRSO consortia, such as VOICE (Voluntary Organizations in Community Enterprise) in Zimbabwe, already involved in primary health care and women's issues, could add family plan-

---

Exhibit 5.4
Family Planning and Safe Motherhood in Africa

Family Care International (FCI), a U.S. PVO that focuses on women's health and safe motherhood, including family planning, is working with seventy organizations, including governments and NGOs, in Ghana, Nigeria, Uganda, Tanzania, and Zimbabwe. By brokering contacts between different organizations, it enables them to better support each other. Although not all of FCI's partners are involved in family planning, family planning partners in Nigeria include the National Association of Nigerian Nurses and Midwives, with 50,000 members, the Medical Women's Association of Nigeria, the Nigerian Association of University Women, the Girl Guides, and the National Council of Women's Societies, with member organizations in nineteen states. International partners include the International Federation of Women Lawyers, Soroptimist International, which is building a market clinic for women which will include family planning, International Inner Wheel, and the African American Institute, as well as the Planned Parenthood Federation of Nigeria. Tanzanian partners include the Association of Gynecologists and Obstetricians in Tanzania, the Tanzania Media Women's Association, the Women's Research and Documentation Project (with twenty-five volunteers), the Christian Medical Board of Tanzania (with fifteen Catholic and non-Catholic groups), the Family Planning Association of Tanzania, and the African Medical Research Foundation, an INGO. (FCI, 1989)

---

ning relatively easily. Although I have found no accounts of GRO networks that are involved in family planning, carefully targeted international assistance might make this possible as well.

Finally, the evidence from Africa and elsewhere suggests that nongovernmental health systems that may not yet be active in grassroots outreach could strengthen networking for family health, including family planning.[75] By strengthening women's organizations, GRSO umbrellas and voluntary health systems, the institutionalization of family planning can be accelerated even though it may not result in rapid declines in fertility. It took some years for the institutions created in Asia in the late 1950s to have a real impact on fertility.

The growth of the population and family planning movement has been heavily dependent on outside donors for inspiration as well as financial support. In contrast, GRSOs focusing on the environment, poverty, and the connections between them, have actually led outside donors toward an enhanced understanding of the connections between poverty and environmental degradation.

Exhibit 5.5
Sustainable Development in Sup Tai

The village of Sup Tai is located near the Khao Yai National Park. By 1984, 10 percent of its people were illegally farming on park land. Wildlife Fund Thailand, the Population and Community Development Association, and the World Wildlife Fund began a project to combine conservation education, agricultural support, and family planning. Low-interest loans provide for income generating activities such as park trekking. A local GRO, the Environmental Protection Society, is engaged in tree planting and road grading. Within one year after the project began, land violations decreased considerably, temporary migration fell, corn and soy production increased significantly, and contraceptive prevalence went from 67 percent to 77 percent. (Conservation Foundation, 1988:3)

SUSTAINABLE DEVELOPMENT: LESSONS LEARNED

Chapter 4 focused on the dramatic growth of GRSOs and their place in the independent sector. This chapter examined their potential for meeting the key obstacles to sustainable development. On this front, the news is both good and bad. GRSOs are broadening the scope of their activities, particularly on the environmental front, and are leading world opinion in their understanding of the connections between poverty and environmental deterioration. Yet, as they move away from thinly spread social services and towards environmentally sustainable economic development, their lack of attention to population growth is noteworthy. The full implications of sustainable development, in other words, have not yet become an organizing principle among most GRSOs.

Case studies of those exceptional GRSOs that integrate concern for poverty, population, and environmental deterioration could spread the word more effectively than can resolutions of international organizations. The Federation des Associations Feminines du Senegal (FAFS) is integrating family planning with cook stove development and tree planting to reduce the use of fuel wood and to assist women. The Kenyan Family Health Association is cooperating in reforestation efforts and is assisting small cooperatives as well as training home health visitors in family planning. In Ghana, Practical Life Education hires and trains family planning workers to work with existing community development programs. An even more comprehensive sustainable development model is being implemented in Thailand. (See Exhibit 5.5.)

The relative scarcity of GRSOs with expertise in population, family planning, and clinical delivery capability makes it unlikely, however, that such examples will spread by word of mouth alone. Donors and GRSOs could, in addition, build on the inherent strengths of the broader universe of GRSOs and other voluntary health organizations that seem to be having an impact on this issue in some countries.

1. Providing demographic and family planning expertise through GRSO networks would be a more effective use of donor funds than sending international experts or trying to promote new family planning NGOs. The international affiliates of IPPF and other GRSOs specializing in family planning could obviously play a key role in this process. But family planning organizations would also improve their capacities for scaling out at the grassroots level by working with GRSOs focusing on poverty and the environment.

2. The rapidly growing women's movement could increasingly spread the message that attention to the reproductive as well as productive roles of women will be central to the achievement of sustainable development. GRSOs that are already enhancing women's productive role could build on an added motivational advantage in promoting reproductive choice and child spacing.

3. The potential for communicating about family planning through GRO networks has barely been tapped. According to Pradervand (1990:72), the Naam peasant organizations "quite spontaneously, started informing its members about birth control" and by 1984 had initiated training sessions in remote areas.

4. These approaches could be tied to programs designed to strengthen nongovernmental health organizations of all types, including strictly charitable organizations, which were important to the initial development of the family planning movement in Asia. The spread of a grassroots support function among many types of voluntary organizations, outlined in Chapter 4, implies that there is considerable potential for adding family planning to existing health systems. Linking existing hospitals and clinics to women's organizations and GRSO networks could rationalize the cost of increasing coverage.

NOTES

1. Ross, 1990, p. 1.

2. Padron, 1988b, p. 51; Landim, 1988; Tongsawate and Tipps, 1985. Even GRSOs working on preschools focus on mothers (IDRC, 1992: 10–11).

3. IRED, 1987, p. 22; Brundtland Bulletin, 1990, p. 41.

4. Trejos, 1992, pp. 34–35.

5. See Tendler, 1987. Albert Hirschman's earlier (1963) writings on "imbalanced" growth provide a conceptual counterpart to this point of view within economic development theory. Peterson (1982), on the other hand, argues that single-sector organizations in an inegalitarian setting tend to become public service contractors.

6. See Tendler, 1987, Annex I:5; Durning, 1989; Hulme, 1990. Similar banks have been organized in Rwanda, Egypt, Kenya, Sudan, and Malawi.

7. McKee, 1989; Tendler, 1987; Durning, 1989, p. 31.

8. Everett and Savara, 1987, p. 7.

9. Interview with the director, Francisca Escoto, May 1989. ODEF is part of a small international network with BEST, another enterprise development organization in Belize and Katalysis, a U.S. PVO in Stockton, California.

10. PACT, 1989, pp. 130–135; Pardo, 1990.

11. Carroll (1992) found productive activities to have a long impact.

12. Mendez Lugo, 1988, pp. 12–13.

13. Ashoka, 1991, p. 142.

14. Discussion with Mario Ganuza, Technoserve, 1989.

15. Leet and Leet, 1989, p. 31.

16. Interview with Vijay Mahajan, June 1989.

17. Ashoka, 1990, p. 4.

18. Valenzuela, 1989, p. 50.

19. Ashoka, 1991, pp. 29–30.

20. IFDA, 1990b, pp. 115–116.

21. de Graaf, 1987, p. 288.

22. Carroll, 1992, p. 76.

23. Ibid, pp. 47, 57.

24. Field visit, Santiago, with Consuela Unduragga of CIDE, September 1991.

25. Assistance is not necessarily focused on village enterprises. The J.N.M. group of Indian companies spends at least 10 percent of pre-tax profits on hospitals, skills training, and medical centers. Enriching and protecting the eco-system has "taken the corporate sector by storm in Bombay" (Dadrawala, 1990:367).

26. Callanta, 1990, p. 249.

27. Brundtland Bulletin, 1990b, p. 16

28. Durning, 1989, p. 15. Other information was obtained from discussions at the Asia Society with Asian environmental activists in May 1991.

29. Clark, 1991, p. 117; and IFDA 1991, p. 110.

30. IFDA 1990b, pp. 102–103.

31. Hiremath, 1991. The case was before the Supreme Court by 1991.

32. Partners of the Americas, 1988; California Institute of Public Affairs, World Environmental Directory, 1989; La Otra, 1991, p. 27. In 1989, I visited one of many community tree nurseries in Costa Rica developed by Arbofilio, not listed in either directory. The growth of the environmental movement makes any such listing extremely difficult.

33. Durning, 1989a, p. 56.

34. Proterra, 1990.

35. Thompson, 1992, p. 19.

36. Landim, 1988b.

37. Cabarle, 1991, p. 8.

38. Muchiru, 1986, p. 113.

39. Ross, 1990. The U.N. Non-Governmental Liaison Service estimated in 1987 that there were 140 indigenous NGOs and 64 INGOS in forestry in Africa.

40. Durning, 1989, p. 39. Six S stands for Se Servir de la Saison Seche en Savane et au Sahel (Making use of the Sahel in the Dry Season).

41. *Brundtland Bulletin*, 1990, p. 52.

42. Williams, 1989a.

43. Proterra, 1990, pp. 39–40. There is a similar organization in Cusco, the Asociation de Derecho Ambiental de la Region Inka (ADARI). Brundtland Bulletin, 1992, p. 35.

44. Cordoba, Novion, and Sachs, 1987, p. 33. CAP also conducts house-to-house counseling on nutrition, health, budgeting, and credit. When villagers raise a problem such as irregular bus service, CAP works with villagers to apply long-term political pressure.

45. Peng, 1983, pp. 30–32; IFDA, 1986, p. 81.

46. The twenty-one member World Commission on Environment and Development, chaired by Prime Minister Gro Harlem Brundtland of Norway, presented its findings in April 1987. The main message of *Our Common Future*, an international bestseller, is that long-term sustainable development and environmental preservation must be pursued jointly. The report gave little attention to the population issue, however.

47. The Socially Appropriate Technology International Information Service (SATIS) grouped forty-one agencies as of 1987, with a secretariat in the Royal Tropical Institute in Amsterdam. The International Service for the Support of Training and Technologies in West Africa/Sahel (AFOTEC) has a wide base of contacts in West Africa and works on reforestation, water, agriculture, public health, credit, and literacy. Its Community Advisers' Committee comprises men and women from the first communities where AFOTEC worked (Non-Governmental Liaison Service, 1988:36).

48. McRobie, 1983.

49. IFDA, 1988c, pp. 73–74 and IFDA, 1990a, p. 104.

50. CET, 1989.

51. IFDA, 1990, p. 109; IFDA, 1989c, p. 70.

52. Ashoka, 1989, p. 138.

53. Coombs, 1980; Tongsawate and Tipps, 1985, pp. 38–39.

54. Agricultural assistance, for example, generally focused on food production rather than crops for market.

55. Ahmed, 1980, p. 196; PACT, 1989, p. 63; Durning, 1989, p. 27.

56. Paul, 1984.

57. Interview with Fred and Alice Bunnell, Vassar College, November 2, 1990.

58. Korten, 1990, p. 191.

59. Soap operas sponsored by Population Communication International helped change attitudes. Fertility declined from 5.75 in 1970 to 3.2 in 1989, and the projected population of 170 million by the end of the century is 50 million fewer than demographers were predicting in 1980 (Brooke, 1989:A1).

60. By 1991 this had begun to change. Women's World Banking, for example, announced plans to become more active in health, nutrition and family planning.

61. 1990 interview with Daniel Pellegrom of the Pathfinder Fund.

62. Clark, 1991, p. 44.

63. Interview with Dr. Hans Groot, Family Planning International Assistance, 1990.

64. Moen (1991:42), for example, found that only about one-fifth of her sample

of thirty-three GRSOs in Tamil Nadu emphasized family planning or population education in annual reports.

65. World Bank, 1989, p. 5; FCI, 1989, p. 70.

66. See FCI, 1989; Interview with Dr. Hans Groot.

67. GRNA also lobbies against female circumcision.

68. Durning, 1989a, p. 59 and World Bank, 1990a, p. 9.

69. FCI, 1989.

70. Lopezllera Mendez, 1988a.

71. BWHC is affiliated with the International Women's Health Coalition, a New York–based INGO.

72. Zeuli, 1991:69.

73. ANGOC, 1986, p. 98; and FCI, 1989.

74. Ashoka, 1991, pp. 112–113.

75. In some countries AIDS organizations that could also strengthen family planning began to proliferate in the early 1990s. In Brazil there were seventy-six AIDS NGOs by 1991 (Landim, 1992).

6

GRSO Networks

I like to think of a network of diverse groups as a tropical rain forest. The more diverse the tropical forest is, the greater its survival rate.

Erna Witoelar, founder of WALHI,
an Indonesian environmental network.[1]

A review of all existing networks in Latin America and the Caribbean confirmed what we suspected: For practically every type of development effort—popular education, credit cooperatives, radiophonic programs, legal services... indigenous organizations have formed their own networks.[2]

Most GRSO networks can be classified as formal or informal. Formal umbrella organizations of GRSOs usually have written constitutions or by-laws, often hold annual meetings, and represent GRSOs as a group in negotiations with governments and international donors. Although they often assist their member organizations through management training or bulk purchases, they tend not to be directly involved in grassroots support. GRSOs in informal networks interact with each other and may provide grassroots support as a group but do not generally create a formal organization of organizations. Networks of both general types may be multisectoral or may focus more narrowly on one development sector, and they may be regional or national in geographical focus.

Although these distinctions represent more of a continuum than rigid categories, it is important to understand them before discussing how well GRSO networks perform. This chapter next deals with GRSO performance in communication, technical assistance, funding, and joint planning and implementation for sustainable development.

PATTERNS OF ORGANIZATION

Formal Networks

At the formal end of the spectrum are networks, also called umbrella organizations or consortia of GRSOs, with paid staff and boards of directors. Formal networks are sometimes promoted and funded by foreign donors. They do not usually serve GROs directly but rather concentrate on providing their GRSO members with services. Although formal networks often have a national image or presence, they rarely, if ever, represent all GRSOs in a country. This has left organizational space for other types of GRSO networks.

Although most formal networks are homogeneous, representing mainly GRSOs, they are often heterogeneous in other respects. The Sri Lankan National NGO Council has Buddhist, Hindu, Christian, and Muslim as well as secular members.[3] In Zaire, collaboration with church sponsored GRSOs has enabled secular GRSOs to be less conspicuous and to avoid state intervention.[4] Some formal networks, like CEDOIS in the Dominican Republic, include universities and other nonprofit organizations as well as GRSOs.[5] Others, like the Federacion de Organizaciones Voluntarias (FOV) in Costa Rica, include both charities and GRSOs.[6] INGOs may or may not be included, and they may be represented by counterpart GRSOs or by expatriate field office personnel.

In Africa there were at least ten to fifteen formal national networks as of early 1987, and after the NGO Conference in Khartoum in 1988, more were organized in Djibouti, Ethiopia, Kenya, Somalia, Gambia, the Sudan, and Uganda.[7] Although African networks also tend to be more closely linked to governments than those in Asia or Latin America, they are not necessarily tools of government policy. The Ghanaian Association of Private Voluntary Organizations in Development (GAPVOD), with forty members, successfully promoted a joint project on the social cost of structural adjustment with donors and the government.[8] African networks do not as yet coexist with many informal networks in most countries. Even successful networks like CONGAT in Togo, which became a deomocratic enclave in a one-party dictatorship, has been called an "effective bureaucracy."[9]

In contrast, formal networks in Asia usually coexist with other types of GRSO networks. Both Bangladesh and Thailand have more than 10 GRSO networks of various kinds. Some formal national networks take advantage of this diversity. The Sri Lankan National NGO Council is a network of networks with 112 members, 35 of which are themselves networks of various types (regional, specialized, formal, and informal), with affiliated memberships of over 500 organizations. Because of this inclusive approach, over 90 percent of GRSOs are members or affiliated members of the Council.[10] The Agricultural Development Agencies in Bangladesh (ADAB), the largest formal network, has over 600 members and links GRSOs to government. ADAB provides organizational training and technical assistance and sets up district-level organizations to survey and provide assistance to other networks, GRSOs, and GROs.

In other Asian countries there may be only one formal national network, adapted to varied regional and sectoral needs.[11] Even Vietnam now has a People's Aid Coordination Committee (PACCOM) attached to the government-sponsored Vietnam Union of Peace, Solidarity and Friendship Organizations (VUPSFO). PACCOM has ten paid professionals, raises most of its own money, and assists thirty organizations, which are mostly counterpart GRSOs or INGOs.[12]

In South America and Mexico there are many regional and informal networks of GRSOs and church-affiliated councils, but fewer examples of formal national networks. The sheer number and diversity of GRSOs as well as geographical separation and diverse political and religious agendas make national networks difficult to organize in the larger Latin American countries, according to Stremlau (1987:220). In Argentina, for example, the Encuentro de Entidades No Gubernamentales para Desarrollo has only thirty members, although it provides technical assistance and publishes a newsletter, while another less-formal network, GADIS (Grupo de Analysis y Desarrollo Institucional y Social), publishes research and a directory on the independent sector. A third network, Confluencia, has only eight members and works with GRSOs in the provinces.[13] Peru had 31 small GRSO networks of various types by 1985, and Mexico had at least 25. Almost all of the 300 Mexican GRSOs are members of at least 1 of these networks.[14] There are, however, 2 major formal networks in Colombia, the Consejo Nacional de Organizaciones No Gubernamentales and the Confederacion Colombiana de Organismos Colombianos.

National networks are obviously easier to organize in the smaller countries of Central America and the Caribbean. Although earlier broad-based groupings failed in Panama and the Caribbean during the 1970s, Panamanian GRSOs are now organized into the Federation of Development Organizations (FODEPA). There are also formal networks in Belize (with sixteen members, including four INGOs), Dominica (ten), Grenada (twelve), St. Vincent (twelve) and the Grenadines (six).[15] The Jamaican Association of Development Agencies, with thirteen members (including four INGOs) is researching different development methods and trying to include GROs.[16] And there are two major national networks in Costa Rica. FOV (Federacion de Organizaciones Voluntarias) has AID funding linked to a loan to the banking system and provides funding for its members, while ACORDE funds GRSO proposals, assisted by a private business sector consultant, the

Costa Rican Coalition for Development Initiatives.[17] GRSO networks such
as CEDOIS in the Dominican Republic, FOPRIDEH in Honduras, ASINDES
in Guatemala, ACORDE in Costa Rica, and HAVA in Haiti have handled
substantial AID monies, yet are diversifying their funding and providing
services to their members.

- Honduras: With over thirty members, FOPRIDEH is a cohesive, member-directed
  network, despite the dominance of AID funding. Although 30 percent of the
  members are INGOs or counterpart GRSOs, about half of these are directed by
  Hondurans. With help from PACT, FOPRIDEH has diversified its international
  funding. It also publishes, provides international scholarships for GRSO staff, has
  good press coverage, and has sponsored international meetings. Evaluations have
  been completed for seven funded field projects carried out by members.
- Guatemala: ASINDES, founded in 1979, with twenty-six members as of 1989,
  has had difficulty attracting new members. ASINDES focuses on productive economic development projects and assists GRSOs in proposal preparation. There is
  tension between professional standards of analysis and the need to approve grants
  and generate commissions that provide for ASINDES's overhead.
- Costa Rica: ACORDE (Costa Rican Association for Development Organizations),
  is more of a project approval committee than a membership organization. As of
  June 1988, ACORDE had funded thirty-two projects at over $1.2 million. During
  the first six months of 1988, ACORDE was able to raise over $40,000 from
  domestic nongovernmental sources, a considerable accomplishment in Central
  America. Women are underrepresented, and more diversity is needed on its board.
- Haiti: HAVA (Haitian Association of Voluntary Agencies) has sixty-seven members, half of which are INGOs. HAVA cooperates with the government but successfully defended development workers against human rights violations. In
  addition to AID, HAVA has received grants from IAF, CEBEMO in Holland, and
  the EEC, but like the Central American networks has not been able to organize
  an effective service program as a means of raising local revenue. HAVA holds
  seminars on such topics as water, theater for development, legal aid, and financial
  management in the interior of the country for both GRSOs and GROs. Since it
  only gives grants to GROs (with a preference for women's organizations), some
  GRSOs feel that it competes with members rather than serving as a network.
  However, highly subsidized interest rates make it is attractive for GRSOs operating
  their own programs to shift their groups to HAVA credit rather than the formal
  banking system, a disadvantage for long-term sustainability.[18]

Given the spread of networks and the almost universal commitment to
development and empowerment, it was probably inevitable that some formal
networks would eventually be established that reflect more-conservative,
strictly charitable impulses.[19] In 1990, 100 Mexican organizations with close
ties to the Catholic Church and to business organized a network for organizations with a "strictly philanthropic conceptual interest."[20] GRSO
leaders criticized the event, arguing that the organizers want to help the

poor without considering the causes of poverty such as unjust wages and the lack of democracy.

On the other hand, charitable organizations are not necessarily in conflict with organizations promoting social change. In Colombia, for example, Arbab (1988:31) argues that GRSOs "face more and more complex social and economic problems throughout their evolution, whether they begin with helping orphans, giving credit, or doing elaborate studies of social forces. . . . However, the real efficacy of this path is not necessarily in the expansion of a single organization but more in the linkages with others." Thus, this "community of organizations" involves even charities in a coordinated development process.

Informal Networks

The GRSOs and other organizations that belong to informal networks communicate directly with each other rather than through an apex or umbrella organization. Informal networks are less likely than formal networks to have paid staff and tend to communicate in the field or through computers rather than through formal annual meetings.[21] Like formal networks, however, they may be regional or national, specialized or multisectoral.

There are two general types of informal networks. Service networks may be large or small, but they are consistently homogeneous, involving mainly GRSOs and perhaps one other member of a different type such as a foundation. Service networks enable GRSOs to exchange and promote each other's professional capacities. Support movements are large, heterogeneous, often amorphous systems of communication including GRSOs, universities, charities, GROs, and some individuals such as journalists or professors interested in grassroots development.

Service networks. Service networks often begin with one GRSO or other organization providing specific assistance to other GRSOs. Staff support is usually provided by the GRSO itself, and may or may not, at least initially, involve contacts between the other GRSOs in the network. Often a GRSO skilled in enterprise development, water systems, or women's rights, attracts other GRSOs and GROs to its orbit, and a service network emerges without initial planning. In Chile, the work of the Development Alternatives Center (CEPAUR) with local OEPs (Popular Economic Organizations) attracted local entrepreneurial and professional groups wanting to take on grassroots support activities as well as established GRSOs. Agua para el Pueblo in Honduras works with both GROs and GRSOs to coordinate agronomy and aquaculture, so that completed water systems can be utilized immediately.[22]

In Asia, non-membership service networks are at least as active as formal networks.[23] A majority of the organizing institutions are themselves GRSOs with specialized experience that has grown out of their ties to GROs. A few have become very large. The Socio-Legal Aid Research and Training Center in Calcutta offers workshops on legal aid, child abuse, street children and women's development to participants from over a hundred other GRSOs and more traditional charities.[24] Among the other Asian examples:

- Nepal: LEADERS specializes in environmental research and grassroots legal action and provides technical and legal support for other GRSOs.[25]

- Bangladesh: Hosne Arakan provides training to other GRSOs on gender and class relations, based on a field program designed to test the idea that women can be elevated in status while improving everyone's well being. Field visits to the projects of other GRSOs provide ongoing support for implementation.

- India: The Society for Participatory Research in Asia, which provides support to GRSOs in several countries and helped create the Voluntary Action Network India (VANI) to serve as an information clearing house and advocacy center.[26]

- Philippines: The Center for People's Law is a legal resource network for GROs and GRSOs working with the urban and rural poor. The Center provides legal resource workshops with GROs and lawyers, legal education at the community level, and legal aid or referral to legal aid societies.

Service networks may also be organized by foundations and other organizations not involved in grassroots support. The Island Resources Foundation in St. Thomas gives mini-grants to GRSOs but also helps them with local institutional development.[27] The Fundacion de Educacion Superior in Colombia offers legal and administrative assistance to many groups, including financial services and organizing the social benefits of salaried employees. FAFIDESS (Foundation of Financial Consulting to Development and Social Service Agencies), established by board members of the Rotary Clubs of Guatemala, assists over forty other organizations in project analysis, proposal writing, fund-raising, and administration.[28]

Service networks organized by GRSOs are more likely than those organized by other institutions to encourage ties between organizations being assisted or even to evolve into formal networks. The Center for Education and Technology (CET) in Chile, with links to eighty communities, is training the staff of 160 other organizations in alternative agricultural techniques, including intensive urban vegetable cultivation.[29] During one training session, the GRSOs attending signed an agreement committing themselves to sharing information, joint staff training, planning, and implementation. Membership networks may also evolve as small groups of GRSOs commit themselves to providing support services for larger numbers of organizations. BRAC, Proshika, and Gonoshsthya Kendra in Bangladesh are the hub of a network jointly providing support services to other GRSOs.[30]

In Guinea a formal membership network evolved as part of a larger service structure. The Guinean Institute of Economic and Social Studies (IGES), founded in 1986, concentrates on reforestation, watershed management, health, gardening, and community development. IGES has three branches, two of which provide management assistance to other GRSOs and implement income-generating activities to support this outreach. The third, The Council of Organizations Supporting Development (COPAD), has become a formal networks.[31]

GRSOs that successfully support other GRSOs usually find that networking both strengthens and is a natural result of other activities. With a staff of thirty-eight professionals, PRADAN in India is able to train new staff members through three-year field consultancies with other organizations.[32] Other trainees join field-based teams assisting several GRSOs (and GROs) in one region. This not only provides them with project skills; it also builds networking into PRADAN when they return. As of 1988, fifty person-years had been spent working with twenty other GRSOs.

The annual report of Seva Mandir, a large GRSO assisted by PRADAN, notes that PRADAN support played a critical role stimulating them to install a computer. "Their sympathetic but critical report goaded us to review our management practices." The complexity of networking is underlined by the fact that Seva Mandir also received help with income-generating projects from the Tribuvandas Foundation in Gujarat.[33]

Cooperation is not, however, inevitable, and GRSOs sometimes compete with each other over finances. In Tamil Nadu, India, Moen (1991:95) found that small GRSOs complained that the big ones monopolized foreign assistance, while the large GRSOs allege that small GRSOs only want addresses of foreign donors.[34]

Support Movements. Support movements are more likely than are formal networks or even service networks to include GROs and GRO networks.[35] Support movements also tend to include individual professionals and universities. Like grassroots movements, support movements are generally more amorphous than federations or networks. Unlike grassroots movements or grassroots networks, however, support movements include GRSOs as members.

Without detailed information about a particular network, it is often difficult to guess whether it is a GRO network with a few attached intellectuals or a support movement involving large number of GROs, GRSOs, and individuals. Bina Swadaya in Indonesia, CIDOB in Bolivia, and FONGS in Senegal are all GRO networks defining and incorporating their own outside assistance, but whether they evolve towards multiple vertical as well as horizontal connections is not yet obvious. Sensitive outside professionals may be reluctant to incorporate more middle-class groups unless the GRO network itself decides that this is necessary.

Support movements are often very large. Lokayan, an Indian support movement, holds workshops for its 2,000 individual and organizational members. Lokayan publications are designed to "end the isolation of various movements for change."[36] As a well established network, Lokayan has some of the characteristics of more-formal networks, including a paid staff, and regional coordinators for those areas not covered by GRSO members. In some states new organizations and movements have come into existence through Lokayan's participative research on topics such as deforestation. An organizational dialogue with SEWA produced a permanent working group of women activists. One observer remarked that "It is through this process that a conventional researcher like me has been exposed to different realities, to stirrings at the grassroots and to collaboration between activity-oriented intellectuals and intellectually oriented activists."[37]

ANADEGES, (Autonomia, Decentralismo, y Gestion) a support movement in Mexico with 400 group and individual members, is based on self-initiated grassroots activity. A "donation" fund of $500,000, designated for peasant groups, has revolved four times, with 95 percent of the original funds redonated. Gustavo Esteva (1987:127–128) describes the origins of ANADEGES:

[GROs and GRO networks are] constantly multiplying and intensifying their horizontal contacts . . . but they have carefully avoided the temptation to federate themselves into bigger "national" organizations. . . . People from the other extreme of the educational scale then began to join them . . . highly decentralized webs of heterogeneous organizations proliferated before our eyes, transforming us into de-professionalized intellectuals. . . . What began as a web has now evolved into a so-called "hammock," which like a web is horizontal and lacks a center but is less likely to trap people and "conforms to the shape of the user."

In addition to support movements that mix GROs, GRSOs and individual professionals, there are several giant, well-established volunteer movements that include both professionals and beneficiaries in self-help development, even though they are dominated by one large GRSO. The best known is the Sarvodaya Shramadana movement in Sri Lanka, founded in 1958 by a young Buddhist science teacher in an upper-class high school in Colombo who led his students to a low-caste village to help villagers build latrines. It is now more formally organized yet continues to mobilize large numbers of middle-class Sri Lankans as well as peasants who want to help communities other than their own. Its programs reach hundreds of Sri Lankan villages, and its founder claims that there are between 2 and 3 million beneficiaries.[38] Sarvodaya organizes village councils, concentrating initially on pre-school and nutrition programs, and then trains and supports farmers in development projects such as methane generators to convert human waste to cooking gas.[39]

A similar network-movement in India is the Association for Sarva Seva Farms. ASSEFA was founded in 1968 in Tamil Nadu by two Indian activists with help from Giovanni Ermiglia, a retired Italian philosophy professor devoted to Gandhian ideals.[40] With help from the European Economic Community, the movement has reached seven states and has regional offices in a number of locations. The ASSEFA network uses local volunteers for well digging, land reclamation, education, animal husbandry, literacy, forestry, and rural industries. ASSEFA has also published a *Practical Management Handbook for Local Development Associations.*[41]

Other informal volunteer movements are more specialized. An early example was the People's Science Movement in Kerala, India, founded in 1962 by volunteer scientists, science writers, teachers, and social workers. It ran an adult literacy program, science clubs for students, promoted action-oriented research, and used social action to undermine scientific elitism. In 1977 volunteers conducted a "long march," traveling over 10,000 kilometers and contacting 500,000 people through 900 public meetings.[42]

SECTORAL FOCUS

The lack of pressure for formal networks in Latin America is partially due to the existence of large numbers of more specialized networks, both formal and informal.[43] Mexico has a number of specialized informal networks on health and education as well as one linking artisans with GRSOs that assist them (Red Artesanal Solidaria). In Paraguay a broad network of GRSOs working in rural areas called Cooperacion de Obras provides space for dialogue and shared insights. Brazilian networks are often issue oriented and may be temporary in nature, although a national network of 108 organizations was formed in 1991.[44]

Sustainable development as an organizing principle has catalyzed the creation of all kinds of environmental networks. Network organizing was further accelerated by preparations for the U.N. Conference on Environment and Development held in Rio in June 1992.[45] New environmental networks sprang up in response to the conference announcement in several African countries such as Chad and Mauritius. In Mauritius, the Council for Development, Environmental Studies and Conservation includes women's GRSOs concentrating on nonformal education as well as environmental organizations. In 1990 the Environmental Management Society in Karachi established the Pakistan Environmental Network, which assists its members in establishing and strengthening environmental impact assessments as well as monitoring and enforcing environmental laws.[46]

During the early 1980s, environmental networks might have been considered "specialized"; today they encompass a wider range of issues, including poverty and population, than do many multisectoral networks. The Management Institute for Social Change in Malaysia (MINSOC) has a newsletter called SUSDEN Malaysia that coordinates a very large sustainable development network. Networks of Islamic and non-Islamic intellectuals in Indonesia have informal links to both grassroots cooperatives and all levels of government. For example, The Institute for Economic and Social Research

---

Exhibit 6.1
A Spin-off Network

SKEPHI was organized following a forest fire in eastern Kalimantan in 1982. SKEPHI, now independent of WALHI, has seven full-time staff members. Initially more confrontational than WALHI, SKEPHI sued a paper complex in Sumatra and won its case with the help of the Indonesian Legal Aid Society, a member of the network. SKEPHI has also analyzed the country's military budget and the ties between exports and environmental degradation. It has worked with international environmental groups against deforestation and plantation monoculture by the Scott Paper Company. (PACT, 1989:65)

---

links a number of GRSOs to the *pesantrens* through environmentally sustainable microenterprise development.[47]

As with individual GRSOs, mergers are occurring between environmental and developmental networks and also between human rights and environmental networks in Asia (see Chapter 4). The smaller number of GRSOs focusing on population and family planning are beginning to be used by some networks to train other members. Although population networks are not common, they are beginning to influence the sustainable development agenda in some countries. The Philippines NGO Council on Population, Health and Welfare, incorporated in 1987, has aggressive membership drives and provides grants and training to build GRSO capacity in population and family planning. Woman Health Philippines is a national support movement of individuals, GRSOs, and other organizations working on the right to health and reproductive freedom through education, policy advocacy, and health support services.[48]

Given their vast environmental agenda, some environmental networks are dividing themselves into specialized subnetworks. Wanana Lingkungan Hidap Indonesia (the Indonesian Environmental Forum or WALHI) links environmentalists and other activist intellectuals to university environmental centers, several hundred GRSOs, arts organizations, local governments, and portions of the private sector. At one point, WALHI had over 500 members, and it therefore divided itself into the Forestry Conservation Network (SKEPHI), the Pesticide Action Network Indonesia (KRAPP), and the Anti-Pollution Network (SKREPP). KRAPP has several organic farming and community seed bank pilot projects, a computerized data bank, and a directory of over 500 NGOs.[49] Even specialized spin-off organizations such as SKEPHI are engaged in larger socioeconomic issues. (See Exhibit 6.1.)

Many other informal networks remain specialized yet are also tied to larger issues. In the Philippines, for example,

- The National Confederation to Support the Urban Poor (NACUPO), includes a number of GRSOs and other cause oriented groups as well as a GRO federation of urban squatters.

- Three established cultural institutions provide a secretariat for the Mindinao Community Theatre Network of sixty groups in eighteen provinces, which is committed to community empowerment through reinstating Philippine cultural traditions.

- Advocacy networks include the Congress for a People's Agrarian Reform and a freedom-from-debt coalition.

- An Ashoka Fellow, Sita Aripurnami, organized the Center for Women's Information to connect women's organizations. The Center researches the condition of women and promotes women for senior government positions.

- Gabriela is a national coalition of women's organizations in the Philippines that also has over 38,000 individual members. (Santiago, 1987:95; IFDA, 1985a:88; Liamzon, 1990; Ashoka, 1988:78)

Formal networks also help promote more-specialized networks, usually tied to the parent body. The Sri Lankan National NGO Council formed eight groups as watchdogs on environmental issues such as soil erosion, pesticides and herbicides, and energy waste management.[50] Autonomous sectoral networks of varying degrees of formality are more common, however, and the variety of sectors covered is remarkable. In Mexico there is a health network, a communications network, a popular education network, a children and family network, an environmental education network, and two other environmental networks.[51] A Theatre for Development Network in Bolivia has representatives from nine provinces. Bolivia also has a National Biogas Network that studies the results of the uses of biogas in different areas of the country and sponsored construction of a new type of biodigester.[52] In Peru one network links organizations caring for children, another specializes in technology for the Andes, and a third links twelve organizations involved in health.[53] The Voluntary Health Association of India has over 100 member organizations.[54]

Some formal specialized networks include GROs as well as GRSOs. KENGO in Kenya provides training in agroforestry, and wood and soil conservation for women's organizations, church groups, and local artisan groups as well as district-level networks and national level GRSOs. In fact, two-thirds of its 130 members are local organizations.[55] The Muslim Women's Conference in Sri Lanka organizes both middle class and poor women, has thirty-four member organizations (both GROs and GRSOs), and concentrates on employment training as well as the health of women and children.

GEOGRAPHICAL FOCUS

Both formal networks and informal networks often represent only certain regions or localities. In large countries such as India and Indonesia local or regional networks of all types are common.[56] The Center for Human Development and Social Change in Madras works with both rural and urban GRSOs in thirty communities in Tamil Nadu, providing them with assistance in education, development training, and biogas technology.[57] WIM is a northern Sumatran network made up of twenty local GRSOs that has received help from the Asia Foundation.[58] Twenty GRSOs working with the Mapuche tribe in the Temuco area of Chile banded together to prevent uncoordinated encroachment by larger Santiago organizations. This "Commission Relating to Non-Governmental Organizations" has developed effective working relationships with the common clientele of the member organizations. Some regional networks are beginning to work together. Five regional networks in Zaire coordinate fund-raising, training programs, and contacts with the government.[59]

GRSO NETWORKS AND INSTITUTIONAL SUSTAINABILITY

Whether a GRSO network is a formal network, an informal network, some mix of the two, or a GRSO serving other GRSOs, there are five major roles it can play in serving its members or affiliates. These include communication and shared facilities and purchases, technical assistance and training, financial assistance, bridging the relationships with donors and governments, and joint planning to coordinate and scale up grassroots development. Few GRSO networks are able to perform all of these roles successfully, yet those that survive tend to accomplish at least some of these purposes and assume new roles over time.

Communication

The most obvious purpose of all kinds of GRSO networks is to enhance communication and cooperation among GRSOs. The informal sharing of ideas through networking is an important source of organizational learning and renewal whether or not networks provide ongoing services for their members. A study of fourteen GRSOs in Argentina, Chile, Uruguay, and Paraguay concluded that networks that include universities as well as other GRSOs can prevent institutional learning from becoming erratic and confined to the parameters of the past development experience of staff members.[60] Carroll's (1992:137) study of thirty IAF-supported GRSOs and MSOs (GRO networks) in Latin America concluded that relationships with other NGOs enhanced the impact of their efforts.

Communication needs may vary considerably in different countries, how-ever. In extensive multiple-island nations even simple communications tech-niques can have a real influence. Sahabat Alam Malaysia (SAM) links GROs and GRSOs from many areas around environmental issues. The 400 or more members of WALHI, working on sustainable development throughout Indonesia communicate through a newsletter called ENVIRONESIA.[61] On the other hand, in the small compact nation of Uruguay, communication involving more-sophisticated forms of information sharing is considered essential. The Instituto de Comunicacion y Desarrollo, founded in 1986, has developed a National Information Service for rural areas of Uruguay and for communicating with other Latin American GRSOs. It also trains GRSO staffs in communications and has installed a computerized network connecting GRSOs to newspapers.[62] Computerization is also occurring in large compact nations such as Brazil, where a computer network called Alternex is active.[63]

The need for communication to the wider society may, in fact, be as important as communication between member organizations. In Bangladesh the Center for Sustainable Development, founded in 1988 in response to the Brundtland Report, runs regional workshops for rural journalists and provides free articles on environmental issues to newspapers (60 percent are printed). In cooperation with the Bangladesh Centre of Advanced Stud-ies, it is assisting twenty-three GRSOs to produce the country's first "state of the environment" report. A specialized network in Trinidad and Tobago called Community Media for Development includes thirty organizations lobbying for broader media ownership.[64]

Technical Assistance and Training

The ability to communicate efficiently can also have an important bearing on a network's training and technical assistance services to its members or constituents. The National NGO Council of Sri Lanka can, as a federation of federations, communicate with a much larger group of organizations and utilize the specialized expertise of smaller networks, its member INGOs, and its affiliated international networks such as the Asian Cultural Forum on Development. The Council has a service center that trains field workers in agriculture, biogas technology, marketing, and many other technical fields. It also holds workshops on project identification and appraisal.[65]

Whether specialized networks are formal or informal, they generally do a better job than do multisectoral networks in providing technical infor-mation and disseminating what members have learned, perhaps because there are fewer conflicting demands.[66] A 1985 PACT survey of seven Latin American countries concluded that at that time the only two networks with a record of continuous service to their members were a specialized health network in Guatemala called ASECA and a Colombian network that distributed information on women, children, and nonformal education to other organizations.[67] Sectoral networks in India "often perform better than their geographical counterparts" and are skilled in dealing with collective management problems.[68] The Voluntary Health Association of India works through its state affiliates to help its 125 members improve training.

Service networks are also good at technical training. GRSOs that provide consulting services on a fee-for-service basis strengthen their own incentive to remain useful and are often responsible for enhancing the institutional sustainability of new GRSOs. Thirty-six of forty-three GRSOs surveyed in Bangladesh had used at least one training or technical service from a "Voluntary Resource Organization" (service network).[69] Training was the service most often used, and two-thirds of those getting help with training had done so from more than one source. The Village Education Resource Center (VERC), for example, has been introducing participatory training methodologies to other GRSOs for many years. VERC also promotes cooperation between village organizations through exchanges.[70] BRAC, Proshika, and Friends in Village Development formed an interorganization resource building group. This phenomenon "is also occurring among sub-national agencies, a most promising trend given the lopsided dominance of Dhaka-based agencies."[71] Among the examples from other countries:

- Thailand: The Rural Reconstruction Movement became a trainer in health, literacy and economic development for many newer organizations.
- Malaysia: The Management Institute for Social Change, founded in 1989, is strengthening the capacities of other GRSOs on sustainable development activities.[72]
- Chile: The Centro de Educacion y Tecnologia (CET) trains other GRSOs in self-help food provision, with each training activity producing something tangible such as a solar food dryer.[73]
- The Philippines: Business for Social Progress provides training and technical assistance to more than 500 GRSOs in housing and microenterprise development.

Appropriate technology research centers such as one in Kumasi, Ghana, use international assistance to provide technical support for GRSOs as well as governments. The Centre de Formation et de Recherches Cooperatives (IWACU) in Rwanda, with IRED support, unites twenty-member GRSOs that work on appropriate technology, and in Lucknow, India there is a national information clearing house concentrating on appropriate technology.[74]

Funding Relationships with Donors and Governments

The advantages of international financial support do not necessarily compromise the goals of GRSO networks. Where networks were originally founded by INGOs, and GRSOs joined later, autonomy sometimes increases as more funding decisions are made locally Some GRSO networks have been able to help members gain access to a diverse range of funding without compromising their own or their members' autonomy.

On the other hand, networks may compromise their autonomy by their close ties to foreign donors. Competition for funds among members may undermine the original values that led GRSOs to organize a network in the first place. If the network actually disperses funding instead of just giving members guidance in seeking their own support, this problem can become serious. "All the research warns that dealing in funds overshadows all other functions and distorts member expectations... [and] conflicts with VRO [Service networks] technical services, since recipient institutions are much less likely to reveal weaknesses when the VRO is also a funding body. Moreover, the VRO may be viewed as more of a donor or government conduit than as an NGO resource."[75]

This is an even more pronounced danger where formal networks have been organized "from above" by major official donors such as AID or the World Bank. Despite the existence of indigenous consortia and other networks that have evolved from INGO networks, large official donors have promoted "umbrella" funding in recent years, particularly in Africa. This type of umbrella network may become little more than a funding channel, according to Brown and Korten (1989:24) since donors are "particularly preoccupied with the disbursement of funds and usually find their own procedures and modes of working ill suited to making grants to dozens, or even hundreds of small scattered organizations."

International donors also tend to focus on assisting formal networks to provide management support for their members. CONGAD (NGO Council Supporting Development) in Senegal has received international assistance to provide GRSOs with help in marketing, feasibility studies, and administrative support. The German NGO EZE promotes networks that advise GRSOs on planning and evaluation.

While much of this help is useful, it tends to strengthen the more formal networks that fit the Western model of the umbrella organization. Informal networks are not always recognized nor are their innovative approaches to coordination understood by outside donors. Informal networking often evolves as organizations discover they have good reasons to cooperate. Informality helps circumvent police repression and the risk of hegemony while preserving diversity and the autonomy of the individual GRSOs.

Financial support from governments can also inhibit network independence. In Egypt, GRSOs relate to each other mainly through the government's Ministry of Social Affairs, and there are few incentives for independent networks to organize. In Thailand the government set up a Coordination Foundation for Rural Development with Thai GRSOs. An evaluation showed that the foundation itself had become the implementing agency, even though Bangkok-based government administrators had an inadequate understanding of field-level problems. GRSO leaders spent so much time carrying out joint projects with government organizers on rural leadership training and rural water projects that coordination between GRSOs was neglected.[76]

Specialized or informal networks seem to be more willing than are formal multipurpose networks to engage governments in dialogue and challenge policy. The National Environmental Societies Trust in Jamaica, an environmental network, has become a major lobbying and liaison organization with the government. Informal networks can form broader coalitions and do not seem loath to take on political and human rights issues. In Bangladesh, the Coordinating Council for Human Rights, (CCHR), a coalition of thirty organizations, is using thousands of volunteers to monitor elections. In Mexico, 120 organizational members of the Convergencia de Organismos Civiles (Convergence of Civic Organizations) has lobbied against taxation of nonprofit organizations.[77]

Some formal networks have been able, on the other hand, to maintain their autonomy and influence governments, particularly where informal networking is less common. FOPRIDEH in Honduras successfully blocked passage of a bill requiring GRSOs to submit annual budgets to the Treasury Ministry.[78] And government sponsorship of networks may have a positive impact, if it is intended to promote communication where no previous networking was occurring. In Argentina, the Alfonsin government organized a conference of 400 GRSOs to promote improved management, cooperation, and closer contacts with GROs.[79]

Joint Planning for Sustainable Development

Most networks do not play a major role in getting GRSOs to coordinate long range planning in relationship to key development issues or bottlenecks for an entire country or region. Padron (1988b:64) found that only five of thirty-one GRSO networks in Peru carried out joint projects. Yet, as a PACT study (1989:54) argues, "Indigenous agencies need ways to expand programmatically—by engaging more and more village and multi-community volunteers, technicians and local resource people in the development cause."

Informal networks with multiple vertical and horizontal connections obviously have some of the resources needed for joint planning and field networking, however. Pushed by the demands of their GRO members or GROs assisted by members of service networks, informal networks tend to pursue network maintenance and housekeeping through joint fieldwork rather than as an end in itself. Service networks organized by smaller numbers of GRSOs that include GROs can also build planning and field coordination into networking. In Pakistan, the Village Development Committees, established by the Rural Development Foundation with other GRSOs, help villages prepare profiles based on a socioeconomic survey.[80] The Inter-American Foundation has promoted this approach by sponsoring regionally linked systems of GRSOs and GROs in Colombia.[81] There are so many GROs (including ethnic communities) in some regions where IAF has sponsored regional networks that "broad programmatic reach and collaboration is relatively easy."[82]

Informal networks are also likely to include organizations such as universities that can provide the technical and analytic resources needed for scaling up successful local innovations or for changing policy. Regional networks, be they formal or informal, allow GRSOs to remain small enough to help GROs empower local communities yet to collaborate with each other in policy advocacy on either the regional or national level.[83] Policy impact can be multiplied by including individual political actors in networks. The Permanent Ecological Assembly in Argentina, which is working on major collective programs to save the environment, includes members of parliament as well as GRSOs. Even small service networks can play an important advocacy role. In Bangladesh, Nigera Kori and five other GRSOs helped create a national organization of the landless.[84]

On the other hand, large, more-formal networks, organized through networking over a number of years, may acquire some of these same advantages. ADAB (the Association of Development Agencies in Bangladesh) is assisting its members to coordinate regional development planning. In India, the Association of Voluntary Agencies in Rural Development (AVARD) had 280 members by the late 1970s covering most states and territories. As early as 1983 it was described as a "unique, vital coordination link between India's growing number of voluntary, private sector organizations working throughout the nation."[85] By 1986 it had over 500 organizational members, was sponsoring regional and specialized conferences and using its newsletter to link hundreds of programs. AVARD's planning and research staff assists GRSOs to formulate district and region specific plans. AVARD has also tackled some of India's most difficult social problems, such as the rehabilitation of former dacoits (criminal gang members) in the Chambal Valley.[86]

Where GRSO networks have already created their own autonomous programmatic linkages, government and foreign donor backing may be useful rather than deleterious for joint planning and implementation. Decade Service, created by Sri Lankan GRSOs in 1983, has received backing from both the government and the United Nations Development Program (UNDP). Decade Service helps GRSOs arrive at strategies for sustaining their work through exchange field visits and joint experiments with different development models. Decade Service also arranges training in participatory methodology and provides nonformal educational materials for linking water and sanitation to community development.[87]

Korten (1990) has underlined the need for networks to transcend the local planning and coordination functions and to influence dramatically national development priorities. For this to occur, however, there needs to be a natural, albeit deliberate, progression from some of the simpler forms of collaboration between GRSOs. In Bolivia, for example, poor information exchange between GRSOs led to problems with community greenhouses and solar covers and the "multiplication of faulty technologies." In 1990, twelve Bolivian GRSOs working in 322 communities in nineteen provinces with a combined field staff of over ninety professionals began coordinating research through a plan that assigns topics and distributes results.[88] GRSO networks that first improve their own capacities for communication and technical exchange will be more able to avoid corruption in collaborating with governments and donors to scale up their efforts.

The unprecedented proliferation of GRSOs and GRSO networks of all types in the Philippines seems to have speeded up this process. In 1990 a network of GRO and GRSO networks called the Green Forum was created in the Philippines, with more than 500 GRO and GRSO members. The Green Forum was specifically designed by its multiple creators to undertake sustainable development planning on a broad scale incorporating related, but diverse, concerns such as agrarian reform, foreign debt, and environmental degradation. "People's habitats," or ecosystems, rather than provinces are to become the primary unit of the economy. What gets produced in each of the 350 river-integrated ecosystems will be suited to that particular environment, and trade between ecosystems will be encouraged.

One river system, organized by locally active GRSOs, has received funds from business and loans from development banks and is cooperating with government reforestation. Local communities have organized five savings and credit societies, and a federation of credit societies from another region provided a loan. As of 1990, there were four biodistrict organizations with community management centers.

According to Philip Camara, one of the Green Forum organizers, "The Community Management Center is a specific example of a new kind of institution that I don't think has been created anywhere in the world. It forces governments to respond to it. It forces businessmen to consider our proposal." As the district organizes itself and elects board members, GRSOs become technical advisers rather than organizers. The Green Forum hopes to attract larger loans from international banks as they demonstrate that community-based regional projects can have a high rate of return.[89]

The bottom line in collaboration between GRSOs is whether it helps the ultimate beneficiaries of assistance. De facto collaboration in the field may not yet be common, but it is clearly crucial if GRSOs and GROs are to continue to learn from each other. The Green Forum is not the only example of this. In small countries, informal networking on a more modest scale is becoming increasingly important. In Guatemala, for example, a community-development organization (ACAD) will borrow a financial analyst from ASINDES (a consortium), a water specialist from Agua del Pueblo, a health trainer from the Berhorst foundation, a microenterprise expert from FUN-DAP, and an appropriate technology expert from CEMAT to support a local GRO initiative.[90] In Brazil the *pastorals* share a common belief in Christianity and participatory methodology. They are tied both to GROs and to each other, although each *pastoral* is tied to a particular group of people such as squatters, landless peasants, or abandoned children. Each *pastoral* connects the work of thousands of lay agents to specific community work. Although most of these GRSOs are obtaining international assistance, GRSOs are also developing ways of collaborating with each other that are independent, autonomous, and probably more effective than consortia organized by donors.

SUSTAINABLE DEVELOPMENT: LESSONS LEARNED

1. Although some GRSO networks are more effective than others, GRSO networking as a general phenomenon obviously increases GRSO (and GRO) capacity and institutional sustainability. An Argentine study concluded that the most effective GRSOs were those actively engaged in networking with each other.[91] Conversely, an earlier study of thirty projects in Burkina Faso found that the failure to cooperate and build linkages was one of the main reasons why only one-fourth had been able to continue once external support was withdrawn.[92] Experimentation with alternative, collegial management styles is often a direct result of networking patterns. PRADAN in India, for example, which has an innovative rotating directorship, began as a network of young professionals interested in development.[93]

2. The causal relationship between effective internal organization and external linkages can flow in two directions, however. Enhanced internal capacity, the subject of the next chapter, often leads lead to an awareness of the need for networking.

3. Specialized consortia of all types, even formal ones, seem to be more effective than formal multisectoral consortia in providing technical assistance and other services for their members.

4. Paradoxically, however, patterns of cooperation are developing that exchange sectoral knowledge and lead to a multisectoral approach based on the idea of sustainable development. Service networks formed by GRSOs are sharing technical information across specialties, although specialized service centers continue to serve GRSOs that have limited contacts with each other. Environmental and poverty-focused networks, like individual GRSOs, are communicating around the sustainable development agenda. The population issue still lags, but networks may prove to be the most powerful force to spread knowledge about population and family planning.

5. What is most striking about GRSO networks is their wide evolutionary variety in organizational patterns and sectoral niches. These develop out of the needs of a wide range of participants, including some outside the in-

dependent sector. Because GRSOs themselves emerged fairly recently in Africa, this evolutionary variety is more evident in Asia and Latin America than in Africa. Such "organic" evolution is also likely to incorporate a shared philosophy of social change, identified as important to the success of networks in a number of studies carried out by PACT.[94] Because it is sometimes difficult for informal networks to obtain foreign assistance, a kind of "survival of the fittest" may be occurring that insures the sustainability of the networking process if not individual networks.

6. In contrast, formal multisectoral consortia, organized and financially supported "from above" by governments or foreign donors, may be less sustainable over the long run. Although individual GRSOs also develop out of the availability of foreign assistance, their direct work with GROs tends to insulate them from the bureaucratic diversion provided by money. Although some formal consortia are organized by GRSOs themselves, an additional layer of bureaucracy buttressed by international donors can easily become a financial funnel without member services. Power dispersion from the international to the national level does not inevitably cascade down to the GRSO and GRO level. In fact, the availability of funding can lead to competition instead of collaboration between GRSOs.

7. Some formal consortia such as ADAB in Bangladesh and the Sri Lankan National NGO Council are learning to tap into the vitality of informal networking and become "networks of networks." The ability to see the larger picture and understand who is doing what and where is a potential comparative advantage for formal national umbrella organizations of GRSOs.

8. Shared planning and practice is the key to unlocking the future potential of GRSO networks to learn from each other, to extend what works, and to challenge the political and societal structures that maintain poverty. In some countries, such as the Philippines, the large-scale creative potential of networks is already emerging. But there are many other examples of shared philosophy, planning, and practice.

SUMMARY

If nothing else, our discussion thus far has conveyed the complexity of the independent sector in the Third World. A general pattern has been outlined that begins with GROs establishing linkages with each other and with GRSOs. GRSOs have also created several types of regional and national networks with each other. And GRSOs have ties with governments and are active in international networking, as we shall see in Volume 2.

Despite the vast and complex institutional picture we have glimpsed thus far, it is as if those involved in it see only a portion of this prodigious reality. Although our discussion is more extensive than most, there has been no way for the information on each organization to be up-to-date, accurate,

or completely objective. Knowledge about GROs, GRSOs, and their horizontal networks can provide activists with a clearer idea of their part in the
whole picture and with ideas for future connections. There is every indi-
cation that the impact of empowerment from below is greater if those
empowered, or empowering others, gain an awareness through networking
of their actual and potential impact on their colleagues and on larger systems.
For their part, international donors need to drop the assumption that their
mission is to "build capacity." Instead, they should engage in enhancing
their knowledge and respect for the considerable organizational capacity
already transforming the Third World.

What is most striking about the phenomenon of networking is the contrast
between authoritarian political superstructures in most countries and innovative cooperation between NGOs. Although GRO and GRSO networks
harken back to traditional, deeply rooted cultural practices, they also provide the expanding space needed to create a new political culture, or what
Latin Americans call "sociedad civil." Ironically, in the United States, the
cultural ethic of competition, so useful in the private economic sphere, may
make broad-based cooperation among social change organizations more
difficult than in the Third World.

Careful, planned support for informal networks could avoid many of the
financial and other difficulties seemingly inherent in formal consortia, particularly those organized from above. Outside money can be used, for example, to support a GRSO assisting other GRSOs with technical assistance
and planning. Great care must be taken, however, not to compromise the
independence and vitality of informal networks.

Thus far we have examined GROs, GRSOs, and their horizontal networks. The next two chapters focus on the factors that promote the sustainability of both empowerment from below and the substance of
sustainable development. Chapter 7 deals with the factors that make GROs
and GRSOs effective as individual organizations. Chapter 8 asks the same
question in relation to the vertical connections between GROs and GRSOs.

NOTES

1. Interview in IMPACT 13 (Winter-Spring 1991): 1.
2. Vetter, 1989, p. 13.
3. IFDA, 1991, p. 110.
4. Schneider, 1985, pp. 140–141. However, in Guatemala COINDE represents
Catholic GRSOs, CONCAD represents Protestant organizations, and ASINDES has
no religious affiliation (Ganuza, 1988). COINDE, according to one account has
been more outspoken against government violence than the other two. (Inter-Hemispheric Resource Center, Guatemala, 1988.)
5. Approximately 56 of CEDOIS's 119 member organizations are GRSOs (Centro Dominicano de Organizaciones de Interes Social, 1988:136).
6. The League of Women Voters Overseas Education Fund was instrumental in

helping FOV organize during the 1960s. FOV has retained a strong interest in women, although training initiated with middle-class women has been replaced by an emphasis on the poor (Yudelman, 1987; Arbab, 1988, p. 31).

7. United Nations, 1988, p. 66, Atang, 1992.

8. In Namibia, the Council of Churches coordinates NGOs (Shaw, 1990). On Ghana, see FCI, 1989.

9. FCI, 1989.

10. IFDA, 1991, p. 110.

11. Stremlau, 1987, p. 221.

12. PACT, 1990, p. 3.

13. Interview with Co-Director Elba Luna, September 1991, Buenos Aires. See GADIS, 1989.

14. FAO/FFHC, 1985, p. 8; Lopezllera Mendez, 1988, p. 6.

15. CNIRD, 1989, pp. 2, 111.

16. IFDA, 1991, p. 111.

17. CINDE, 1986.

18. Checci and Co., 1989; HAVA 1987/88, p. 1.

19. Other well-established charitable consortia, such as the Council of Voluntary Social Services in Jamaica, include GRSOs.

20. Interaction, 1990.

21. The PACT studies in Asia used the term *Voluntary Resource Organization* to denote all networks serving GRSOs (PACT, 1989).

22. Max Neef, 1985; Weber, 1990, p. 8.

23. PACT, 1989, p. 13.

24. IFDA, 1989e, p. 82.

25. Case study done for Beyond Boundaries: Issues in Asian and American Environmental Activism. April 24–26, 1991, Asia Society, New York.

26. Brown and Korten, 1989, p. 14.

27. Towle and Potter, 1989, p. 81.

28. Arbab, 1988, p. 55; FUNDESA, 1989.

29. CET, 1989.

30. PACT, 1989, p. 13.

31. United Nations, 1987a, p. 33.

32. Interview with Vijay Mahajan, July, 1989.

33. Seva Mandir, 1988–89, p. 56.

34. Moen, 1991, p. 95.

35. KENGO in Kenya is an example of a formal consortia with GRO members. Another more formal example is the Council for People's Development, in Quezon City, Philippines, which incorporates twenty-seven GRO and GRSO networks from thirty provinces. Its quarterly publication, *Kabalikat*, deals with sustainable development (Brundtland, 1989a, p. 45).

36. IFDA, 1984, pp. 37–50.

37. Sheth, 1983, p. 11.

38. Ariyaratne, 1986; Goulet, 1988, p. 71; IRED, 1987a, p. 8.

39. An earlier observer of Sarvodaya (Ratnapala, 1980:469–523) argued that leadership training courses were merged to a predetermined pattern of local organization, and that villages multiplied tenfold between 1968 and 1978 with no increase in organizers or resources despite the use of volunteers. Ratnapala commends

Sarvodaya for seeking out the poorest villages and for helping to reduce caste discrimination but argues that the organization had a top-down approach. One village had a pre-school, a batik center that could not sell its product, and a grocery stall. The village remained "steeped in poverty," and there was little evidence that the people themselves were empowered to take further steps (p. 520). Whether or not this situation still prevails or whether it was even representative at the time, Sarvodaya does seem to have had a more ideological approach than other organizations such as BRAC in Bangladesh that have also suceeded in reaching large numbers of people.

40. The ASSEFA network was the child of the Bhoodan land movement, founded by Acharya Vinoba Bhave (1895–1982), who spent fourteen years walking through rural India to persuade landlords to donate land to the landless. His goal was to obtain 50 million acres, but he only suceeded in achieving 4 million. To become a *Graamdan* village, a community had to agree to hold land collectively. (IFDA, 1987).

41. OECD, 1988, p. 64; IRED, 1986a; interview with Jeya Pragasam, June 30, 1992.

42. Kannan, 1981, pp. 37–40. I have not been able to update this.

43. Fernandes, 1988, p. 21; Brown, 1990, p. 5.

44. Lopezllera Mendez, 1988; FAO/FFHC, 1987b, p. 102.

45. Environmental networking was already a pronounced trend in some countries even before the announcement of the conference, however. Three hundred organizations from twenty-two Indian states attended a national conference on the World Bank and the Environment in December 1988 to launch a national alliance of environmental groups.

46. *Brundtland Bulletin*, 1990a, p. 44; 1990b, p. 54.

47. Eldridge, 1984–85; PACT, 1989, p. 65.

48. Booklet published for the International Women and Health Meeting in the Philippines, November 3–9, 1990.

49. Case study produced for the Asia Society Conference, April 1991.

50. IFDA, 1991, p. 110.

51. Lopezllera Mendez, 1988a, pp. 19, 191.

52. IRED, 1988, p. 13; IRED, 1987, p. 20.

53. IRED, 1987a, p. 11.

54. Interview with P. V. Rajgoapal, Interaction Forum, Baltimore, 1990.

55. United Nations, 1988, pp. 26–27; Postel and Heise, 1988, p. 40.

56. Amir Effendia is creating local consortia in Indonesia, according to Fred and Alice Bunnell (interview, November 25, 1990).

57. Cordoba, Novion, and Sachs, 1987, p. 21; IFDA, 1987b, pp. 66–67.

58. PACT, 1989, p. 91.

59. IRED, 1988, p. 23; Secretariat ONG/Zaire, 1988, p. 8.

60. Martinez Nogueira, 1987.

61. IRED, 1988, p. 19. Indonesian GRSOs are, nevertheless, suspcious of governmental corralling and like the idea of looser networks that allow each member to place a priority on their field work and maintain their own identities. (PACT, 1989:64).

62. IFDA, 1988a, pp. 70–71.

63. Garrison, 1989, pp. 48–49.

64. Rush, 1991, p. 191; IFDA, 1989b, p. 81.

65. Interview with L. M. Samarasinghe, chairman of the National NGO Council of Sri Lanka, Interaction Forum, Danvers, Massachusetts, 1989. See also PACT, 1989 and IFDA, 1991, p. 110.

66. Stremlau, 1987; Brown, 1990, p. 16.

67. Aruda, 1985; Smith, 1990.

68. PRADAN, 1988, p. 32.

69. PACT, 1989.

70. IRED, 1986a; PACT, 1989, p. 13.

71. PACT, 1989, p. 31.

72. *Brundtland Bulletin*, 1990, p. 53.

73. FAO/FFHC, 1987, p. 5. See also Carroll, 1992, pp. 241–245.

74. IRED, 1986a, 1987a, p. 68, Alliband, 1983. IRED (Development Innovations and Networks) is an international network located in Geneva.

75. PACT, 1989, p. 11.

76. Tongsawate and Tipps, 1985, pp. 2, 52.

77. *Brundtland Bulletin*, 1990, p. 54; Monday Developments, 1990a, p. 5.

78. Inter-Hemispheric Education Resource Center, Honduras, 1988, p. 14.

79. Andres Thompson, speech at City University of New York, Spring 1989.

80. IFDA, 1988a, p. 72. RDF also sponsors seminars and development research and initiates discussions with government and foreign donors.

81. Ritchey Vance, 1991.

82. Carroll, 1992, pp. 130, 137, found the regional approach to be tied to performance.

83. Carroll, 1992, p. 131.

84. FAO/FFHC, 1984, p. 13.

85. Alliband, 1983, p. 50.

86. Shadab, 1987, p. 17.

87. PACT, 1989, p. 147.

88. Bebbington, 1991, p. 28.

89. See PACT, 1990, and IMPACT, 1990. The Green Forum grew out of a visit by Philippine GRSOs to the United States. As of March 1990 over 500 NGOs were members. An urban group, Green Forum Manila, has 155 members.

90. Interview with Mario Ganuza at Technoserve, 1989.

91. Martinez Nogueira, 1987.

92. Gueneau, 1984.

93. Interview with Vijay Mahajan, July 1989.

94. Stremlau, 1987, p. 221.

7

What Works: Assessing the Performance of GROs and GRSOs

MEASURING ACHIEVEMENT

Most observers believe that nongovernmental organizations have at least a potential comparative advantage over governments and official donors as agents of grassroots development.[1] In organizational terms, comparative advantage means, according to Fowler (1988:5), "that an organization has traits or features which make it more suitable for achieving a particular purpose than an organization which has the same purpose but does not possess these traits or features." GROs are knowledgeable about local resources. GRSOs do not need to organize themselves bureaucratically and can adapt more easily than government agencies to the varied needs of local communities.[2] INGOs relate more easily than official donors to GROs and GRSOs. There is also evidence that nongovernmental costs are lower as well.[3] (See Exhibit 7.1.)

The measurement of development outcomes, essential to flagging the actual achievement of this potential, has proven to be both difficult and complex, however. The debate over what to measure continues to reflect macroeconomic controversies over the continuing utility of per capita GNP versus measurements such as the Physical Quality of Life Index (PQLI) that attempt to measure progress in reducing inequality.[4]

Even Northern observers who are sensitive to the debate about inequality tend to stress the need for economic, quantitative baseline performance measures such as wage increases, a decline in the profits of local money lenders, or an increase in primary school enrollment ratios as measures of performance.[5] Tendler (1987) argues that credit provides the clearest measure of single organizational performance, since clients can withdraw their savings if organizations do not perform adequately.[6]

Exhibit 7.1
The Cost of Housing in Costa Rica

A nongovernmental housing program in Costa Rica built 1,300 houses in two
years at final construction costs that were 40 to 50 percent lower than houses
of comparable quality built by either government or the private sector. The
program achieved economies of scale in the purchase of materials and administrative costs were only about 5 percent of the total cost of materials and
labor (excluding volunteers). Since paid labor was buttressed by trained self-
help on a massive scale, it was very cost effective. Ordinary people learned
to erect prefabricated walls and to use computers for accounting, planning,
and compiling data on members.[7]

Third World professionals, on the other hand, are more likely to stress
qualitative empowerment indicators such as networking or impact on
policy.[8] In this spirit, Cotter (1988:40) proposes that process indicators be
developed to measure an organization's ability to reach the exceptionally
disadvantaged, generate spin-offs, broaden financial responsibility, access
available resources through collaboration, and promote decentralization
and local autonomy. Moran (1991:20) argues for more specific measures
of impact on economic subgroups such as the landless.

And, finally, the nature of the insider-outsider relationship almost guarantees that the goals of GROs will not coincide with those of governments,
INGOs, or even GRSOs. Not all GROs organize around the provision of
credit. Newly established GROs, in particular, may want to concentrate on
organizational survival and they may be more sensitive than outsiders to
the differences between short- and long-term objectives.

The quantitative/qualitative discussion also focuses on evaluation methods. Although Fowler (1988:6) is critical of Esman and Uphoff's (1984)
reliance on "post factum assessments of performance ... [that] rely on the
inter-subjectivity of those analyzing source studies whose structures and
contents differ widely," intersubjectivity can be useful when combined with
intensive field visits. Alliband (1983) spent ten months visiting twenty GRSO
development programs in India. By using key informants, he was able to
evaluate both the pace of activity as a part of village life and integration
between different parts of the program.[9]

Qualitative descriptions may buttress quantitative indicators, particularly
if empowerment methodologies are integral to the continual tracking of
economic objectives. In Honduras, for example, the gravity-flow water systems developed by Agua para el Pueblo (Water for the People) are very
efficient and cost one-tenth of government systems, yet the real key to their
overall success is not technical, but human. "What makes them unusual ...

is their view that water can be used to raise community consciousness...
in much the same way Paulo Freire uses literacy."[10] Involving GROs from
the beginning in "participatory evaluation" is becoming a key form of
training as well as an effective way of measuring progress. FORMA, which
provides technical assistance to artisan workshops in Santiago, is experimenting with an evaluation system involving European donors, GROs, and
GRSOs in initial implementation and periodic reviews of progress.[11]

Increased environmental awareness has added proposals to measure environmental impact, including resource use, to this already complicated
debate. Evaluations frequently measure yields, but not what is happening
to soil or the opportunity cost of using land for sugar cane.[12] For example,
more water may be required for high-yield crops than for traditional crops.
High-yield crops also lack thatch, a by-product of traditional crops used by
villagers for many purposes.

The academic nature of this entire discussion is underlined by the failure,
until relatively recently, of either "Northern" or "Southern" NGOs to actually measure their accomplishments, failures, and learning processes. Cotter (1988:31) notes, "Although I have spent many years working in
development offices with learning and/or evaluation mandates, I know of
no comparative application of standardized PVO performance criteria." In
Africa, according to Fowler (1990), most studies are internal documents,
not validated by field observations. Even highly rated GRSOs such as the
Country Women's Association in Nigeria lack adequate documentation of
their results.[13] Nor has there been much interest in assessing the broader
impacts of development projects. None of the thirty-six Colombian GRSOs
surveyed by Smith (1990:264) carried out impact audits related to changes
occurring in the wider environment of grassroots development projects,
including policy consequences or spin-offs.

Recognition of the need for measurements and tools that relate to sustainable development is increasing. The purpose of this and the next chapter
is to contribute to this debate by offering some guidelines for evaluating
GROs and GRSOs both as discrete organizations and in their relationships
with each other and to identify those characteristics likely to be related to
the actual attainment of their potential comparative advantage in promoting
empowerment and development. Descriptions of the characteristics most
closely related to high performance inevitably merge into prescriptions for
change. The examples chosen, however, are illustrative and are not intended
to replace the detailed mutual exploration of ends and means by GROs and
GRSOs working in a particular environment.

This chapter proceeds with a discussion of sustainable empowerment and
development as the most common general goals of GROs, GRSOs, and
other outsiders. This is followed by a discussion of those characteristics of
GROs and of GRSOs that appear to promote these goals.

SUSTAINABLE DEVELOPMENT AND EMPOWERMENT

Although GROs and GRSOs are sectorally, culturally, ethnically, and religiously diverse, most of them share a commitment to the long-run goals of sustainable socioeconomic development and empowerment, however these are measured. In Chapter 1 it was argued that as institutions specifically concerned with development and development policy, GROs and GRSOs have the potential to integrate political development with socioeconomic development at least on a micro level. In other words, participation promotes institutional sustainability, which makes it possible to implement sustainable economic and social development, which in turn promotes participation. "With participation we can expect higher interest in the good operation and maintenance of projects, a higher proclivity to engender follow-on activities, and a host of changes in social and political perceptions which are highly constructive to fostering development in general and pluralistic development in particular."[14]

We have defined sustainable development as a process that does not compromise the resources needed for future development. Empowerment can be defined as a process enabling the poor "who have been traditionally powerless, to become protagonists or subjects of their own and society's development."[15] Empowerment may be achieved by an individual, a group, or a larger organization and may relate to the political system, social relationships, gender relationships, or the economic system.

Yet if sustainable development and empowerment are understood as long-term societal objectives, then socioeconomic gains and participation can be analyzed as proximate goals, usually, but not inevitably tied to positive long-term results. One village's economic gain may undermine another village's natural resources. Participation may be used by governments or others for pacification or public relations with little impact on the poor. When NGOs and others understand and self-consciously take advantage of the interrelationships between participation and sustainable socioeconomic achievements, however, they can advance rather than undermine long-term goals as well.[16]

Evidence of the causal flow from participation to socioeconomic development is considerable, whether participation emerges spontaneously from below or is promoted by GRSOs, INGOs, or official donors. An analysis of 50 programs for introducing technical change found that popular participation was the only consistently effective development strategy.[17] Thirteen of twenty-five World Bank projects evaluated after completion failed a long-term sustainability test, defined as an acceptable net flow of benefits from the project's investments after completion. First among the main causes of failure was not involving GROs to enhance beneficiary participation. Successful projects, on the other hand, had in common a "clear attempt by design, to enhance the institutional capacity in some form" and were based on partnerships with existing GROs.[18] Other factors related to success, such as technical improvements, socioeconomic compatibility, favorable policy environment, and recurrent cost financing/recovery, were all strongly related to institutional development as well.

A later World Bank report (1989a), however, while also praising participation, unselfconsciously argues that the costs of participation are "high" when projects such as big dams are involved. The assumption that such projects should proceed, however they will affect the lives of those participating, is still ingrained in the Bank's institutional psychology, dependent as it is on members' governments. The report also points out, with some insight, that undemocratic local structures lower the benefits of participation. The benefits of the Bank's work with some herder and livestock GROs, for example, have been captured by elites. And the report honestly acknowledges that participatory approaches are still the exception in Bank projects.

The gains from participation are many, but the most obvious are the quality of information and a lowering of project costs. Bridges built in the Philippines, Nepal, and Mexico washed out after farmer warnings about high seasonal crests were ignored by engineers. Construction committees in Nepal organized as GROs by the local Panchayats or community councils built sixty-two dams at one-fourth the cost of construction by the government.[19] A World Bank study of fifty projects in urban housing, health, and irrigation linked community participation to cost sharing and project effectiveness, defined as the smooth achievement of objectives without delays.[20]

On the other hand, if participation is promoted or encouraged in isolation from sustainable socioeconomic achievements, then potential for mutual reinforcement is as neglected as if participation were ignored. The causal flow from development to participation is twofold. First, the desire to continue participating can be sparked by even limited socioeconomic advancements, such as learning to maintain irrigation canals. Second, *economic participation*, even before *economic results* are achieved, can have a spin-off effect on political participation. Members of the women's clubs in Colombia organized by Save the Children first ventured out of their homes to attend club meetings and apply for microenterprise credits. Next they began to attend and even speak out in LDA meetings.

Despite the potential for positive reinforcement between economic achievement and participation, many integrated rural development projects ignore income generation, although they may empower participants and achieve some marginal improvements in health or agriculture. The increasing interest in microenterprise development has only partially overcome this deficiency, despite growing numbers of participants. Women who are relatively better off may become the self-selected participants in women's enterprise projects because they can afford to volunteer their time and labor.[21]

GRSOs such as PRADAN in India, which promote larger community based enterprises and work consciously to alter wider marketing structures, are still the exception to the rule.

The arguments for focusing on economic development need not imply an abandonment of social development goals. Indeed, social development investments by NGOs or governments can have important economic or political spin-offs. Literate farmers in the Third World generally produce more than do illiterate farmers. When the health of women improves and they can choose the number of children they want, enormous economic energies can be liberated. In Indonesia, productivity in a major factory increased substantially after workers were treated for debilitating parasitic disease. And a study of Latin American GRSOs found a strong correlation between "poverty reach" and participation, either because the poorest people were easier to organize or because those GRSOs targeting the poorest of the poor were more participatory in their approach.[22]

It is not enough, however, to argue that "growth and equity are more complementary than competitive."[23] It is also that the particular social or economic focus chosen should have the maximum number of spin-offs or potential overlaps between the numerous goals that comprise the daunting sustainable development agenda.[24] If there was a problem with the much needed emphasis on "basic needs" that emerged during the 1970s, it was the assumption that integrated rural development at the community level could close the gap in governmental social investment. A well-targeted, narrow, but massive governmental social initiative with potential spin-offs (providing health and family planning services to women of child-bearing age or making it illegal for banks to deny credit to women), can have a more substantial impact than social development, thinly spread.

The causal relationships between social, economic, and political development often extend into decades or even generations. Despite the strong correlation between material outcomes and quality of organization and participation, they are rarely achieved simultaneously. Several observers have concluded that major socioeconomic and political advances have only occurred simultaneously where GROs and their networks have established their programs in the "teeth of opposition" from such groups as money-lenders or powerful landowners.[25] On the other hand, an Ashoka Fellow in Java, Amir Panzuri, is building a GRSO that promotes enterprises owned by the poor that produce goods desired by their wealthier neighbors. The project also includes social services for both groups, including school tutoring.[26]

Complicating the relationships between development and empowerment is the need for NGOs to promote institutional as well as environmental sustainability. Defined as an organization's continuing capacity to learn and adapt, institutional sustainability then becomes the key to understanding and taking advantage of this complex, interrelated, and apparently overwhelming agenda. In addition to devoting a great deal of attention to vertical and horizontal connections, GRSOs and even some GROs are focusing on the effectiveness of their own internal management, partially in response to international donor interest in "capacity building."

WHAT MAKES GROs SUCCESSFUL?

Esman and Uphoff (1984) studied 150 local organizations in Asia, Africa, and Latin America and rated their overall performance in terms of economic gains, social benefits, equity effects, and reduced discrimination.[27] They found that local organizations operating under "adverse or indifferent normative conditions" were less successful than the average "*unless* they are highly participatory and egalitarian in their operations—and then they showed much more success than the average."[28]

Why are some GROs more egalitarian than others? Most obvious is equity of ownership and productive assets. Cooperatives and rural LDAs dominated by local elites are less egalitarian and less likely to encourage participation. In contrast, urban neighborhood associations benefit from the relative homogeneity of squatter settlements.

One of the major reasons for the success of women's groups in the Third World is that they are more likely than male-dominated groups to be socioeconomically homogeneous.[29] The 800 communal kitchens in Lima, for example, involve 16,000 women in preparing meals for 80,000 people.[30] Well-established mothers' clubs in Bolivia are so successful that men are moving to "women's villages" where women control the land. A mothers' club in La Loma, Cochabamba, has built a five-room clinic, a well, and pays the local teacher. All of the women in the village belong to the club.[31]

Donors or GRSOs who lump male farmers with landless women in organizing GROs not only forego these advantages but also "virtually guarantee that the men will reap the bulk of rewards."[32] Yet GROs organized by women from below or by outsiders as strictly women's groups seem to be able to include men at a later stage without being dominated by them. Arguments for mixed groups make more sense once women have had the chance to strengthen their own autonomy and self-confidence. Uphoff (1986:154) argues that an optimum strategy for change in many villages might involve a combination of women's, men's, and mixed groups.

If members of GROs become aware of the local as well as national power structures that constrain them and learn how to empower themselves, the organization is much less likely to become the tool of a few members or the elite within a community.[33] Where local vested interests are strong and inequality extreme, this awareness can be promoted by GRSOs that sponsor alternative GROs such as landless organizations. "Pressures for fairness can be built up through discussions among farmers," according to a Sri Lankan organizer quoted by Uphoff (1992:86) who had also noted that "It is hard to be selfish in public." While outsiders wrestle with the dilemma of involving elites without allowing them to exclude others, GROs sometimes find their own ways to deal with inequality. Water users' associations in the Philippines, for example, have evolved a system in which the communal land from which the association officials earn income is located downstream. This provides an incentive for the leadership to ensure that upstream farmers do not monopolize irrigation water. It also promotes maintenance and conservation.[34]

After spending three years visiting rural villages in Senegal, Mali, Burkina Faso, Kenya, and Zimbabwe, Pradervand (1990:126) concludes that there is another major reason for GRO success. "Evidence strongly suggests—and I did not come across a single exception—that the commitment and the efficacy of the peasant groups is in direct proportion to the severity of the admission criteria; the more demanding the criteria, the better a group functions." In Bamba Tialene, Senegal, for example, where the Entente (common ground), or regional network, originated, prospective members must agree to devote sixty days per year to communal activities, must accept the group's rules, and must pay a significant yearly contribution. A leading member told Pradervand that this also decreases the cash available to members who would otherwise waste it on tobacco, green tea, and other stimulants.

A number of other factors have been linked to the success of GROs. Esman and Uphoff (1984) found that GROs were generally more successful in Asia than in Latin America or Africa as measured by a series of defined performances in planning, conflict management, resource mobilization, provision of services, integrating services to bureaucracies, and claim making.[35] After surveying the literature, they also concluded that self-help is a more important learning process than is resource mobilization from outside, but that the former helps promote the latter. In addition, "the process of planning may be more important to their [GRO] success than the specific outputs of that process." In other words, the ends and means of empowerment are not easily separable. Clearly, as Diaz Albertini (1989:97) suggests, more attention should also be focused on the conditions, often spontaneous, that create or maintain social energy. A number of studies of squatter neighborhood organizations in Latin America suggest that organizational capacity may lay dormant and then be reactivated when needed.[36]

Esman and Uphoff's strongest finding, however, was the positive correlation of 0.29 between overall performance of the local organizations they studied and their horizontal linkages with other GROs, either within or between communities. A World Bank study linked sustainability to "organizational density" within one community.[37] The grassroots horizontal networks described in Chapter 3 are the most powerful recent trend affecting GROs and may well outweigh other factors affecting performance, except for differences in leadership quality.

Despite all the possible factors affecting GRO performance and sustainability, the differences between communities with and without functioning grassroots organizations are probably far greater than the differences among GROs. A World Bank (1988:28) study of twenty-five projects concluded that "when such organizations existed, they acted as enduring structures supporting the project initiated activities long after project completion." Although some GROs are dominated by local elites, stories of development assistance benefiting only the few frequently originate from villages where no local organization existed before a project began or where the existing organization was bypassed by outsiders. Uphoff (1986:33) found that local institutions in communities where traditional norms still predominated were capable of managing natural resources equitably and successfully.

Not even traditional GROs inevitably mirror society as a whole. Gamer (1982) describes neighborhood associations as part of the patron-client network in Latin America. With the exception of Mexico and some parts of Brazil, however, neighborhood associations are far more active in self-help and lobbying for neighborhood assistance than in promoting the fortunes of individuals. And even in Mexico the neighborhood associations are becoming more independent of the official PRI party.[38]

EVALUATING GRSOs

The present climate of ample, sometimes competitive, international funding allows ineffective as well as effective GRSOs to survive. Differences in performance may be tied to individual personalities, motivation, or organizational culture as well as the strength or weakness of ties to GROs. It is surprising, therefore, that, as noted in Chapter 4, the most common characterizations of GRSOs are quite positive.

Despite this encouraging picture, there are major differences between public service contractors (either honest or opportunistic) on the one hand and GRSOs committed to development from below on the other. Public service contractors seem to be more prevalent in Africa than in Asia or Latin America, since GRSOs are often INGO counterparts, or young organizations that were created and often defined by the dominance of particular international donors in relation to government.[39]

GRSOs committed to participatory development generally anchor their beliefs in the writings of Paulo Freire, Saul Alinsky, Frantz Fanon, and other writings about community organization.[40] However, this commitment also grows out of *previous* linkages with GROs.[41] In the words of a Brazilian active in the Grassroots Education Movement, "Today we are no longer working with schools or literacy programmes. Now [our work] is related more to land and labour organization problems ... the purpose is to come closer to the social movement in the countryside, to begin to prepare material based on our own experiences in the communities." A survey of twenty-two nonformal education GRSOs in Brazil concluded that almost all were producing materials written by community members. "The phrases are their own . . . the agent connects the phrases and occasionally makes additions."[42] Arruda (1985) argues that activists no longer teach, but rather "learn-teach-learn." In practical terms this commitment is manifested by willingness to accept low pay and work under adverse conditions.

Participatory development goes beyond earlier concepts of community development by contending that people at the grassroots level are not only capable of defining their needs, they can and should also plan, implement, and evaluate their own development process. Outsiders can serve as development catalysts, but if training is successful the people themselves become further empowered, take over the development process and begin to determine how and when they will make use of outsiders.[43]

The need to "learn-teach-learn" from the poor while maintaining organizational self-consciousness and what Martinez Nogueira (1987:172) calls "the necessary professional distance in relation to the grassroots group" is a difficult balancing act. Without directing the process of planning, outsiders can sometimes assist the process by foreseeing consequences such as the long-term indebtedness of villagers who decide to build a new water system. This advisory rather than supervisory relationship with GROs has spread to a number of countries in recent years.[44]

A first step in finding GRSOs committed to participatory development is to look at women's organizations. Although the philosophy of participatory development is widespread among all GRSOs, it is practically universal among GRSOs organized by women, including those that have evolved from middle-class women's movements in Latin America.

However, there are GRSOs of many other types committed not only to this philosophy, but also to "feeding the creative thinking of the poor."[45] This concept extends beyond the training of organizers by foreign donors that fueled the growth of GROs in Africa or even the diffusion of productive skills in the Dominican Republic that fueled the growth of many kinds of NGOs:

- The Morelia Training Program for Social Action and Research (PRAXIS) utilizes participatory action research to unite GRSO and GRO participants into a university of the grassroots. PRAXIS gives degrees to organizers of all backgrounds, with support from the Western Technological Institute of Higher Studies in Guadalajara and the University of Paris. Local groups differ considerably, but all use participatory action research. In a village near Puebla, for example, a team was assisting three GROs, including an association for coffee processing and marketing, a handicraft cooperative, and an economic association.[46]

- A rural university (FUNDAEC) was founded in Cali, Colombia, in 1974 by a group of professors who saw that the green revolution was only helping plantation owners. One of the founders, Dr. Farzam Arbad, argues that technical knowledge is part of the participatory process. *"What is usually taken to the peasants is information, not knowledge. It is a rare kind of institution because we make the creation of knowledge the basic issue. A rural population needs a university, not just primary or technical schools, to act as its learning institution."*[47]

Without this philosophical commitment there is a real danger that institutionalization at the intermediate level may siphon off development funds and help create a new nongovernmental elite.[48] Although rhetoric can mask a different reality, it can still be used as a kind of rough measure, particularly in combination with other indicators of effectiveness. GRSOs without even the rhetorical commitment to empowerment may not necessarily be opportunistic or narrow, however. They may themselves be less self-conscious or empowered. As Mario Padron (1987) writes about the hundreds of Peruvian GRSOs:

At a rough estimate...no more than one-third...are truly aware of their real institutional nature. The majority...do not distinguish themselves clearly from the GROs with (or for) whom they work and are unlikely to accept being considered as institutions. They prefer to be seen as part of the popular sectors.

The autonomy as well as accountability of GRSOs ultimately depends on their success in implementing the philosophy of participatory development and empowering people at the grassroots level. What Uphoff calls this "troublesome circularity" means that local institutional development "is not something that can be promoted in neat, sequential fashion...increased capacity of intermediate level institutions is to be welcomed so long as they do not stifle local institutions." (1986:227) Before examining the relationships between GRSOs and GROs in more detail in the next chapter, we turn to this "increased capacity" of GRSOs as intermediate level organizations.

GRSO Management: Finances

GRSOs face what Fowler (1988:19) calls "multiple accountabilities" to their financial donors, to their staffs, and to their intended beneficiaries. For example, major international donors may insist on priorities or reporting requirements that conflict with the goals of GROs. Those organizations that deal effectively with the competing pressures conditioned by money are obviously more able to concentrate on their accountability to beneficiaries. Because finances are tied to so many other management problems, looking at how a GRSO deals with money is a good indicator of its general performance. (See Exhibit 7.2.)

GRSOs share many management problems, including financial uncertainty, with their counterparts in the developed countries. However, the complexities and implications that predominantly external financial support

---

Exhibit 7.2
Managing a GRSO in the Solomon Islands

"The executive director of the Solomon Island Development Trust, a group dedicated to village awareness training, must understand the mentality and conditions of a Melanesian village, know how and with whom to deal in government ministries, how to juggle support from several foreign donors (different development philosophies, different nations, different currencies, different accounting systems), as well as run the organization with a certain degree of finesse (management information systems, staff development, and financial management). He or she must also have skills and credibility in the relevant technical area (in this case as an educator) and be a leader of people in often trying circumstances. All of this he or she must do in an economic and political climate that is far more changeable than that of an American town. Even the meteorological climate...can play havoc with the program or open up needs for unanticipated sources of development funding."[49]

---

raise are unique to the Third World. A survey of seventy Thai organizations concluded that national sources constituted an average of only 15 to 20 percent of their budgets.[50] In Africa dependency rates on foreign funding typically exceed 90 percent of organizational budgets.[51] Even more important is how long organizations remain dependent. An African survey concluded that only 25 percent of the projects surveyed will eventually become self-supporting.[52]

However, the widespread creation of GRSOs in response to the availability of foreign funding does not necessarily or universally translate into high dependency rates. In Nigeria, where GRSOs rely on membership dues and individual donations, only 11.5 percent of a sample were dependent on international donors. Only 31.4 percent of 261 NGOs in a Guatemalan survey received foreign support.[53] Geographical contrasts in dependency are also common within large countries. A survey of Indian GRSOs concluded that, overall, they received about 50 percent of their budgets from foreign donations, 30 percent from local contributions, and 20 percent from the government. However, dependency rates in South India were higher than the national average.[54]

Dependence on foreign assistance as the major if not exclusive source of funding can, nonetheless, lead to administrative delays and project discontinuity. Grant raising takes time and energy, even in a resource-rich environment, leaving less of both for the catalytic and supportive roles of GRSOs. Dependence can also decrease learning and reflective capability, since organizations tend to alter their programs based on what they think the donor wants. Support for participatory planning may be needed before donors can obtain the kind of long-term detailed plans they usually require.[55]

Finally, some GRSOs worry about the political strings attached by large bilateral donors. "Many politically sensitive NGOs in Latin America steer clear of U.S. NGOs which are heavily funded by USAID."[56]

Although diversification of funding may require even more administrative time than does a single funding source, it increases GRSO autonomy by diluting the strength of donor agendas. Not surprisingly, a common diversification method is to obtain assistance from several foreign donors. As early as the 1970s, Gonoshasthaya Kendra, a Bangladesh GRSO, was receiving help from Oxfam for their health program, Inter-Pares for health and vocational training, Terre des Hommes for an alternative elementary school, War on Want and a private French group for agricultural extension, and Bread for the World for an integrated women's project.[57] FUDECO in the Dominican Republic has secured grants from four external sources as well as the Dominican government. And in Kenya, the Greenbelt Movement has built on the extensive international publicity surrounding tree planting to add new donors.

Domestic Fund-raising. Until recently, it has been less common for GRSOs to raise funds locally. A few organizations, however, have begun to do so because in spite of foreign assistance, growing numbers of GRSOs attempting to scale out have increased the demands for donor support. Yet in many countries GRSOs are faced with weak philanthropic traditions, further undermined by poorly designed and administered tax systems. Even in countries that inherited tax-exempt legislation from the British, this can be a problem. In Sri Lanka, where only 2 percent of the people pay income taxes, nonprofit organizations must pay 20 percent of their income in taxes. Less than half of 261 nonprofit organizations surveyed in Guatemala reported receiving benefits from fiscal exemptions or other tax privileges.[58]

Ironically, philanthropic traditions are strongest in the Middle East, where NGOs are weakest. The traditional bequest, or *wafg*, channels the profits from a farm or business to charity. Egyptian GRSOs, however, are becoming more autonomous from the Ministry of Social Affairs and are expanding their appeal to local donors such as religious societies and local mosques. Religious leaders in Jordan have announced that mosque *zakat* funds, one of the five pillars of Islam, can be devoted to development.[59]

Even where GRSOs coexist with philanthropic traditions, however, they may not receive much financial support. Although religious foundations and charitable trusts are numerous and well established in India, access by social activists to these funds is difficult.[60] In Argentina, individual donations tend to be cast in the patron-client mold, with donors buying clients by funding them.[61]

Some GRSOs have middle- and upper-class members who make financial contributions. The Malayan Nature Society, one of the oldest environmental organizations in Asia, has 3,000 dues-paying members and is planning an endowment fund.[62] The results of a survey of Guatemalan GRSOs and charities suggest that support for GRSOs may be wider than is usually assumed. Only 22 organizations out of a sample of 178 had ten or less "member sponsors." An environmental organization (Amigos del Bosque) involved in rural nurseries and social services has over 1,000 "member sponsors" who contribute either money or volunteer time.[63] There are, however, few accounts in the literature of fund-raising events that solicit small donations from larger numbers of people.

GRSOs created by professional membership organizations and those that emerge from GRO networks have built-in financial support. In Indonesia the Legal Aid Institute for Women and Families (LKBHWK) established in 1979 by Moslem women professionals, supports information desks for women at religious courts through fifty "First Lady" donors as well as consultancies to other agencies.[64] Membership dues strengthen GRO networks such as the National Farmer's Association in Zimbabwe.[65] Cooperative and credit union federations that are evolving into GRSOs also depend on member dues.

Interest in corporate or business donors is probably most advanced among counterpart GRSOs that focus on enterprise development. ACAO, the Brazilian counterpart of Accion, a U.S. PVO, has over 300 corporate sponsors. However, interest in private-sector donations is also growing among other GRSOs and networks. WALHI, the Indonesian environmental network, has board members from local businesses and from multinationals such as IBM.[66] Philippine Business for Social Progress, founded in 1970, has over 145 member companies and has worked with 700 NGOs on 1,200 projects with an impact on 1 million people. Although business membership donations account for only about 20 percent of its budget, smaller businesses are beginning to contribute on a local level. PBSP was modeled on the Dividendo Voluntario para la Comunidad in Venezuela.[67]

Despite these apparent trends, the substantial barriers to domestic fund-raising in most countries have pushed GRSOs, toward for-profit activities. Some sources of income have little impact on grassroots support or are unrelated to the main mission of the organization. After a fund-raising campaign, the YMCA in Kitwe, Zambia, built a block of shops that are rented out. The Federation of Ghanaian Business and Professional Women runs a bakery and food fair.[68]

In other cases, however, fees for services and profitable activities strengthen the grassroots support mission more directly and allow for cost recovery. A study of preventive health care organizations funded by the World Bank in a number of countries gave them high ratings in ethics and commitment because their dependence on modest fees for services maintains accountability.[69]

Among the other examples:

• Tototo Homes Industries in Kenya not only has a profitable retail shop, it also charges modest fees for vocational training to help support work with women's GROs and does consulting for other development agencies.[70]

- Jam Khed, a health organization in Maharashtra, has become self supporting by serving 175 villages with a population of 200,000 on a modest fee-for-service basis.[71]

- The Institute of Indonesian Studies accepts no foreign funds, has an all-volunteer professional staff, and works through local governments, investors, and banks on market schemes and housing projects to provide the poor with housing and business opportunities. It earns brokerage fees on loans to local cooperatives and consulting fees from developers.

- Technoserve Costa Rica works through a GRO network in Tarrazú that runs a reforestation nursery and sells thousands of seedlings at low prices to low-income farmers.[72]

- In Senegal the Federation of NGOs of Senegal (FONGS, a federation of GROs, despite its name) buys cereal from peasant groups and sells it to urban GROs to create a revolving loan fund for development, using the profits to help maintain its programs.

- The Association Africaine D'Education Pour Le Developpement (ASAFED) in Togo publishes *Famille et Developpement*, read in forty different countries, with 400,000 subscribers.[73]

- The Proshika Human Development Center in Bangladesh has rehabilitated and sold abandoned government tubewells through providing loans to landless groups.[74]

- Honduras: Agua para el Pueblo helped develop a local tax base through which each household pays $1–2 per month for water. APP also makes community loans for its inputs. After repayment, 25 percent of the utility fee is designated for maintaining the new water system and the rest is invested in expanded service or a new development activity.[75]

Unfortunately, government policies can disrupt this natural mesh between the for-profit and not-for-profit activities. During the 1970s the Community Based Family Planning Service in Thailand (now the Population and Community Development Association) sold contraceptives at very low prices, yet the program was so extensive that these fees supported 60 percent of the entire budget of the organization. In addition, the accounting and record keeping required for the business operation imposed a financial discipline on the entire organization. When the government began providing free contraceptives, new outside funding had to be found.[76]

GRSOs also connect for-profit activities to their wider societal mission of promoting sustainable development. Clovis Ricardo Borges, an Ashoka Fellow in Brazil, created the Wildlife Research and Environmental Education Society, which is partially supported by its own environmental consulting to business, government, and other organizations.[77] Among the other examples of income producing activities are BRAC's printing business, which gives it power within the wider societal dialogue.

As independent sector organizations, GRSOs are usually not skilled in linking up with or borrowing techniques from the business sector. However,

---

Exhibit 7.3
The Rural Industries Innovation Center in Botswana (RIIC)

RIIC redesigned a small Canadian device for removing hulls from dryland grain by adding a trap door so that a small amount could be processed. With service milling in the morning and commercial in the afternoon, the new mill's total capacity equalled larger commercial mills, became a commercial venture that supported RIIC's training and research programs in appropriate technology, and gave small farmers, particularly women, access to the mill for small amounts of sorghum. Through connections to the private sector, RIIC convinced two local companies to begin building de-hullers. RIIC provides technical assistance and remains responsible for marketing and servicing in other areas. By 1987 there were thirty-six small-scale mills in operation in Botswana, each with an engine, and one or more dehullers, which provided more than 250 jobs. RIIC has also trained researchers from Kenya, Mali, Senegal, Tanzania, Uganda, and Zimbabwe. A Zimbabwean GRSO (ENDA) has launched a four year project to develop and disseminate the de-huller there, where the population is more dispersed than in Botswana.[78]

---

by marketing appropriate technologies that replace scarce or environmentally damaging capital with the intensive use of knowledge and organization, GRSOs such as Development Alternatives in India can promote sustainable development and also become partially self-supporting. (See also Exhibit 7.3.)

Controlling Costs. Controlling costs is the flip side of financial sustainability for GRSOs. When AID ended support for a Nigerian vocational training center (OIC), the organization deliberately kept costs at a level that could be sustained by contributions from trainee families. The Associacion Para el Desarrollo de Empresa (ADEMI) in the Dominican Republic provided only credit for some years. As of 1989, it was able to explore expansion of its capacities since it had become 100 percent financed by locally generated support, had been keeping excellent records of inputs and impacts, and had initiated short- and medium-term planning.[79] FUNDESA's (1989) study of Guatemalan GRSOs and charities concluded that operations and management costs averaged only 20 percent.

Another way to control costs is to use volunteers.[80] The use of relatively small numbers of volunteers appears to be widespread in the Third World. One of the few quantitative studies estimated that 66 percent of those working with Guatemalan NGOs are volunteers and 34 percent are paid, with the majority of organizations having fewer than twenty volunteers. Seventeen of seventy organizations surveyed in Thailand used only volunteers.[81] Inflationary pressures may make volunteering difficult, however, even in countries such as Brazil and Argentina, which have large middle classes.

The use of massive numbers of volunteers seem to be more common in Asia than in Latin America or Africa. Not only are Asian GRSOs likely to use grassroots as well as middle-class volunteers, they have also developed volunteer incentives to fulfill their enormous outreach needs.

- Sri Lanka: The Lanka Mahila Samiti Movement, founded in 1930, provides a five month training course for each volunteer. In return the volunteer pledges to work for the organization for a minimum of two years.[82]
- India: The nationalized bank invited its clerks to volunteer for two years in village development work of their choice without the loss of seniority. This triggered numerous innovative experiments and lead to an increased supply of volunteers for established GRSOs.[83]
- Bangladesh: Service Civil International (ABESH) has 2,500 members, twenty-nine local units, and a volunteer board of executives. It raises funds from member subscriptions and solicits contributions. Volunteer members participate in service projects, study camps, and a placement service. Its youth section runs camps focusing on the environment.[84]

The ratio of volunteers to paid workers is particularly high in Asian health and family planning organizations that enlist thousands of village health workers. The Population and Community Development Association in Thailand has 12,000 volunteers, compared to 618 paid staff. The Federation of Family Planning Associations in Malaysia has 2,162 volunteers compared to 187 staff. There are over 40,000 grassroots field volunteers tied to the Family Planning Association of Sri Lanka, compared to 130 paid staff and 75 "management volunteers."[85]

Some women's GRSOs in Latin America are also building large volunteer bases out of the desire of rural women to escape the heavy constraints on their lives. Rede Mulher in Brazil, with 11 paid staff members, has over 2,000 volunteers and concentrates on women's rights through popular theater. The middle-class volunteers who founded Accion un Maestro Mas (Action for One More Teacher) in Bolivia in 1967 spread their concept of rural farm schools to hundreds of rural communities through local parent organizations.[86]

Other Management Issues

Management skills are spread very unevenly among GRSOs. On the plus side, Cotter (1988) estimates that 20 percent of the BINGOs (Big NGOs) in Indonesia had excellent overall managerial capacity and 60 percent could be rated as "adequate," with only 20 percent "inadequate." He even rated the Little NGOs (LINGOs) as half adequate and half inadequate. Perhaps more typical in its conclusions was PRADAN's study of other Indian GRSOs: "Well developed systems of accounting, reporting and personnel management are the exception. . . . The more skilled persons joining voluntary action do so to participate in the core activities rather than in administration, whereas the job seekers attracted to administrative positions at inherently low salaries are not of very high quality."[87]

Nonetheless, the pervasive image of the need for managerial "capacity building," supplied by Western donors who have their own set of managerial problems, can be damaging as well as misleading. Many GRSOs would benefit from training in accounting, or fundraising, or personnel management. Yet, as noted in Chapter 6, they are more effective at networking and sharing what they have learned with each other than most Northern NGOs. Assistance from other GRSOs can be more powerful than donor management assistance, given the processes of organizational change and networking already underway. The advisors sent by PRADAN to assist other Indian GRSOs found that with increasing professionalization and networking, GRSOs became less dogmatic, with better articulated long-run strategies and coherent programs. PRADAN's study assisted other GRSOs to identify their own managerial needs and led to a number of proposed innovations. PRADAN helped other GRSOs implement personal growth, leadership development, and advanced degree opportunities for staff, as well as internships to promote horizontal mobility between the government, private, and independent sectors.[88] The resulting Action Consultancy Programme also promotes skill exchanges of all types between GRSOs. One organization provides consulting assistance in geohydrological investigations for ground water and another, Dastkar, shares its knowledge of handicrafts marketing.

Some donors are beginning to understand the crucial role of networking. A USAID study (1989:13) of twenty-eight GRSOs in different countries concluded that the "charismatic leadership syndrome" inhibiting the spread of leadership skills was less of a problem than anticipated, in part because of the sharing of ideas locally and internationally.[89] In addition, the organizations had capable leaders, the ability to retain good staff, a community base of support, institutional vision, goals, strategies, and a diversified portfolio of financial support.

Process documentation through computers is another method for merging improved management of GRSOs with empowerment objectives. Seva Mandir in Rajasthan found that involving GROs in the computerization of information on village resources, beneficiaries and those left out, as well as health, forestry, payroll, and financial data, significantly reduced internal factionalism and friction.[90] With computerization, many Indonesian GRSOs acquired the ability to maintain in-depth profiles of beneficiaries, data on loan repayments, market data, follow-up and profitability data, needs assessment in health projects, profile information on treatment, impact data on reduced malnutrition, housing, infrastructure support systems, property values, cost of expanding standard models, ability to integrate community support services, agricultural yields, and the ratio of organic to chemical pesticides. The result of all of this baseline information was better management through constant monitoring.[91]

The need to reach ever larger numbers of beneficiaries has led to other dramatic management innovations, particularly in Asia. The Grameen Bank has consistently searched for its most successful field workers and tried to learn from them and replicate their strategies. An early example was a branch of the bank with no defaults. Instead of a prescriptive evaluation, Grameen used what they learned from the best parts of the program to improve the whole. Rigorous long-term training and a number of opportunities for self-screening have resulted in an excellent, highly motivated staff of over 8,000. Trainees are given questions that they have to answer in the field before the next class.[92]

Cotter (1988) was particularly impressed with the innovative managerial abilities of the Philippine GRSOs obtaining assistance from USAID. They produce quality development publications and successfully highlight the role of women and ethnic minorities. They use community volunteers to build local development teams and GROs. Among their other achievements:

- highly sophisticated health and community development monitoring systems, continuously updated by community workers;
- income-generation and credit programs with high repayment rates and potentially sustainable designs;
- community mobilization . . . under the most challenging conditions;
- agricultural projects with sophisticated crop diversification, market strategies, innovative processing, technical innovation, [reduction of] fertilizer and pesticide costs and levels, ecological sensitivity and high levels of beneficiary management;
- women with wealthy and influential family connections who network effectively and also bring high levels of technical competence to program/project implementation;
- Philippine Business for Social Progress has successfully involved the Philippine business community in a highly professional set of inter-related development initiatives that has significant cost-effective growth potential.

Although the Philippine GRSOs may be exceptionally capable, high quality managerial skills exist almost everywhere. The challenge is to enhance institutional sustainability by spreading them around.

SUSTAINABLE DEVELOPMENT: LESSONS LEARNED

Despite their nonbureaucratic advantages, building GROs and GRSOs that can both sustain themselves and promote sustainable development is complex and difficult. Given the magnitude of the task, no organization can successfully promote participation, economic development, social development, and environmental sustainability all at once. Yet an organization that trains women to care for and sell tree seedlings builds both care for the environment and the empowerment of women into the initial design for change. If this then leads participants to demand health care and family planning, it can also have a spin-off effect as a GRSO seeks out another GRSO to provide it.

1. The case is strong for qualitative as well as quantitative evaluation tools that depend on what people at the grassroots level learn about assessing their own progress. This implies that the best evaluations may need to be long run, with a built in focus on unexpected spin-offs, local innovations, learning from mistakes, networking, and changes in the larger environment.

2. The process of participatory development (planning, evaluating, etc., by people at the grassroots level) often has more serendipitous spin-off effects than the planned results obtained. In other words, institutional sustainability based on bottom-up participation and the ideas and contributions of ordinary people have particularly powerful, long-run impacts on other goals.

3. GROs that are highly participatory and egalitarian seem to be unusually successful, with women's organizations disproportionately represented. Linkages with other GROs have an additive impact. Outsiders could seek out innovative methods used by GROs to enhance equality and promote wider adoption through GRO networks.

4. GRSO sustainability over the long run depends on decreasing their dependence on one or even more foreign donors. GRSOs are developing a number of creative ways of tying for-profit activities to grassroots support. Particularly noteworthy are modest fees for services that depend on reaching tens of thousands of people, become a significant source of income and build in accountability.

5. Given the weak philanthropic traditions in the Third World, it is difficult for GRSOs to broaden their domestic contributors. Although there are few accounts of GRSOs organizing specific fund-raising events, this might be one avenue for INGO assistance.[93] Government-to-government assistance might include help for reforming tax codes to encourage domestic contributors.

6. GRSOs are also becoming paid consultants to governments and other development agencies. In some cases they are developing innovative linkages with the private sector. Although this can promote the wider awareness of sustainable development and the adoption of environmentally sustainable technologies, it also risks attenuating the mission of organizations with weak grassroots ties.

7. Controlling costs and the use of volunteers can extend the reach and efficiency of a GRSO, but in most cases does little, by itself, to lessen dependence on foreign donors.

8. Facile assumptions by northern donors about the management needs of GRSOs are not very useful. Not only are GRSOs developing innovative

managerial capacities, they are also beginning to exchange these with each other through GRSO networks. Rather than providing specific management skills, Northern NGOs could become supporters and facilitators of this exchange. They could, for example, support research on sustainable technologies, including lessons learned in adapting them to the field, and then support dissemination of results to other GRSOs.[94]

Now that we have examined the capabilities of GROs and GRSOs, we turn, in the final chapter, to the core of grassroots support—the vertical relationships between them.

NOTES

1. See, for example, Fowler, 1988, and OECD, 1988. Carroll (1992) notes that they may not be able to compete with government in service delivery.

2. Fowler, 1988.

3. See Arbab, 1988, p.65; Ahmed, 1980, pp. 89–91. Administrative costs declined as a percentage of total budget in Carroll's (1992) study of Latin American GRSOs. On the other hand, Williams (1990:32) found that GRSO and government salaries in Bangladesh were often comparable.

4. The PQLI, by giving equal weight to literacy, life expectancy, and infant mortality may also be misleading.

5. A better educational indicator, rarely used, would be female primary completion rates.

6. The repayment rate, by itself, would be an inadequate measure without data on increased income, profitability, or increases in employment.

7. Ruiz Zuniga and Morgan Ball, 1989, p. 9. Interview in Costa Rica with Ruiz Zuniga, 1989.

8. Ritchey Vance, 1991, pp. 117–118.

9. The key informants included other researchers, donors, and program directors (as a source of information about other programs).

10. Herman, 1990, pp. 8, 304. Technoserve and its counterpart GRSOs have developed a cost-effectiveness model that gives numerical weight to noneconomic as well as economic benefits.

11. Lovemen, 1991, p. 14.

12. Speech by Atherton Martin at the University of Iowa, Spring 1990.

13. Zeuli, 1991.

14. Berg, 1987, p. 10.

15. Diaz Albertini, 1989, p. 24.

16. Carroll's (1992:36) study of thirty Latin American GRSOs (including three Member Support Organizations or GRO networks) concluded that "harder" economic goals and "softer" organizational objectives are compatible if properly implemented and can also be "mutually reinforcing."

17. Lance and McKenna, 1975. See also Cheema, 1986, for urban examples.

18. Cernea, 1987, p. 5. See also Cernea's citations.

19. Uphoff, 1986, pp. 63, 284.

20. Paul, 1987, p. 3. The "intensity" of participation was related to information

sharing, shared decision-making, and the degree to which actions were initiated by beneficiaries.

21. Buvinic, 1989, p. 1052.

22. Carroll, 1992, pp. 34, 67. Organizations gained experience assisting people who were slightly better off, then extended their reach to poorer people. Also positively correlated were providing services and innovation.

23. Lewis, 1986, p. 26.

24. Similarly, Carroll (1992:36–37) notes that the strongest GRSOs in his Latin American sample invented development innovations that took advantage of "synergy" in apparently conflicting development objectives. The Centro de Educacion y Technologia in Chile, for example, uses regionally tailored family gardening for home consumption as a wedge for participation.

25. Eldridge, 1984–85, pp. 414–415; Hyden, 1981. Hollnsteiner (1979:409) argues, "Tactics against the powerful should be within the experience of the powerless and outside the experience of the powerful."

26. Ashoka, 1989, p. 142.

27. Among the institutional evaluation indicators that can be used to assess GROs are the number and composition of its members, whether it has a substantial number of women members, and the percent of the very poor who participate. If members have left, why? Was this discussed in the group? Is responsibility shared in running the group? Are members, including women, becoming more articulate? Is the group undertaking joint economic activities? And, finally, are they networking with other groups? (FAO/FFHC, 1985:18).

28. Esman and Uphoff, 1984, p. 159.

29. Esman and Uphoff, 1974; Tinker, 1986.

30. Diaz Albertini, 1990, pp. 49, 51. A GRSO founded in 1984 helps kitchens purchase food wholesale from peasant cooperatives.

31. Presentation by Amy Baker, University of Illinois, Association for Women in Development Conference, Washington, D.C., 1989.

32. Durning, 1989, p. 19.

33. Hollnsteiner, 1979; Coombs, 1980; Freire, 1970; Esman and Uphoff, 1984.

34. F. Korten, 1983, pp. 193–194.

35. The reasons for this geographical distinction are unclear. However, one could hypothesize that Asian GROs are older and more experienced.

36. See Fisher, 1984, p. 67.

37. Cernea, 1987, p. 12. See also Merschrod, 1980.

38. See Fisher, 1977, 1984, p. 75.

39. Fowler, 1990.

40. Elliott, 1987, p. 64.

41. Arbab, 1988, p. 65.

42. Moita, 1985, p. 4.

43. Fals Borda (1988) gives a more detailed descripton of participatory research.

44. Ahmed, 1991, p. 11, calls BRAC's ties to GROs "collegial."

45. Millwood and Gazelius, 1985, p. 196.

46. Haubert, 1986; Lopezllera Mendez, 1988a.

47. AIRD News, 1987, p. 11. Emphasis added.

48. Smith, 1990.

49. USAID, 1989, p. 12.

50. Tongsawate and Tipps, 1985.

51. Mwangi, 1986.

52. Guneau and Morrisson, 1985.

53. See Anheier, 1987a, p. 8 and FUNDESA, 1989, p. 140. Foreign contributions to Guatemalan organizations in 1988 exceeded $46 million, compared to approximately $20 million from the government.

54. McCarthy, 1989; Dadrawala, 1990, p. 369.

55. See Fernando, 1986, for an account of a project funded in Sri Lanka by Save the Children that was given initial planning support.

56. Fox, 1987.

57. Gonoshasthaya Kendra, 1980, p. 26.

58. FUNDESA, 1990, p. 14.

59. Ibrahim, 1990, p. 352.

60. Dadrawala, 1990, pp. 364–365.

61. McCarthy, 1989, pp. 12, 22.

62. Discussions with Gurmit Singh, Avadhani Popuri Nageswara and Kishokumar at the Asia Society, April 1991.

63. FUNDESA, 1989, pp. 20, 116.

64. Eldridge, 1988, p. 23.

65. Bratton, 1989, pp. 29, 39.

66. McCarthy, 1989, p. 7.

67. Garilao, 1992.

68. Leonard, 1982, p. 203; McCarthy, 1989.

69. Cernea, 1988, p. 32. The study covered all World Bank financed primary health care GRSOs.

70. Leach, McCormack, and Nelson, 1988.

71. Clark, 1991, p. 87.

72. I visited the project, which has received assistance from Technoserve, in 1989.

73. International Tree Project Clearinghouse, 1987, p. 184.

74. Tendler, 1987.

75. Weber, 1990, p. 8.

76. Ahmed, 1980a, p. 203.

77. Ashoka, 1988, p. 3.

78. Schmidt and Toomey, 1987, pp. 4–5; Non-Governmental Liaison Service, 1987, p. 16.

79. USAID, 1989, pp. 18–19.

80. Estelle James studied eighteen Sri Lankan organizations (mostly charities plus a few GRSOs) and estimated that volunteers contributed 2,525 full-time equivalent people years, "approximately the same as the number of full-time paid employees" (James, 1982:303).

81. FUNDESA, 1989; Tongsawate and Tipps, 1985.

82. Lokniti, n.d.

83. Gupta, 1990, p. 12.

84. IFDA, 1990c, p. 106; *Brundtland Bulletin*, 1990, March, WP1.

85. Population Institute, 1988, pp. 94, 77, 91.

86. IFDA, 1990, pp. 99–100.

87. See PRADAN, 1988, p. 15. PRADAN's nine-member task force visited thirty-

six varied GRSOs in eight Indian states, interviewing staff, community members, and leadership. See also Muttreja, 1990, p. 12.

88. PRADAN, 1988, p. 26.

89. Carroll (1992), on the other hand, sees overdependence on charismatic leaders as a continuing problem with many Latin American GRSOs.

90. Seva Mandir, 1988–89.

91. Cotter, 1988.

92. Ross, 1990, pp. 1–2.

93. This topic will be explained more fully in Volume 2.

94. See Carroll, 1992, p. 119.

8

GRO-GRSO Linkages

You have changed my life forever. I have never thought about the
connection between power and behavior before. One year from today
I am going to be powerful.

A Kenyan woman[1]

Intellectuals, when isolated from the social movement, become sterile.
... Contrarily, when intellectuals become an integral, organic part of
the social movement, they have a crucial catalytic effect on it, in a
mutually fertilizing, creative relationship ... indispensable for the social
movement to make qualitative leaps forward.[2]

Influencing people to build capacity to act on their own behalf, originally
described by David McClelland (1970), has been called the "central paradox
of social development."[3] The top-down–bottom-up relationship, designed
to empower, is itself based on unequal power.

Previous chapters have dealt with the building blocks of this insider-
outsider relationship: GROs, GRSOs, their horizontal networks, and, finally, what makes GROs and GRSOs able as individual organizations to
achieve sustainable development and empowerment. This chapter focuses
on the relationships between NGOs that are tied most closely to the resolution of this "central paradox."

Outsiders, whether they represent governments, INGOs, the World Bank,
or GRSOs, all confront this dilemma, although not all take full account of
it. Before dealing with the unique characteristics of GRO-GRSO relationships and the institutional relationships that affect organizational perfor-

mance, we shall explore some general lessons learned about the process of linking sustainable development to empowerment. These could apply to any top-down–bottom-up relationship, although we use GRO-GRSO examples.

PROMOTING EMPOWERMENT AND DEVELOPMENT

Nonformal Education

All communities in the Third World have individual human resources that need to be enhanced if development is to be sustainable and, in the long run, autonomous. All communities, including those without GROs, also have some organizational resources. By buying into the development process as individuals, local people also buy into existing or emerging local institutions, whether they are microenterprises, schools, or GROs.

There are many hands-on participatory learning techniques that can include almost everyone in a community. These include regular democratic meetings, community celebrations to inaugurate concrete achievements (with outsiders invited), or organizing a GRO as a legal entity that can then apply for credit. Seva Mandir in India uses poets, playwrights, folk singers, and puppeteers as volunteer teachers.[4] The Departamento de Educacion Popular Permanente de Chimborazo in Ecuador uses street theater in Quechua to build self-awareness. A housing cooperative president in Buenos Aires explained his own method:

> People get tired of meeting and discussing. On the other hand, if one begins to unite people through a party, another state of animation arises. I define a party as being able to invite others . . . everyone brings something . . . once people are happy they can think about solutions to their problems . . . We've also gotten help in training people in journalism and other communication techniques such as public speaking.[5]

Mass educational approaches can have a long-term but equally positive impact on community organization. A GRSO called Accion Cultural Popular Hondurena (ACPH) began conducting adult education through radio schools in 1960. Founded by the Bishop of Tegucigalpa, the programs initially covered such topics as literacy, health, agriculture, and home economics. Later an accelerated primary school correspondence degree and an agricultural development program were added. "The subsequent growth and strength of *campesino* movements, especially the National Campesino Union (UNC), are a measure of ACPH's success in grassroots organizing."[6]

Nonformal adult education also has to focus on the diffusion of individual skills. Providing local members of a community with training in practical development skills is so obvious that it is sometimes overlooked by enthusiastic advocates of participation. Consultores del Campo in Michoacan, Mexico, has achieved a 50 percent increase in agricultural yields by "highly participatory testing and diffusion of innovations" that have been tailored to that locality and incorporate production risk.[7]

That the people already know a great deal is undeniable, but that some people can and should learn to become paramedics or accountants is also true. The Aguaruna Huambisa Council of the Marañon river in Peru trains and supplies community mechanics to repair motorboats, for example.[8] The Fondo Ecuatoriano Populorum Progresso trains farmers as extension agents by using their own land.[9] Alliband (1984) spent a year visiting the programs of GRSOs in India and concluded that the single most powerful factor promoting measurable results was the training and support of villagers as paraprofessional extension workers, or paramedics.

The Asian GRSOs that pioneered large-scale approaches to family planning and health built their programs on paraprofessional training. Gonoshasthaya Kendra (People's Health Center) in Bangladesh developed a health care, family planning, and nutrition program using trained village auxiliaries. By 1980, it served approximately 100,000 people. A rough cost-benefit analysis done in that year suggested that its cost per beneficiary more than favorably compared with government health program still centered on curative medicine and hospitals.[10]

Longer term education for technical careers in development can contribute even more to organizational sustainability. Agua del Pueblo in Guatemala provides a two-year intensive training course for rural sanitation technicians who will work with many other GROs and GRSOs. FUNDAEC, the rural university in Colombia, concentrates on careers related to development "selected and integrated in new ways so that individuals can comprehend it at different levels of competence," in contrast to other Colombian university graduates "trained to function in a modern society in which only a small number can participate."[11]

Nonformal education can also be tied to local leadership and management skills, which Clark (1991) considers to be the most powerful factor determining the success of NGOs. Paraprofessional training can include problem solving and organizing skills as well. An example is the wasteland unit of Seva Mandir in Rajasthan that trained paraprofessionals in forestry and community organizing. Each of these "barefoot foresters" supervised the plantings of fifty families. Within fifteen months, 23 million saplings were planted.[12]

Organizational skills such as management and accounting strengthen technical education and can be spread among a number of group members. These skills allow GROs to recognize the need to systematically develop a plan of action and, through "process documentation," gather data about their own communities, measure performance, and make informed decisions. (See Exhibit 8.1.)

Process documentation, even more powerful if computers are available, is both training and a form of implementation. In Kenya, for example, the

---

Exhibit 8.1
Process Documentation in the Philippines

The Community Information and Planning System in the Philippines was organized by Phildhrra. Each community agrees on the process, local research groups are trained, and the research reports are presented to the community, which suggests a plan of action. An organizational planning committee draws up an implementation plan, which is submitted back to the community a number of times, with periodic reports on participation, equity, and increases in income. Once implementation begins, the community organization can draw on technical help from a network of specialized agencies such as the Agency for Community Education in Luzon on conflict resolution, the Muslim-Christian Agency for Rural Development (MUCARD) in Mindinao on income generation, the Visayas Cooperative Development Center in Cebu, or the Institute of Primary Health Care (IPHC) in Davao.[13]

---

most successful GROs linked to Tototo had a system of facilitator and coordinator log books filled with data from extensive participant surveys and interviews. As a management training device, the books had "a striking impact on collective work aimed either at income generation or community development" and led to the development of a bakery, poultry projects, rabbits, a firewood business, and a nursery school.[14] Data collection need not apply solely to the GRO itself. Unpaid data gatherers from GROs tied to two Chilean research organizations (Programa de Economia para el Trabajo and Centro de Investigaciones para el Desarrollo Educativo) planned and recommended a practical manual on establishing and maintaining revolving loan funds. It was published and distributed among 100 other organizations.[15]

There are real pitfalls in education for development, however. Trained "leaders" may leave their communities because they are now able to obtain jobs elsewhere. GRSO professionals, particularly those trained in the developed world, may leave for more lucrative positions. The National Council of Churches in Kenya lost two of every three foreign trained staff within two years.[16] University professors may have their own private agendas despite their rhetorical commitment to the poor. Expectations may far exceed educational resources. The demand for training by the Savings Development Movement in Zimbabwe could not be supplied by three professionals.[17]

Yet such problems can be foreseen or can trigger innovative responses once they occur. The Colombian counterpart to Save the Children began training married, middle-aged women after a majority of the young unmarried women's group coordinators left for jobs in the city.[18] Fasle Abed, the founder and director of BRAC sought the best university graduates from the beginning and offered them contracts for three years, including time for field work on a doctorate. Although this was at first considered risky, the staff members learned about development management at the village level and BRAC's middle and senior management is now considered "exceptional."[19]

Sometimes the positive results of training are not planned. BRAC's high turnover *after* the three-year contract provides other GRSOs with high-caliber staff.[20] An Inter-American Foundation study of the Guatemalan Centro de Autoformacion Promotores Sociales concluded that the training of 16,000 paraprofessionals "radiates outward, it doesn't trickle up or down. One graduate, for example, manages a national federation of small farmers."[21]

Also crucial to education for institutional sustainability is the ability to learn from less than satisfactory results. FUNDASAL in El Salvador found that after six years of operation only 5 of their 22 associated communities were well consolidated in terms of participation, administration, and maintenance of roads, clinics, housing, and income generation. FUNDASAL's own evaluation concluded that it was attempting to maintain too much control.[22] After reducing its staff by two-thirds, FUNDASAL established looser and more flexible relationships with 350 communities centered on community leadership training in health, enterprise development, and community administration.[23] The Association of New Alchemists (ANAI) in Costa Rica learned that tree nursery groups with more than fifteen members were more successful. They also found that they needed to upgrade their own professional skills in forestry at a tropical agricultural research center.[24]

Learning from failure may apply on a broader scale as well. Guatemalan GRSOs sponsored by the Inter-American Foundation have learned that GROs need up front funding to sort themselves out and develop their own plans.[25] In Peru, GRSOs have shifted from education and consciousness raising to promoting practical political and technical skills. (See Exhibit 8.2.)

Promoting Autonomy

In addition to being willing to "learn-teach-learn," outsiders have to really want to work themselves out of a job and know when to do it. If a GRSO or other outside agency pulls out too soon, they may leave little behind. If they stay too long, they may establish a pattern of dependency.[26] Some GRSOs now plan their own departure. DESEC in Bolivia begins working intensively in a rural community but then sets up community centers and specialized committees which eventually become linked to a regional federation of community centers and a national federation that assumes a stronger assistance role. GROs are encouraged to work with other development organizations and programs.[27] The Center for Research and De-

---

Exhibit 8.2
The GRSO Learning Curve in Peru

Between 1975 and 1982, Peruvian GRSOs concentrated on consciousness raising, popular education, leadership training, and alternative communication more often than they directly addressed the material needs of the poor. Problems such as water and sewage were discussed through radio, but few alternatives were provided. According to Diaz Albertini (1990), there were few attempts to evaluate results.

Having learned from earlier failures, Peruvian GRSOs are now focusing on self-government for villages and squatter settlements. They have become more technically oriented and have incorporated architects, engineers, and lawyers into their staffs. The ebb and flow of popular participation was recognized and GRSO practice adapted by supporting GROs "at the crest of mobilization and retiring when it slowed down." Some GRSOs worked with up to 12,000 families and covered larger geographical areas. In addition to providing legal aid, urban GRSOs supported LDA contacts with construction firms. GRSOs also became brokers between GROs such as street vendors' associations and the housing ministry.

Exhibit 8.3
Splitting the Nucleus of the Social Atom

The Center works through married couples, trained in support group methodology, for a cost of $10 U.S. The Center found it is easier to teach illiterate peasants than educated teachers to be monitors for family support groups. Both volunteer monitors and coordinators receive a small payment to organize local support groups. "The handover to groups is accomplished not by professionals but by monitors...the point at which the latent social forces begin to be deployed—which Fals Borda compared with the potential unleashed at the moment when the nucleus of an atom is split—comes when the monitors start work." The objective is to increase demands for what the program cannot provide such as jobs, schools, and housing. "This demands a non-traditional evaluation of costs and benefits, since the most important effects are not those proposed by the program but are rather those achieved by the participants. In fact, the processes are more important than the results achieved."[28]

---

velopment in Chile uses community monitors for this transition. (See Exhibit 8.3.)

Sometimes it is necessary to pull out because a project may not be sustainable, or accept the fact that not all GROs succeed. The Penny Foundation in Guatemala limits loans and technical assistance to local groups to four years and does not try to assure that all groups survive. By stressing its own limited financial resources and setting limits on credit, it discourages dependency. By being willing to accept some failures it may actually increase the percentage of organizations that survive and prosper. It also preserves an option for the poor—that of allowing them to desert an organization no longer serving their needs.[29]

Finally, empowerment depends on encouraging people to buy in to their own development through contributions in labor or money to the common task. One study concluded that the most successful GRSOs in India were those that require token payment and/or a work requirement from even the poorest people.[30] Modest fees increasing the likelihood of cost recovery and the ability to scale out do not seem to deter vast memberships, even in very poor countries. The Associacion Vive le Paysanne in Burkina Faso helped organize a GRO network from forty-two villages in Sapone that charges an entrance fee of $2 for men and $1 for women. Over 1,500 people have joined, and 30,000 have worked in agriculture, adult education, and health projects.[31] Poor communities sometimes contribute more-substantial funds. A GRO network near Oaxaca, Mexico, paid to educate a forester from their region. One community alone had previously contributed over $12,000 for outside technical assistance in forestry and was able to pay a smaller amount as their contribution to his salary.[32] Outsiders can also charge GROs for their services. Technoserve's counterpart organizations in Latin America and Africa require that a small percentage (usually 5 percent) of its costs be paid by the cooperatives being assisted.

GRO networks tied to GRSOs are, in some cases, achieving a more difficult goal—financial independence. In Northeastern Thailand, the Saccakorn groups organized a regional movement with assistance from ThaiDHRRA (The Thai Foundation for the Development of Human Resources in Rural Areas). With only six full-time staff members and limited funds, however, ThaiDHRRA's desire to help the movement support itself and expand was a real challenge. In 1980 a grant from Christian Aid, London, was used to form a collateral fund. This allowed banks located near the GROs to secure a large overdraft in the form of an additional fixed deposit dependent on group savings. The deposit earns 13 percent interest, the group borrows at 15 percent from ThaiDHRRA, with the 2 percent supporting administrative expenses, and makes loans to its members at 18 percent. Loans are approved and administered by the GROs, and have a 98 percent payback rate. By 1987 there were twenty-one groups with over 1,000 members, with savings over $100,000.[33]

THE COMPARATIVE ADVANTAGES OF GROs AND GRSOs

Just as certain strategies help promote development and empowerment, regardless of outsider identity, so also do top-down–bottom-up linkages of all kinds (whatever their function) have an independent impact on development. A study of agrarian reforms in twenty-five countries concluded that governmental linkages with, and devolution of authority to, local governments or GROs were more likely to increase peasant income than centralized processes or the use of national government extension workers. Devolution was also more likely to increase income than either technical aid or credit.[34] In Esman and Uphoff's (1984) study, local organizations with horizontal and vertical linkages had the highest overall performance ratings, although horizontal linkages were the more powerful of the two explanatory variables. "Field level officials, when confronted with an active [GRO], begin performing their duties better, keeping office hours more regularly, making requested visits to the field, coming up with suggestions of possible higher level assistance."[35] Linkages, in other words, increase the possibilities for learning and create "multiple channels of action."[36]

Although linkages strengthen many types of governmental and nongovernmental organizations, GROs and GRSOs have some particular comparative advantages in relation to empowerment that complement each other. According to an Inter-American Foundation study of the organizations they have funded, GRSOs have the capacity for "organizational, economic or technological innovation, as well as for rapid response to unforeseen opportunities. Yet membership organizations (GROs) have the potential (albeit often unrealized) to have a much deeper, and potentially more far-reaching social impact."[37] GRSOs may have the greatest grassroots development impact by providing services which strengthen GROs as membership organizations. In some cases they encourage GROs that would not otherwise have done so to organize networks.

GRSOs both link GROs to the outside world and protect them from it. Argentine GRSOs have protected GROs from the full impact of the economic crisis. Bolivian GRSOs have helped unemployed tin miners cope with structural adjustment by organizing food buying cooperatives. Stallholder and hawker cooperatives in Indonesia obtain legal and political protection as well as capital from GRSOs.[38]

With this protection from middle-class outsiders, GROs are more apt to challenge local injustice. BRAC interviewed the landless in ten Bangladesh villages, and recorded land grabs and unfair loans and bribes as a way of mapping corruption. Single events were not news to the poor, but as the numbers added up, they became intensely interested, and BRAC used this interest as an organizing vehicle for landless groups. GRSOs in the Dominican Republic help coffee farmers export coffee directly and bypass middlemen.[39] GRO networks that assume the role of GRSOs can have much the same impact. ACOOPELLI, a federation of livestock producers' associations in Zaire helps herdsmen defend their interests, curbs rustling, manages communal pasture, and represents the herders with donors and the government.[40]

Table 8.1
Modes of Support for Local Institutional Development

EXISTING LOCAL
INSTITUTIONAL CAPACITY

SOURCE OF INITIATIVE	Strong	Weak
Local	— ASSISTANCE — — — — — — — — — — —	
Shared	— — — — — — FACILITATION — — — — — —	
Outside	— — — — — — — — — — — PROMOTION —	

Source: Uphoff, 1986, p. 189.

GROs provide GRSOs with the principal means of accomplishing their objectives and the raw material of development needed to ensure flexibility and innovation. Linkages with GROs also tend to prevent GRSOs from becoming narrow and exclusionary service providers.[41] Yet the impact of GROs on GRSOs is very often greater than their impact on governments or other donors. What is consistently striking about nongovernmental vertical linkages is the evolutionary impact of GROs on GRSOs.

GRSOs, in other words, are more likely to overcome the "central paradox" of development than are other outsiders. There are several reasons for this stronger-than-average impact. The first is the widespread strong GRSO commitment to participatory development, which emerges from previous grassroots experience. The second is that GRSOs are more likely than other outsiders to seek out existing GROs, preferably strong ones.[42] Where GRSOs (or other outsiders) work with an established GRO, the "central paradox" may have less validity, even when linkages are first established. Uphoff (1986:189) shows in Table 8.1 how outside support evolves as local organizations become stronger.

When GRSOs work with weaker GROs, their commitment to participatory development makes them more likely than other outsiders to give priority to group empowerment over immediate service provision. Carroll's (1992:217) Latin American study concluded that GRSOs that focused on promoting the capacity of GROs had the highest potential for performance. The Centro de Autoformacion para Promotores Sociales (CAPS) in Guatemala and the Association of New Alchemists (ANAI) in Costa Rica provide credit to groups only after intensive empowerment training and the accomplishment of tasks not dependent on external input.

As a newly established or weak GRO becomes more effective, the mode of GRSO support tends to shift from promotion to facilitation to assistance. What is not illustrated above, however, is the impact of the GRO-GRSO

Table 8.2
Existing Capacity of GRSOs to Learn and Adapt

SOURCE OF INITIATIVE	IMPACT OF GROs ON GRSOs
Outside (weak GRO)	LITTLE IMPACT — — — — — — — — — — — — —
Shared	— — — — — — FACILITATES — — — — — — — LEARNING
Local (strong GRO)	— — — — — — — — — — — — EMPOWERS — GRSOs

relationship on the GRSO. When a GRSO can begin working with a strong, established GRO, the impact of the relationship may be stronger on the GRSO than on the GRO (see Table 8.2). Even when GROs are weak or newly established the impact on GRSOs may begin but not end with the gradual shift in modes of assistance.

Vertical connections between GROs and GRSOs enable or permit such learning to occur on both sides, but do not ensure that it will happen. What factors increase the likelihood that the potential comparative advantages of GRO-GRSO combinations will actually be able to promote sustainable development and empowerment? The functional differences *among* GRO-GRSO linkages have only begun to be reviewed statistically, so we can only hypothesize based on available evidence.[43] We know that networking among both GROs and GRSOs strengthens their potential to scale out and learn from each other. And we know that GROs and GRSOs have some unique comparative advantages that can complement each other. But do we know which patterns of networking are most likely to lead to development that is economically, environmentally, and institutionally sustainable? The next section outlines some general institutional indicators in the relationships between GRSOs and GROs that appear to warrant further study as "better performing" vertical linkages.[44]

INTERORGANIZATIONAL INDICATORS OF HIGH PERFORMANCE

There are two major reasons for discussing those types of GRO-GRSO linkages that appear to be more likely to lead to empowerment and sustainable development. The first is that this will help indicate directions for further research. The second is to provide potential donors with initial indicators for selection among GRSOs as well as potential strategies for institutional sustainability and scaling out.

Working with Existing GROs

An initial obvious but major indicator is the use of existing GROs. In Senegal, the Union for Solidarity and Mutual Help grants assistance to an LDA (called Village Development Associations or AVDs) if it has the ability to take over a project. With ties to 350 AVDs, it provides "discreet and appropriate backstopping through the provision of modest and simple funding and materials over a limited period of time."[45] In Haiti, an agro-forestry project working through GRSOs and *groupmans*, the local peasant organizations with seven to twelve members, reached not the 6,000 peasants planned but 75,000, who planted 20 million trees within four years.[46]

Because GRSOs can skip the difficult first stage of the "central paradox"— trying to create an organization from above—planning and evaluation techniques to provide a community with additional tools for determining its own future can be initiated sooner. As GRO members learn to write down their observations on how their organization is performing or could be improved, GRSOs also deepen their awareness of what they can learn as well as teach.

Sometimes the role of a traditional GRO may be apparently unrelated to development. However, the relationship of the Six S Association in Burkina Faso to the traditional *Naams* shows that roles can change and that there are enormous advantages in building on what is already in the village. Six S chose the *Naams* because, as youth organizations, they were the only traditional groups among the *Mossi* with no social inequality. As the "first African creation of a society that is neither a copy of Western ideas nor a return to ancestral custom," Six S works through the *Naams* to safeguard positive traditional values such as mutual help and its philosophy is "development without damaging."[47]

Although it is not always obvious where to draw the line between traditional local institutions and those that may have evolved from the earlier efforts of outsiders, Wali (1990:12) asserts that "organic forms of local social organization are prerequisites to successful development." The work of two Chilean GRSOs, SOPRODER and TER, illustrates the potentially important role of anthropologists in supporting indigenous peoples and their environments. (See Exhibit 8.4.)

Unfortunately, there are also examples of GRSOs and other outsiders who fail to make the effort to understand and work with indigenous institutions. According to Cusicanqui (1990), the traditional indigenous Bolivian communities, *allyus*, have been undermined by "the left and NGOs as well as the government" in Potosi. Yet this occurred simultaneously with the rise of a grassroots peasant movement elsewhere in Bolivia that successfully combined peasant union and *allyu* forms of authority.

Rotating credit societies and other pre-cooperatives are among the most widely utilized GROs. Fundacion Centavo (The Penny Foundation) in Gua-

---

Exhibit 8.4
Preserving a Fragile Ecology

Both SOPRODER (*Sociedad de Profesionales para el Desarrollo Rural*), a GRSO that works with the Mapuche, and TER (*Taller de Estudios Rurales*), which works with the Aymara, include anthropologists. SOPRODER's approach is based on an understanding of the reciprocal exchanges of resources and labor that helped the Mapuche redistribute resources and protect fragile lands before forced deed registration by the government in 1979 led to migration and began unraveling the complex web of mutual obligation. SOPRODER encourages local Mapuche groups to become experts on wheat production, animal husbandry, and health, to meet with groups from other villages, and to organize a horizontal federation. TER has found that preserving the *allyu* is essential to preserving the fragile ecology of the altiplano and compatible with both horizontal networking and intelligent modification of traditional technologies.[48]

---

temala gives enterprise credit to existing groups as well as to many that it has organized itself. Unlike government programs, which have certain criteria for "graduating" organizations from pre-cooperative to cooperative status, the Fundacion supports groups that continue to function informally. "This has been seen by some evaluators as a deficiency . . . but formalization should not be equated with institutionalization. To the extent that people's needs are being met through these organizations, they will become and remain institutions even if not legally constituted."[49] The Cameroon Credit Union League has supported the *njangi* or rotating credit associations while simultaneously founding primary credit unions. Linkages have begun to develop between the two types of groups, and the *Njangi* often become members of the local credit union.[50] In Paraguay, the Centro Paraguayo de Cooperativistas consciously avoids formal cooperatives in favor of small problem-solving committees of farmers, including women and the poorest of the poor. Peruvian GRSOs are moving away from supporting formal cooperatives and experimenting with indigenous informal groups such as water users' associations.[51]

Linkages with traditional institutions do not, of course, provide any guarantees. The Credit Unions in Cameroon kept their funds in banks that have subsequently failed. And the more sustainable *Njangi* have returned to ties with other traditional organizations.[52]

Where GROs or other local organizations do not exist, GRSOs can provide some creative substitute techniques. For example, the Kottar Social Service Agency in India only enters a community if asked. It is then in a far better position to work with local people to facilitate the creation of cooperatives.[53] BRAC in Bangladesh began by creating GROs, but the movement of landless groups that it helped to launch is now self-sustaining enough that BRAC is able to work with many new groups that it has not created.[54] The Centre pour le Developpement Auto-Centre in Cameroon encourages the creation of new groups as well as the strengthening of established ones by setting priorities by date of requests for assistance, the cohesion of the group, and the unfolding amount of participation. The Centre carries out rural training in health and agriculture through a wide range of GROs including women's groups, rotating credit funds, and work groups.[55] Not all GRSOs even try to work through local groups, however. Some Latin American GRSOs focus almost entirely on individual entrepreneurs, and therefore have less impact on empowerment.[56]

Working with GRO Networks

A second indicator of better performance linkage between GRSOs and GROs is the use of existing GRO networks rather than unrelated collections of GROs. Of course, this may involve some self-selection of innovative GROs that are also likely to link up with others, both horizontally and vertically. GRO networks do, however, have some other inherent advantages. GRSOs can assist GRO networks to empower themselves even when GRSOs are themselves reluctant or unable to confront local or national power structures. Networks are also a powerful mechanism, for scaling out even though particular approaches to development may or may not be sustainable on a larger scale. Because they spread leadership skills and reduce dependence on a few dynamic local community leaders, GRO networks enhance institutional sustainability.[57] They also help equalize the top-down power differential that maintains the "central paradox."

Some GRSOs promote networking among similar GROs. For example, the Foro Nacional de Colombia, composed of professional architects and housing experts, promotes networks among neighborhood improvement associations. However, network promotion in Colombia also includes finding common ground among diverse groups. CEPAS–San Gil and CINEP, Jesuit-sponsored research and popular education institutes in Bogota, have helped form a unified confederation (USITRAS) in Santander among student groups, women's groups, and small farmer and landless peasant organizations, including affiliates with different political tendencies. The groundwork for this was laid by CEPAS sponsorship of COOPCENTRAL, a federation of cooperatives, small farmer organizations, and local unions, which by the mid-1980s united 300,000 people or almost 60 percent of the population of the diocese of Socorro and San Gil. CEPAS runs a regional congress, offers training, and publishes a monthly paper expressing peasant views.[58]

The time invested in strengthening a GRO network is often considerable, and network promotion may not always be a practical initial strategy. Regional training institutes, such as CESAO and INADES in West and

Central Africa, started assisting emerging village groups in Burkina Faso, Mali, and Senegal in 1970–75. Between 1975 and 1980 the first GRO networks were formed by those trained earlier, but they still faced the need to include additional villages, reassure local authorities, and establish their own programs.[59] In urban Rwanda, JOC–Kigali (Young Catholic Workers) spent three years promoting the establishment of craft associations, training members, and establishing a line of credit from member savings. Only after that were they able to assist the craft associations with networking. Lecomte (1986) notes that donors, because of the up-front time needed, are often reluctant to fund the transition from "scattered and hesitant local initiatives" to regional networks. "Yet it is here that some of the prime benefits of independent supra-village associations are to be found."[60]

If a GRSO begins working in an area where there are no existing GROs, then promoting regional networking may have to be postponed for some time. The Palawan Center for Appropriate Rural Technology in the Philippines has formed eight village-level peasant associations among slash-and-burn farmers that work on agriculture, education, and health and have formed an intermediate peasant association affiliated with the National Peasant Association. Appropriate technology is used as the "entry point," followed by consciousness raising. Yet Belamide (1986) noted that the associations were not seen by the farmers as their own because too much emphasis had been placed on leadership training and not enough on mass education.

As an investment in sustainability, even having to promote a horizontal network is more productive than equal time spent organizing a single community organization. DESCO, a Peruvian GRSO, initially set up ties with thirty-six peasant community organizations. After four years of support to peasant organizations and the formation of the Inter-Communal Committee for Development, a project was designed and directly assumed by the intercommunal organization, although the advisory relationship with DESCO continued.[61] Ritchey Vance's (1991:67) field observation of the vast SEPAS network in Santander suggest that the regional infrastructure is now in place for the kind of developmental "transformation" being promoted by the Green Forum in the Philippines.

The Six S Association in Burkina Faso, Mali, and Senegal has made horizontal federation among neighboring village Naams a condition of assistance. Nine years after Six S was founded, levels of funding to the Naams had declined, providing evidence of sustainability.[62] (See Exhibit 8.5.)

When a GRSO can locate a very dynamic group of GROs or an existing network, faster results are sometimes possible. The railway authorities in Bombay asked SPARC to assist with the relocation of thousands of squatter families living too close to the railway tracks. When the SPARC relocation program began, the families had already met with a network of pavement dweller or homeless organizations called Mahila Milan (originally trained

---

Exhibit 8.5
Networking in the Sahel During the Dry Season

To qualify for Six S assistance, networks must work solely with their own resources for two years. Support is provided for regional cohesion and responsibility and only indirectly for particular activities. By avoiding dispersion and inexperienced beginners, Six S has been able to follow a "minimalist" approach and thereby reach large numbers of people. By 1983–84 there were twenty-one zones, ten in Senegal, two in mali, and nine in Burkina, encompassing 1,000 groups and 500 villages. By 1987 the number of peasant groups had reached 3,000, with 400,000 members.

Not surprisingly, technical assistance from Six S is spread thin, but this is accepted philosophically by local groups, since dry season activities such as catchment dams do not threaten productive activities taking place during the rainy winter season. Area committees or networks produce their own educational tools on such topics as soap making, solar drying, agro-forestry, and cereal banks. The organizational/educational process ignited by Six S may actually be strengthened because peasants are allowed to learn from failure and need to seek out technical assistance from each other as well as from outsiders.[63]

---

by SPARC in the early 1980s) and had used the GRO network's contacts and signatures to establish over 1,000 individual bank accounts. SPARC built on what had already happened by collaborating with the National Slum Dwellers Federation and the railway dwellers in relocation planning with the women themselves. SPARC also works with National Slum Dwellers Federation.[64] Linkages with GRO networks also evolve out of grassroots organizing without being planned. Nijera Kori in Bangladesh had organized 1,800 GROs by 1982 with a total membership of 50,000 by acquiring twenty-three organizers from another GRSO.[65] UNIDAD's use of theater in Ecuador led to the unplanned formation of five regional federations of Indian communities.[66]

Ties with GRSOs may also facilitate politically unpleasant tasks. A Paraguayan GRSO was able to remove the top tier of a peasant federation that had lost touch with its members.[67] Yet such efficiency may also have its downside. The Country Women's Association of Nigeria (COWAN) is a relatively formal multilayered network at the regional, state, and national levels, based on local groups of approximately 20 members. Total national membership is over 15,000. Once local groups make an initial contribution and join the national organization, they are eligible to borrow from a revolving loan fund, which has promoted solid income-generating activity. Zeuli (1991:60–61) describes the organization, however, as a "maximum effort from below organized from above" that is overly dependent on its founder.

Specialized Support

A third pattern to look for is a GRSO that provides specialized help to large numbers of GROs that may or may not be affiliated with each other. By specializing and by spreading specialized knowledge as widely as possible, GRSOs dilute the top-down–bottom-up power disparity. In some cases this leads to new networks, with the GRSO role limited to that of initial catalyst:

- In Paraguay BASE/ISEC (Investigacion, Sociales, Educacion, y Communicacion) is researching the roles of all kinds of GROs in political participation in the absence of effective parties. Their action program includes leadership training and helping groups communicate with each other for mutual aid.[68]
- In Senegal, a Senegalese GRSO and a French NGO promote meetings for peasants from entire regions of the country without delineating the contents of the meetings in advance. Meetings are initially given some structure through such questions as "What do you want in the way of development?" and "How do you mean to achieve it?" and then proceed to cost-benefit discussions and the use of existing resources such as rotating credit associations. The reports of the meetings are widely distributed. The Casamance Association of Young Farmers grew out of these meetings and includes forty groups.[69]

In other cases, specialized help is not intended to promote networking. CENPRODES, a GRSO tied to the Episcopal Conference of Colombia, seeks out and helps GROs prepare funding proposals for European NGOs. Since its founding in 1974, CENPRODES has helped over 700 GROs obtain funding. The percent of assisted projects designed and operated by recipients themselves increased from 8 percent in the first three years to 29 percent between 1981 and 1983.[70]

Far better known are large GRSOs such as the Grameen Bank that work with hundreds or even thousands of borrowers' groups that are not usually tied to each other. Although Grameen's administrative costs are high and cross-subsidized by interest rate earnings from depositing concessionary loans with other banks, the benefits have been enormous for the people most difficult to reach.[71] Only 4.2 percent of the loans have been granted to borrowers with more than half an acre of land. Yet incomes of borrowers' groups are 43 percent higher than those of comparable groups in non-Grameen Bank villages, and 28 percent higher than non-Bank members in the same villages. Of 975 loans surveyed, only 0.5 percent were more than a year overdue. Despite this minimalist credit approach, many groups have organized their own additional projects such as vegetable gardens or schools.[72]

The Grameen Bank model has spread to Malaysia, where AIM (Amanah

Ikhtiar Malaysia), in deference to Islamic values, charges a fixed management fee rather than interest. The Malawi Mudzi Fund, also modeled on Grameen, had organized over 500 borrowers groups by 1990. Other banks similar to Grameen have been organized in the Philippines, Guinea, Chile (CONTIGO), Peru (Accion Comunitaria del Peru), and Instituto de Desarrollo del Sector Informal (IDESI).

Although borrowers' groups are not generally linked into networks, word about the opportunities they provide spreads rapidly among neighboring communities. Working Women's Forum in Madras was founded in 1978 by Jaya Arunachalam, a social worker and political activist. Its purpose was to provide credit to the urban informal sector. By 1983, membership in Madras alone was over 40,000 in 2,000 neighborhoods, and membership had reached 12,000 in the countryside. "The most astonishing aspect of all this has been the ability of illiterate and extremely poor women to pass on the word and extend their movement to other districts, towns and states in India."[73] Leaders rose from the ranks who set up groups to raise funds, build up savings, negotiate bank loans, and provide for members' welfare needs.

Organizing these specialized economic groups allows them to become active participants in marketing, input supply, technical training, and credit. McKee (1989) argues that this is more effective than using area-focused strategies based on horizontal networking. However, this sectoral strategy narrows the range of development approaches to strictly economic ones. Trade groups might not be as effective as regionally linked LDAs in coping with an environmental crisis or family planning and health care.

GRSO service networks that provide specialized assistance to other GRSOs can also have an indirect impact on large numbers of GROs. They may, for example, be able to provide well-established "minimalist credit" GRSOs with additional capacities at a relatively low cost. The GRSOs in the Philippines that are assisting other GRSOs to incorporate family planning into their programs are a good example.

Creating GRSOs from Below

Creating GRSOs from below can actually by-pass the unequal relationship between insiders and outsiders. A fourth powerful indicator of better performance is the evolution of a GRO network into a GRSO, described in Chapter 3.

Sometimes the metamorphosis from GRO federation to GRSO is quite dramatic. Bina Swadaya (formerly The Peasants Socio-Economic Development Foundation) in Indonesia grew out of a horizontal farmers' movement organized in the 1960s. It works through LDAs called Usaha Bersama to help villages organize cooperatives and market their products. Bina stimulates local savings by providing soft credit pegged at four times the amount that a group saves on its own. It has also trained family planning workers for the Indonesian government. As of 1985, Bina Swadaya had assisted in the development of 17,830 Usaha Bersama, which consisted of 381 groups organized by Bina, 1,112 "consultative" groups that had organized themselves, 300 groups in cooperation with other GRSOs and INGOs in eight provinces, and 16,037 groups in cooperation with government departments and agencies. It is now the largest single development network in Indonesia.[74]

Among the other examples are a farmers' association among the Tiv in Nigeria that was built on traditional rotating credit arrangements. It has created 200 base centers grouped in eight regional and one national council.[75] In the eastern lowlands of Bolivia, an Indian federation (CIDOB) provides organizational and technical support to consumer and credit cooperatives as well as to subsistence farmers. Although timber companies have been logging in the region since the 1950s, the group runs its own logging company, which avoids clear cutting. The Federation of Farmers' Associations of Senegal (FONGS), founded in 1978 with help from French and Dutch NGOs, represents over 1 million people.[76] FONGS provides training in accounting and management as well as a savings and credit program for its member organizations. Many of its trainers are women.

When entrepreneurs or managers hire specialists, it is usually assumed to be a top-down process. But if GROs federating with each other are the entrepreneurs, then the notion of hierarchy as usually understood is stood on its head when they hire their own experts. Since a functional definition of hierarchy is determined by who works for whom, a bottom-up hierarchy, while challenging existing class structures, is not a contradiction in terms.[77] Also challenged by these patterns is the notion that outside linkages necessarily increase GRO dependency.[78] Although this pattern has become more common in recent years, some cooperative federations in Bolivia that are still active and autonomous were advertising for and hiring European technical experts in the 1970s.[79]

The spread of GRSOs created from below has accelerated since the late 1980s. Mexico's large number of federations, for example, includes the Confederacion Mexicana de Cajas Populares (a federation of 200 credit cooperatives), the Frente Autentico de Trabajo, which emerged from the independent labor movement, CEDESA (Centro de Desarrollo Social y Agropecuario en Dolores Hidalgo) in Guerrero made of up of peasant women, CEPOCATE (Centro Popular de Capacitacion Tecnica) in Leon, Guanajuato, comprising urban workers and other activists, the Asociacion de Mircoempresarios Mexicanos (MIMEXA) in Monterrey, and the Centro Owen in Tacambo, Michoacan, plus many local cooperatives and cooperative federations that are now able to provide technical assistance to others. According to Lopezllera Mendez (1988a:34) it is not always easy to distinguish the point at which an organization is mainly "introverted" and at what point it becomes a "micro GRSO." Nevertheless, the trend is re-markable for Mexico, where governmental co-optation is a fine art, and most independent GRSOs are founded by middle-class intellectuals.

GRSOs also emerge from below as a direct or indirect consequence of development projects implemented from above. The Rural Women's Advancement Society in West Bengal was organized by women in an ILO (International Labor Organization) camp for environmental refugees from deforestation in 1980. The organizers hired technical assistance but continued to direct the organization themselves, promoting group enterprises for sustainable forest products. They challenged the middlemen and by 1982 were represented on the marketing agency board. The group originally claimed 9 acres but now own 350 forested acres, including trees for silk worms. They have also organized other groups "like a wave" and act as arbiters in village disputes within a large area.[80]

A formal variation on this general theme are credit union federations that provide technical assistance to their member organizations and organize new credit unions. The Multi-Coop Association in India groups thousands of credit societies, rural banks, and agricultural cooperatives. MCA and an equivalent association of urban Thrift Coops (TCA) have created a joint cooperative development fund and a GRSO to manage it and provide professional training.[81] In Malaysia the Credit Union Promotion Club has 150 credit union members, three regional offices, and five full-time promoters who train new credit union organizers.[82]

Returning Exiles

A fifth frequently identified indicator of effective GRO-GRSO combinations occurs when one or more individuals leave their village, obtain an education, and then found a GRSO to assist their home village or region. Although power disparities inevitably emerge once people depart, returnees tend to be more accountable to their origins than other outsiders. In Chapter 2 we mentioned the six young Harijan women who have founded a large GRSO with a wide impact in Tamil Nadu. In Colombia a group of ten educated young men of campesino origin provide their communities with effective organizational and agricultural assistance.[83]

This pattern is particularly common in Africa where grassroots development activists have typically traveled outside their communities and then returned. According to Lecomte (1986:84), the majority of innovators are from communities "where they are a driving force and are yet in a way outside it, determined to play a transformative role in their own village." Exiles returning to the Middle Valley of Senegal helped boost school attendance. They also created the Association for the Renovation of Ndioum, which has achieved "spectacular success" by distributing audio cassettes questioning the old caste system and exposing exploitation.[84] A more dra-

matic example was the return of Dr. Ben Nzeribe from Cornell University
to his home village in Nigeria. The organization he founded in the Agwu
area has introduced new strains of rice, helped villages plant cashew trees,
and built a hospital and a school.[85]

Sometimes returning villagers create GRO networks. Twenty migrants
from the Kayes region in Mali returned and created a network of fifteen
cooperatives called URCAK (Regional Union of Agricultural Cooperatives
of Kayes) with help from a French NGO. URCAK provides agricultural
inputs as well as production and marketing services for its members. It also
supplies electricity and is promoting pilot villages to spread new ideas.[86]

The hometown or provincial associations described in Chapter 2 often
represent a kind of halfway point in the development of this type of GRSO,
since they initially provide intermittent charitable or even development assistance to their home town. In Senegal, emigrants are the largest financial
contributors to LDAs (called AVDs or Village Development Associations).[87]
Once a few members move back home many of these organizations evolve
into "highly efficient" GRSOs.[88] In Burkina Faso the "Regional Development Associations" in the cities began exerting political pressure to ensure
supplies to certain localities after the peasants began to suffer the ill effects
of poor harvests. With the 1973 famine, they provided more direct help
and later financed small village development projects. In the village of Wuro-
Sogi in Senegal, over one-fourth of the labor force migrated either to France
or to Dakar. In the 1960s these migrants set up a mutual assistance fund
for their village that provided a motor pump during a drought and trained
villagers to maintain it. With the help of these former exiles the village
assembly has made plans for literacy courses and school improvements and
established contacts with the Senegalese government, INGOs, the Federation
of Farmers' Associations of Senegal (FONGS), and the GRSO consortia,
CONGAD.[89]

Support Movements

The multiple horizontal and vertical linkages of the informal networks
described in Chapter 6 dilute power relationships, maximize learning potential, and constitute a sixth type of better performing linkage. Support
movements, like other GRO-GRSO combinations, include people helping
their own community and people helping other communities. Yet they are
continually evolving and developing more complex forms of interaction.
Lokoyan in India, for example, with over 2,000 individual and institutional
members, provides GROs with many varied and diffuse forms of assistance.
With the rise of the environmental movement, new networks are being

created that can provide GROs with specific knowledge about resource sustainability. Support movements also enhance GRO autonomy and make it more difficult for a particular GRSO to become corrupt or beholden to elites. Service networks organized by GRSOs also promote GRO autonomy and provide GROs with a wide range of technical assistance. As a PACT evaluation of Asian networks concludes, "indigenous agencies need ways to expand, not institutionally, but *programmatically*—by engaging more and more village and multi-community volunteers, technicians, and local resource people in the development cause. The net cost . . . should be much less than hiring additional field workers."[90]

Ties to Universities

Finally, if one were to map the development institutions in a given country, it would be worthwhile to pay special attention to GRSOs that are tied to universities or spin-offs of university groups not only because of their intellectual and technical resources but also because they have tended to be committed to other effective linkage patterns as well as participatory research and evaluation.[91] Sometimes, like Praxis (see p. 172), they create new rural universities. In other cases the graduates of development study centers within universities create GRSOs after they graduate. Lopezllera Mendez (1988:35, 50–51) considers only ten of the forty-five university development programs in Mexico to be "very good," and notes that they are often insufficiently autonomous from their universities. Nonetheless, their graduates have created "many innovative and very able GRSOs." Umar Husein, an Ashoka Fellow in Sumatra, Indonesia, is helping universities get their undergraduate students involved in community work. His organization later unites graduates and low-income groups, but the idea is initially spread through the Islamic Student's Association.[92]

CONCLUSIONS: SUSTAINABILITY AND SCALING OUT

This book has focused on the institutional sustainability of GROs, GRSOs, and their networks. Chapter 7 reviewed GROs and GRSOs as discrete organizations. This chapter has viewed empowerment strategies that can be utilized in any top-down—bottom-up relationship and then explored the comparative advantages of the GRO-GRSO relationship. We next hypothesized that there are "better performing" linkages between GROs and GRSOs. To summarize, there are at least seven indicators useful for initial identification of effective GRO-GRSO relationships:

- the use of existing GROs
- the use of horizontal GRO networks
- specialized help to large numbers of GROs
- the evolution of a GRO network into a GRSO

- people who return to their communities ready to help
- informal GRSO networks
- ties to universities

Although the results and long-term sustainability of these approaches have not been systematically evaluated, they do achieve at least four important preconditions for long-term and widespread impact. First, they promote networking and enhance the possibilities for continual feedback and organizational learning. Second, they can help support and sustain effective innovations. Third, they provide the organizational mechanisms if not necessarily the substance of sustainability and the scaling out of new ideas. Fourth, they dilute or even eliminate inequities characteristically inherent in the "central paradox of development."

The *probability* of sustainable development is another story, however. If sustainable economic development is a precondition for GRSOs eventually being able to move out and assist new communities, and for GROs to assist the poorer members of their networks, then there is a strong argument for those GRSOs described in chapters 5 and 6 that focus on income generation, community-based enterprise development, and supporting alternative economic networks that build on economic expansion through bypassing exploitative middlemen. Economic networks that create their own GRSO or obtain outside technical assistance can further enhance the probability of achieving economic sustainability. For example, the Potato Producers Association of Cochabamba, a network of 360 Bolivian communities, is administering a revolving loan fund with assistance from CEDEAGRO (a Bolivian GRSO) and capital from a consortium of European and U.S. donors.[93]

The combined impact of networks and an economic approach to development is also flagged in a summary of evaluations on small enterprise development.[94] Key institutional factors promoting success included support for GROs, linkages to public and private bodies (governments and GRSOs), managerial skills emerging from participation, and networking where institutions maintain a high level of autonomy and coherence in goals and strategy. Autonomy and the lack of elite dominance were in turn related to a democratic context and linkages to other indigenous and external agencies such as informal networks.

Once microenterprises or cooperatives enter the wider market, of course, a whole new set of problems emerges that cannot be solved merely by the self-confidence and feeling of control that small-scale enterprise can engender. For this reason, Tototo in Kenya decided to hire business trainers for its network of women's groups, despite their initial success in microenterprise[95]

Despite the difficulties and complexities of implementing development that is environmentally as well as economically sustainable, there are few if any examples of NGOs implementing the destructive kinds of "development" often promoted by governments, multinationals, and official development agencies. This is partly because investment in human capital, be it training nurse midwives or providing credit for microentrepreneurs, is the least environmentally destructive form of development. Yet it is also because NGOs, including thousands of GROs, have become both the vanguard of the global environmental movement and the testing ground for environmentally sustainable development strategies. The unmet challenge for Third World NGOs is to also incorporate awareness of the population crisis, which threatens to undermine both their environmental and economic progress.

Perhaps the most difficult challenge of all is to extend the reach of sustainable development. Ironically, both scaling up to affect policy and scaling out regionally begin at the micro level, when awareness of the larger impact is built in to participatory planning or when women receiving credit are also involved in a campaign to dramatize the failure of the banking system to lend to women at all. According to Khan (1991), the 20,000 or more GROs with ties to Proshika proliferated because village leaders visited other villages where groups were already organizing. Given the spread of GRO and GRSO networks, it is obvious that the need for an impact on wider systems is widely understood among activists.

Replication generally means "the spread of a particular project's positive results."[96] And single ideas have replicated themselves many times in the past. The forests surrounding Addis Ababa grew rapidly after foreign missions imported a large variety of seedlings in the 1890s. Foreign subsidies were only temporary, yet the idea proved sustainable and easily replicable by entrepreneurs.[97] During the 1920s and 1930s in China, over 100,000 people became literacy volunteers, organized by Dr. James Yen. The minimalist credit approach has spread not only from village to village but also beyond GRSOs such as Grameen and SEWA to other GRSOs in other countries.

There are many other types of replicability, or, perhaps more accurately, scaling out or scaling up. Dichter (1989) describes the most important of these as unintended desirable consequences (serendipity), successful replication of an unsuccessful initial project, or integration at a higher policy level. In Volume 2 the impact on policy of interactions between NGOs and governments will be examined. The evidence presented in this volume, however, suggests that "policy" integration may also be horizontal or both horizontal and vertical within the independent sector.

Tendler (1987) argued that the constraints on NGO expansion and replicability include trade-offs between smallness and homogeneity as a comparative advantage and competition with governments and other NGOs for donor resources, conflict with the state, relatively high costs per beneficiary, and lack of a desire to serve large numbers of clients. Since the mid-1980s, however, networks have allowed the "better performing" organizations that overcame these obstacles to expansion to increase in numbers. Smallness and homogeneity are no longer seen as advantages by some GRSOs, and a growing number are not content to serve small numbers of beneficiaries. Others realize they can use networking to retain a local impact and yet extend their reach. In most countries GRSOs, if not INGOs, cooperate with each other in some form and are developing mutually beneficial relationships with portions of governments (see Volume 2). Moreover, the idea of networking, even particular forms of networking, has itself become contagious. Six S, for example, which began in Burkina Faso, is promoting indigenous GRO networks in Chad, Gambia, Guinea Bissau, Mali, Mauritania, Niger, Senegal, and Togo.

Scaling out is, of course, also intertwined with sustainability. Although GROs are tied to the resources of specific areas, it is hard to imagine a sustainable GRO isolated from both vertical and horizontal development networks over the long run. Institutional sustainability depends on relationships that may not always replicate but necessarily take into account what others are doing. Networks also encourage GRSOs to make impact, and therefore sustainability is "a function of strategy rather than size or money."[98] However, scaling out through networks still depends on the sustainability of most of its member organizations.

Chapter 2 concluded that success in sustainable development ultimately depends on GROs, the strongest and broadest part of the organizational pyramid. In subsequent chapters we tied sustainability to GRO networks, GRSOs, GRSO networks and to particular characteristics of GROs and GRSOs. Finally, we examined the content of institutional sustainability and linked it to education for development, learning from mistakes, knowing when to pull out, and encouraging beneficiaries to "buy in" to development. Enterprise development coupled to better performing institutional linkages can make sustainability probable and not just possible. If this can be tied to awareness of resource constraints, including the impact of population growth, then NGOs could help lead the entire world away from environmental catastrophe.

Robert Michels' (1915) iron law of oligarchy has understandably conditioned the thinking of at least three generations of societal observers. The evidence presented, however, indicates that the link between individual "human nature" and oligarchic behavior is not inevitable. Since it has become nearly impossible in many countries for individuals to advance themselves, they have begun to organize collectively in ways which both pre- and postdate industrial bureaucracies.[99] Although individual GROs and GRSOs can become sources of privilege and patronage for the few, the linkages between NGOs, coupled to the computer revolution, provide enormously enhanced capabilities for implementing sustainable development.

NOTES

1. Pezzullo, 1986, p. 29.
2. FAO/FFHC, 1987b, p. 101.
3. Korten, 1983, p. 220.
4. Seva Mandir, 1988–89.
5. Interview with Guillermo Voss, President of the Cooperativa de Vivienda, Credito y Consumo San Telmo, Ltd., Buenos Aires, September 1991. Included are quotes from a cooperative bulletin.
6. According to Inda (1980:10), the early dedication of the local organizers and moderators of adult radio groups gradually eroded as the organization became more bureaucratized. However, the continued vitality of the *campesino* movement in Honduras today is further evidence of Hirschman's (1984) principle of the preservation and conservation of social energy (Millet, 1987:410).
7. Carroll, 1992, p. 48.
8. Smith, 1987, p. 12.
9. Bebbington, 1991, p. 24.
10. Ahmed, 1980, pp. 89–91.
11. Arbab, 1988, p. 67.
12. Seva Mandir, 1988–89.
13. IFDA, 1989b, p. 71.
14. Leach, McCormack, and Nelson, 1988, p. 10.
15. Swartz, 1990, p. 12.
16. Elliot, 1987, p. 61.
17. Bratton, 1989, p. 12–16.
18. Fisher, 1986.
19. Elliot, 1987, p. 62.
20. Clark, 1991, p. 83.
21. Van Orman, 1989, p. 7. The study was done by Gerland Murray of the University of Florida, Gainesville.
22. Stein, 1990, p. 26. Korten (1990) points out that NGOs with extensive grassroots programs such as the International Planned Parenthood Federation or Dr. Yen's literacy movement in China have tended to increase control and become more bureaucratized.
23. FUNDASAL's original staff was funded by a World Bank grant in 1979.
24. Carroll, 1992, p. 101.
25. Carroll, 1992, p. 101, from a letter written by Denise Humphreys.
26. Norman Uphoff, in a letter to the author, pointed out that the appropriate length of stay also depends on how outsiders conduct themselves.
27. Uphoff, 1986, p. 335.
28. Cariola and Rojas, 1989, pp. 22–24. By 1991 the program had lost funding although it had been sucessful. The methodologies are used in the Center's urban enterprise projects, however. Interview with Patricio Cariola, S.J., Santiago, September 1991.
29. Uphoff, 1986, p. 336; Peterson, 1982, p. 141.
30. Panini, 1987. See also Esman and Uphoff, 1984, pp. 155–158.
31. Interview with Andre Eugen Ilboudo at Save the Children, 1989.

32. Bray, 1991.

33. From an unpublished case study, written by Heather Clark, December 21, 1989, mailed from Thailand to J. E. Austin Associates, Cambridge, Mass.

34. Montgomery, 1972.

35. Esman and Uphoff, 1984, p. 259.

36. Uphoff, 1988, pp. 53–57. Other characteristics identified included projects that focused on sustainable resource mobilization and worked with, rather than for, the poor. They also used local organizations, a catalytic approach, indigenous technology, paraprofessionals, management innovations, and a "learning process" rather than a blueprint approach.

37. Fox and Butler, 1987, p. 4.

38. Clark, 1991, p. 175; Eldridge, 1988, p. 17.

39. Durning, 1989a, p. 61; Clark, 1991. GROs may not always want to lose protection or assume new functions, however. See Swartz, 1990; Arbab, 1988; and Eldridge, 1988, p. 17.

40. Salmen and Eaves, 1989, p. 62. This federation was actually catalyzed by project implementation units of the World Bank in Zaire, yet has been enthusiastically adopted by the herders themselves.

41. Kramer (1981:284) describes many U.S. voluntary service providers as being "narrow and exclusionary."

42. I have concluded from my reasearch that the "strongest" GROs may emerge from terrible adversity and may not necessarily represent the better-off poor. See Chapter 2.

43. Carroll's (1992) study of Latin American GRSOs is an important recent contribution, although it focuses more on GRSO strategies than on institutional patterns. Carroll defines GRSOs that focus almost exclusively on group empowerment as "cooperators." Other types, only partially within this empowerment or "capacity domain," include "retailers," that work with individual (or group) entrepreneurs; community developers, that use general nonformal educational approaches such as radio, "aggregators" (GRO networks) and "advocates" that may combine empowerment with policy advocacy. Although these categories emerged from a large study of thirty organizations, organizations partially within the capacity domain may find their empowerment strategies strengthened by other activities. And once GROs are active in networking and advocacy these activities may further strengthen group capacity. The Asian environmental movement is a good example.

44. Judith Tendler (1987) uses the phrase "better performing" to describe single organizations. I use the term "indicator," not as a quantitative gauge, but, as defined by Webster's Dictionary, as a sign, token, or pointer.

45. Ba, 1990, pp. 92, 100.

46. Murray, 1986.

47. Ouedraogo, 1986, p. 89.

48. Wali, 1990, p. 16. With the return to democracy in Chile, the government has created decentralized corporations called Condicion Especial de Pueblos Indigenas (CEPI) to funnel loans and resources. This is being organized by Jose Bengoa, an anthropologist who has worked with SOPRODER.

49. Uphoff, 1986, p. 36.

50. Uphoff, 1986, p. 353.

51. Carroll, 1992, pp. 106–107.

52. This update was obtained from Elizabeth Thompson, a graduate student at Yale who lived in the Cameroon.

53. Uphoff, 1986, p. 190.

54. On the other hand, many smaller GRSOs have copied the BRAC model of group formation, functional education, savings and credit, and income generation mechanistically, without understanding the need to adapt to local conditions and institutions (PACT, 1989:32).

55. From a pamphlet, no date, p. 15.

56. Carroll, 1992, p. 97. Carroll calls these "retailers."

57. Esman and Uphoff, 1984, p. 226.

58. Smith, 1990, p. 246. The updated figures are from Ritchey Vance, 1991.

59. OECD, 1987, p. 43.

60. Lecomte, 1986, p. 92.

61. Padron, 1983, p. 85.

62. In Mali the GROs that work with Six S are called *Tons* and in Senegal, *N'Bataye*. (Buell, 1987).

63. Lecomte, 1986, IRED, 1987, p. 4, OECD, 1988, p. 45. Although Six S was founded by a Burkinabe sociologist, Bernard Ouedrago, it has a fund-raising office in Geneva and receives assistance from the Swiss government and several Swiss, German, and French NGOs.

64. Daswani and D'Cruz, 1990:31–36; Gahlot, 1991, pp. 8–10.

65. Ideas and Action, 1984, p. 10.

66. Carroll, 1992, p. 61.

67. Carroll, 1992, p. 89.

68. IFDA 1987, pp. 15–24.

69. AFDI, 1987, pp. 9–13.

70. Smith, 1990, p. 245.

71. Grameen has attracted professional volunteers seconded from the Central Bank. Nonetheless, one observer (Jatoba, 1987:130) contends that overhead costs are "significant" in Grameen and in a similar Venezuelan bank called Funda Comun where the cost per job created is higher than those of other urban employment projects. Other benefits such as institution building and empowerment may not stem from other projects, however, and costs may decline over time.

72. Hulme, 1990; Durning, 1989, p. 31.

73. Lecomte, 1986, p. 118. See also Tendler, 1987.

74. IFDA, 1989c, pp. 15–23.

75. Uphoff, 1986, p. 216.

76. OECD, 1988, p. 48.

77. I am indebted to my husband, Richard Peck, for this idea.

78. See, for example, Esman and Uphoff, 1984.

79. Tolles, 1981, p. 3.

80. Talk given by Monoshi Mitra, Association for Women in Development, 1989.

81. IFDA, 1985, p. 78.

82. Asian Confederation of Credit Unions, 1986.

83. Hirschman, 1984, p. 52.

84. Ba, 1990, p. 90.

85. McCord and McCord, 1986, p. 55.

86. See IRED, 1987b, p. 9; IRED, 1988, p. 11; and Rouille d'Orfeuil, 1984.

87. Ba, 1990, pp. 92, 100.

88. Sawadogo, 1990, p. 60.

89. OECD, 1988, pp. 46–47.

90. PACT, 1989, p. 54.

91. Carroll (1992:137) found that GRSOs with regular ties or contacts with universities or government agencies, especially at the regional level, scored higher on performance than did those without such contacts.

92. Ashoka, 1989, pp. 134–135.

93. Smith, 1987, p. 11.

94. Hunt, 1984, p. 183.

95. Leach, McCormack, and Nelson, 1988, p. 15.

96. Dichter, 1989.

97. Ellis, 1984, pp. 204–205.

98. Although he was not writing about networks, Dichter's (1989) discussion of replicability includes this description of being "systems minded" as an underlying principle of grassroots development.

99. Uphoff (1992:287) observes that the most interesting challenge is how "zero-sum exchanges can be converted into positive-sum exchanges by changing the value that people attribute to each other's well being."

Glossary

Grassroots organizations (GROs): Third World membership organizations that work to improve and develop their own communities. Also called people's organizations or base groups. There are three major types of GROs in most countries. Local Development Associations (LDAs) such as village councils or neighborhood associations work on many development issues that concern the entire community. Interest Associations are more limited in membership, and tend to work on particular issues. Among the examples are women's groups and water users' associations. Pre-cooperatives, cooperatives, and other community-based enterprises are a third type of GRO, distinguishable from other for profit organizations by their broad based ownership and participation in wider community development activities.

Local organizations: A broader term including GROs, as well as other membership organizations such as burial societies and kinship groups.

GRO networks: Horizontal linkages among GROs, regionally based.

Grassroots support organizations (GRSOs): Nationally or regionally based development assistance organizations, usually composed of paid professionals that work with GROs in communities other than their own. Also called intermediary NGOs, nongovernmental development organizations (NGDOs), voluntary development organizations (VDOs), etc. GRSOs are nonprofit organizations, that may or may not have members.

GRSO networks: Based on horizontal linkages among GRSOs. These include formal umbrella organizations or consortia, informal service networks that exchange expertise and cooperate in the field and broader support movements that may include individual professionals and activists as well as GRSOs.

Nongovernmental organizations (NGOs): Organizations that work on development, relief, education, and advocacy in the Third World. As used here this term means indigenous NGOs and includes grassroots organizations (GROs), grassroots support organizations (GRSOs), GRO networks, and GRSO networks. It can also be used to include both indigenous or Southern NGOs and international or Northern NGOs. Except for some GROs (pre-cooperatives and co-operatives) most NGOs are nonprofit organizations.

International NGOs (INGOs): Organizations carrying out development assistance whose central headquarters are not based in the countries where they work. Also called "Northern" NGOs.

Counterpart GRSOs: GRSOs founded by Northern NGOs, with all national staffs, that follow a model promoted by the Northern partner.

Sustainable development: Development in the present that does not destroy the resources needed for future development.

Bibliography

ABACED (Association des Bachiliers pour l'Emploi et le Developpement). N.d. Pamphlet. Dakar, Senegal, B.P. 12135.

Abate, Alula, and Fassil G. Kiros. 1983. "Agrarian Reform, Structural Changes and Rural Development in Ethiopia." In Ghose, ed., pp. 141–184.

Acuna Gomez, Antonio; Lismaco Duran Perez; Gustavo Pacheco Rosso; Denise Roca de Mendez; and Cecilia Rojas Rodriguez. 1979. "Community Development and Improved Social Services in the Southeastern Zone of Cartagena, Colombia: The Evolution of This Experience and a Few of Its Implications." United Nations Children's Fund, Special Meeting: Children in Latin America and the Caribbean, with Particular Reference to Their Situation and Development in Rural and Urban Marginal Areas, Mexico City.

Adams, Richard H. 1986. "Bureaucrats, Peasants and the Dominant Coalition: An Egyptian Case Study." *The Journal of Development Studies* 22, no. 2:336–354.

Adelman, Irma, and Cynthia Taft Morris. 1982. "National and International Measure in Support of Equitable Growth in Developing Countries: A Proposal." Working Paper No. 78–13, University of Maryland.

Aeppel, Timothy. 1987. "Bold Plan to Save Brazil's Amazon Forest." *The Christian Science Monitor*, May 20.

AFDI (Association des Agriculteurs Français et Developppment International). 1987. "Communications between Peasants in Different Parts of Senegal." *Ideas and Action*, no. 173, pp. 9–13.

Ahmed, Fauzia. 1991. "The Will to Overcome." *Oxfam America News*, Summer-Fall.

Ahmed, Manzoor. 1980a. "Introduction." In Coombs, pp. 196–206.

―――. 1980b. "The Savar Project: Meeting the Rural Health Crisis in Bangladesh." In Coombs, pp. 42–102.

AIRD News. 1987. Asian Institute for Rural Development, vol. 6, no. 3, p. 11.

Alauddin, Mohammed. N.d. "A Survey of Income Generating/Employment Creating Activities of Thirty NGOs in Bangladesh." Institute of Social Welfare and Research, University of Dhaka, Dhaka, Bangladesh. Cited in Van der Heijden, 1985.

Aldrich, Brian C. 1980. "Neighborhood Social Organization in Five Southeast Asian Cities." *International Journal of Comparative Sociology* 21, nos. 3–4 (September-December):118–130.

Ali, Shaikh Maqsood. 1986. "Government as an Agent of Social Development: Lessons from the Bangladesh Experience." In Korten, pp. 247–259.

Alliband, Terry. 1983. *Catalysts of Development: Voluntary Agencies in India.* Hartford, Conn.: Kumarian Press.

Almond, Gabriel A., and G. Bingham Powell. 1966. *Comparative Politics: A Developmental Approach.* New York: Little, Brown.

Anacleti, A. Odhiambo. 1986. "Rural Groupings and Organizations—With Special Reference to Tanzania." *The Courier,* no. 99, September-October.

ANGOC (Asian NGO Coalition for Agrarian Reform and Rural Development). 1986. *NGO Initiatives in Rural Nutrition and Health.* ANGOC, September.

Anheier, Helmut K. 1987. "Private Voluntary Organizations and Development in Africa: A Research Agenda." Paper presented at the International Symposium on the Nonprofit Sector and the Welfare State, Bad Honeff, West Germany, June.

―――. 1987a "Indigenous Voluntary Associations, Non-Profits, and Development in Africa." In Powell, pp. 416–433.

―――. 1987b "Private Voluntary Organizations and Development in West Africa: Comparative Perspectives." Draft paper.

―――. 1990. "Themes in International Research on the Nonprofit Sector." *Nonprofit and Voluntary Sector Quarterly* 19, no. 4:371–391.

Annis, Sheldon. 1987. "The Next World Bank? Financing Development from the Bottom Up." *Grassroots Development* 11, no. 1: 24–29.

―――. 1987a. "Reorganization at the Grassroots: Its Origins and Meaning." *Grassroots Development* 11, no. 2: 21–25.

―――. 1987b. "Can Small Scale Development Be a Large Scale Policy? The Case of Latin America." *World Development* 15 (Supplement, Autumn).

―――. 1989. "Can Small Scale Development Be Large-Scale Policy?" In Annis and Hakim, eds., pp. 209–218.

Annis, Sheldon, and Jeffrey Franks. 1989. "The Idea, Ideology, and Economics of the Informal Sector: The Case of Peru." *Grassroots Development* 13, no. 1:9–22.

Annis, Sheldon, and Peter Hakim, eds. 1989. *Direct to the Poor: Grassroots Development in Latin America.* Boulder, Colo.: Lynn Rienner.

Arbab, Farzzam. 1988. *The Governmental Development Organizations: Report of a Learning Project.* Cali: CELATER/PACT.

Ariyaratne, A. T. 1986. "Asian Values as a Basis for Asian Development." In Korten, pp. 32–39.

Arruda, Marcos. 1985. "The Role of Latin American Non-Governmental Organizations in the Perspective of Participatory Democracy." Rome: Third International Consultation, Freedom from Hunger Campaign/Action for Development, September 3–6.

Ashoka (1200 North Nash. Street, Arlington, Virginia). 1985. "The New Fellows— Early 1985." *Changemakers.*

———. 1986. "Ashoka Fellows-Brazil." Paper. Winter.

———. 1988. "Profiles of the Ashoka Fellows." Paper.

———. 1989. "Profiles of the Ashoka Fellows." Paper.

———. 1990. "Ten Years Impact." Paper.

———. 1991. "Profiles of Ashoka Fellows." Paper.

Asian Confederation of Credit Unions. 1986. *Report and Directory, 1985–1986.* Bangkok, Thailand.

Atang, Christopher Ivo. 1992. "The Expanded Role of Non-Governmental Organizations in the Welfare of Women and the Disadvantaged in Developing Countries." Paper presented to the Third International Conference of Research on Voluntary and Non-profit Organizations, Bloomington, Indiana University, March 11–13.

Attir, M. O., et al., eds. 1982. *Directions of Change: Modernization Theory, Research and Realities.* Boulder, Colo.: Westview Press.

Attwood, Donald W., Thomas C. Bruneau, and John G. Galaty, eds. 1988. *Power and Poverty: Development and Development Projects in the Third World.* Boulder, Colo.: Westview Press.

Aziz, Sartaj. 1988. "A Turning Point in Pakistan's Rural Development Strategy." In Lewis and Contributors, pp. 111–120.

Ba, Hassan. 1990. "Village Associations on the Riverbanks of Senegal: The New Development Actors." *Voices from Africa,* no. 2, United Nations Non-Governmental Liaison Service, Geneva, pp. 83–104.

Bagadion, Benjamin U., and Frances F. Korten. 1985. "Developing Irrigators' Organizations: A Learning Process Approach." In Cernea, ed., pp. 52–90.

Bangladesh Rural Advancement Committee. 1987. "Household Strategies in Bonkura Village." In Korten, pp. 62–77.

Baquedano, Manuel. 1989. "Socially Appropriate Technologies and Their Contribution to the Design and Implementation of Social Policies in Chile." In Downs et al., pp. 113–133.

Barkan, Joel, and Frank Holmquist. 1989. "Peasant-State Relations and the Social Base of Self-Help in Kenya." *World Politics* 16, no. 3:359–380.

Barreiro, Fernando, and Anabel Cruz. 1990. *Organizaciones No Gubernamentales de Uruguay: Analisis y Repertorio.* Montevideo: Institucion de Comunicacion y Desarrollo.

Barrig, Maruja. 1990. "Women and Development in Peru: Old Models, New Actors." *Community Development Journal* 25, no. 4:377–385.

Bartone, Carl. 1986. "Recycling Waste: The World Bank Project on Resource Recovery." *Development,* no. 4.

Bebbington, Anthony. 1991. "Sharecropping Agricultural Development: The Potential for GSO-Government Cooperation." *Grassroots Development,* no. 2 15:21–30.

Belamide, Eileen. 1986. "Building Self-Help Groups: The Philippine Experience." *Ideas and Action,* no. 171, pp. 13–18.

Bendahmane, Diane B. 1989. "Reviving the Small Farmer Sector in Uruguay." *Grassroots Development*, 13, no. 2:32–35.

Berg, Robert. 1987. "Non-Governmental Organizations: New Force in Third World Development and Politics." CASID Distinguished Speakers Series No. 2. Michigan State University, Center for Advanced Study of International Development.

Berg, Robert, and Jennifer Seymour Whitaker, eds. 1986. *Strategies for African Development*. Berkeley: University of California Press.

Blackburn, Nigel. 1992. "UNCED and the Role of Business." *Rio Reviews*. Centre for Our Common Future, Geneva, pp. 5–7.

Bletzer, Keith V. 1977. "Transition to Cooperativism in a Panamanian Rural Community." *Land Tenure Center Newsletter*, January-March, University of Wisconsin.

Booth, John A., and Mitchell A. Seligson. 1979. "Images of Political Participation." In Booth and Seligson, eds. *Political Participation in Latin America*. Volume 1. New York: Holmes and Meier.

Bratton, Michael. 1983. "Farmer Organizations in the Communal Areas of Zimbabwe: Preliminary Findings." Unpublished paper, Departments of Land Mangement and Political and Administrative Studies, University of Zimbabwe, Harare. Cited in Uphoff, 1986, p. 147.

———. 1986. "Farmer Organization and Food Production in Zimbabwe," *World Development*, March.

———. 1989. "Poverty, Organization and Public Policy: Towards a Voice for Africa's Rural Poor." Paper presented at the Conference on the Voluntary Sector Overseas, Center for the Study of Philanthropy, City University of New York, April 26.

Bray, David Barton. 1991. "The Struggle for the Forest: Conservation and Development in the Sierra Juarez." *Grassroots Development* 15, no. 3: 13–25.

Brooke, James. 1986. *The New York Times*, November 9, p. 18.

———. 1989. "Births in Brazil Are on Decline, Easing Worries." *The New York Times*, August 8.

Brown, L. David. 1990. "Bridging Organizations and Sustainable Development." IDR Working Paper No. 8. Boston: Institute for Development Research and Boston University School of Mangement.

Brown, L. David, and David Korten. 1989. "The Role of Voluntary Organizations in Development." Boston: Institute for Development Research.

Brundtland Bulletin. Number 5, September 1989.

———. Number 7, March 1990.

———. Number 8, June 1990a.

———. Number 9/10, September-December 1990b.

———. Number 11, March 1991.

———. Number 15, March 1992.

Buell, Rebecca. 1987. "Grassroots Development: A Question of Empowerment." *Cultural Survival* 11, no. 1:34–37.

Bunch, Roland. 1982. *Two Ears of Corn: A Guide to People Centered Agricultural Improvement*. Oklahoma City: World Neighbors.

Burstein, John. 1986. "Development Notes." *Grassroots Development* 10, no. 1:48–51.

Buvinic, Mayra. 1989. "Investing in Poor Women: The Psychology of Donor Support." *World Development* 17, no. 7:1045–1057.

Cabarle, Bruce. 1991. "Community Forestry and the Social Ecology of Development." *Grassroots Development* 15, no. 3:3–9.

Calavan, Michael. 1986. "Community Management in Rural Northeastern Thailand." In Korten, 1986, pp. 93–104.

California Institute of Public Affairs. 1989. *World Directory of Environmental Organizations.* 3d ed. Edited by Thaddeus C. Trzyna with Ilze M. Gotelli. Claremont. (Published in cooperation with the Sierra Club and the World Conservation Union)

Callanta, Ruth. 1990. "The Management of Corporate Philanthropy in the Philippines." In Independent Sector, pp. 245–258.

Centre pour le Developpement Auto-Centre. N.d. Pamphlet from Sangelima, Cameroon.

Cantori, Louis J., and Iliya Harik. 1984. *Local Politics and Development in the Middle East.* Boulder, Colo.: Westview Press.

Caplan, Patricia. 1985. *Class and Gender in India: Women and Their Organizations in a South Asian City.* London: Tavistock.

Cariola, Patricio, S.J., and Alfredo Rojas. 1989. "Experiments in Community Education and Some Thoughts on How to Extend It on a Mass Scale." In Downs et al., pp. 9–30.

Carroll, Thomas F. 1992. *Intermediary NGOs: The Supporting Link in Development.* Hartford, Conn.: Kumarian Press.

CEDIME. 1984. "Se forma el centro de documentación e información de los movimientos sociales del Ecuador (CEDIME)." *Revista Ciencias Sociales.* Universidad del Ecuador, Quito, no. 5, pp. 15–16.

Centre for Our Common Future (Geneva). 1992. *Networks '92,* no. 18, June-July, pp. 8–9.

Centro de Orientacion Familiar. 1985. *Grupos Asociativos Femininos con Fines Economicos: Inventorio Nacional,* San Jose, Costa Rica.

Centro Dominicano de Organizaciones de Interes Social (CEDOIS). 1988. *Directorio de Instituciones Privadas de Interes Social de la Republica Dominicana:1986–1988.* Santo Domingo.

Centro Mexicano de Instituciones Filantropicas (CMIF). 1990. *Directorio de Instituciones Filantropicas.*

Cernea, Michael. 1982. "Modernization and Development Potential of Traditional Grass Roots Organizations." In Attir et al., eds., pp. 121–139.

———, ed. 1985. *Putting People First: Sociological Variables in Rural Development.* New York: Oxford University Press.

———. 1987. "Farmer Organizations and Institution Building for Sustainable Development." *Regional Development Dialogue* 8, no. 2:1–24.

———. 1988. "Non-Governmental Organizations and Local Development." World Bank Discussion Papers No. 40.

Centre de Formation et de Recherche Cooperatives. 1987. *Rapport D'Activities 1987.* Kigali, Rwanda: Pallotti-Presse.

CET (Center for Education and Technology). 1989. "Organic Agriculture: Questions and Challenges." In Downs et al., pp. 135–148.

Charlick, Robert. 1984. Animation Rurale Revisited: Participatory Tecniques for

Improving Agriculture and Social Services in Five Francophone Nations. Ithaca, N.Y.: Rural Development Committee. Cited in Uphoff, 1986.

Checci and Company Consulting, Inc. 1989. *Final Report: Evaluation of Experience of USAID Missions with PVO Umbrella Groups in Costa Rica, Guatemala, Honduras and Haiti. Submitted to Office of Development Programs, Latin American Caribbean Bureau, Agency for International Development,* Washington, D.C.

Cheema, G. Shabbir, ed. 1986. *Reaching the Urban Poor: Project Implementation in Developing Countries.* Boulder, Colo.: Westview Press.

Chimedza, Ruvimbo. 1986. "Saving Together, Spending Together: Zimbabwe's Rural Savings Clubs." *The Courier,* no. 99, September-October.

Chira, Susan. 1987. "Seoul Journal: It's Clubby, It's Thrifty and It Can Cover Bills." *The New York Times,* November 19.

Christian, Shirley. 1986. "Democracy Calling: It's Women's New Selling Job." *The New York Times,* November 20.

CIDA (Canadian International Development Agency). 1988. *LDAP and Thai Non-Government Organization in Local Development.* Summary Report.

CINDE (Coalition Costarricense de Initiativas des Desarrollo). 1986. *Directorio Parcial de Organizaciones Privadas Voluntarias.* San Jose, Costa Rica.

Clark, John. 1991. *Democratizing Development: The Role of Voluntary Organizations.* Hartford, Conn.: Kumarian Press.

CNIRO (Caribbean Network for Integrated Rural Development). 1989. *Developing the Rural Network: A Directory of Rural Development Resources in the Caribbean.* St. Augustine, Trinidad, and Tobago.

Cohen, John M., and Norman T. Uphoff. 1980. "Participation's Place in Rural Development: Seeking Clarity through Specificity." *World Development* 8, no. 2 (February).

Conservation Foundation Letter. 1988. No 3. Conservation Foundation, Washington, D.C.

Coombs, Philip H. 1980. *Meeting the Basic Needs of the Rural Poor.* New York: Pergamon Press.

Cooperation for Development. 1987. "What's New?" Vol. 3, no. 1. (Chesham, United Kingdom)

Cordoba-Novion, Cesar, and Celine Sachs. 1987. *Urban Self-Reliance Directory.* Nyon, Switzerland: International Foundation for Development Alternatives, January.

Cotter, Jim. 1988. "USAID-Financed PVO Co-Financing Projects in the Philippines and Indonesia: Reshaping the Terms of PVO Collaboration." The American University, December.

Craig, Susan. 1985 "Political Patronage and Community Resistance: Community Councils in Trinidad and Tobago." In Gomes, ed.

Crossette, Barbara. 1988. "Indonesian Moslems Search for a Middle Way." *The New York Times,* March 15, p. A13.

———. 1988a. "In Vietnam, Craft Project Breaks Mold." *The New York Times,* May 2.

———. 1991. "Village Committees Learn to Guard Endangered Forest in Bangladesh." *The New York Times,* August 6, p. C4.

Cusicanqui, Silvia Rivera. 1990. "Liberal Democracy and the Allyu Democracy in

Bolivia: The Case of Northern Potosi." *The Journal of Development Studies* 26, no.4:97–121.

CVSS (The Council of Voluntary Social Services). 1987. *A Handbook of the Social Services in Jamaica.* Kingston.

Dadrawala, Noshir A. 1990. "The Role of Philanthropy in India." In Independent Sector pp. 361–372.

Daswani, Mona, and Celine D'Cruz. 1990. "The Right Track: A Case Study of Resettlement Initiatives by Women in Bombay." *Community Development Journal* 25, no.1:31-36.

de Graaf, Martin. 1987. "Context, Constraint or Control? Zimbabwean NGOs and Their Environment." *Development Policy Review* 5(3):277–301.

Deshpande, V. D., S. P. Salunke, and David Korten. 1986. "Water for People." In Korten, 1986, pp. 183–200.

De Soto, Hernando. 1989. *The Other Path: The Invisible Revolution in the Third World.* New York: Harper and Row.

Dhungel, Dipak P. 1986. "The People's Movement and Experiment in Nepal." *Community Development Journal* 21, no.3:217–225.

Diaz-Albertini, Javier. 1989. "Development as Grassroots Empowerment: The Case of NGOs in Lima, Peru." Unpublished manuscript submitted to the Yale Program on Non-Profit Organizations.

———. 1990. "Development as Grassroots Empowerment: An Analytical Review of NGDO Programs in Lima, Peru." PONPO Working Paper No. 157 and ISPS Working Paper No. 2157.

Dichter, Thomas W. 1989. "NGOs and the Replication Trap." Technoserve, Findings '80.

Dichter, Thomas W., and Scott Zesch. 1989. *Savings and Credit Societies in Kenya: Insights into Management Transformation and Institutional Modernization.* Sector Study Series. Technoserve, Case Histories in Enterprise Development.

Douglas, James. 1983. *Why Charity? The Case for a Third Sector.* Newbury Park, Calif.: Sage.

Downs, Charles, Giorgio Solimano, Carlos Vergara, and Luis Zuniga. 1989. *Social Policy from the Grassroots: Nongovernmental Organizations in Chile.* Boulder, Colo.: Westview Press.

Durning, Alan B. 1989. "Action at the Grassroots: Fighting Poverty and Environmental Decline." Worldwatch Paper No. 88. The Worldwatch Institute.

———. 1989a. "Poverty and the Environment: Reversing the Downward Spiral." Worldwatch Paper No. 89. The Worldwatch Institute.

———. 1989b "People Power and Development." *Foreign Policy*, no. 76 (Fall):66–83.

Dyson-Hudson, Neville. 1985. "Pastoral Production Systems and Livestock and Livestock Development Projects: An East African Perspective." In Cernea, ed., pp. 157–186.

Edel, Matthew D. 1969. "The Colombian Community Action Program: Costs and Benefits." Yale Economic Essays 9, no. 2

El-Baz, Shahida. 1992. "Historical and Instituional Development of Arab NGOs." Third International Conference of Research on Voluntary and Nonprofit Organizations, University of Indiana, March 11–13.

Eldridge, Philip. 1984–85. "The Political Role of Community Action Groups in

India and Indonesia: In Search of a General Theory." *Alternatives: A Journal of World Policy* 10 (Winter).

———. 1988. "Non-Government Organisations and the Role of the State in Indonesia." Paper presented to the Conference on The State and Civil Society in Contemporary Indonesia, November 25–27, Centre for Southeast Asian Studies/Department of Indonesian and Chinese Studies, Monash University, Melbourne, Australia.

Elliot, Charles. 1987. "Some Aspects of Relations Between the North and South in the NGO Sector." *World Development* 15 (Supplement): 57–68.

Ellis, Gene. 1984. "Making PVO's Count More: A Proposal." In Gorman. ed.

Enge, Kjell, and Scott Whiteford. 1989. *The Keepers of Water and Earth: Mexican Rural Social Organization and Irrigation.* Austin: University of Texas Press.

Ergas, Zaki. 1986. "In Search of Development: Some Directions for Further Investigation." *The Journal of Modern African Studies* 24, no. 2:303–334.

Esman, Milton J., and Norman T. Uphoff. 1974. "Local Organization for Rural Development: Analysis of Asian Experience." U.S. Agency for International Development.

———. 1984. *Local Organizations: Intermediaries in Local Development.* Ithaca, N.Y.: Cornell University Press.

Esteva, Gustavo. 1987. "Regenerating People's Space," *Alternatives* 12, no. 1 (January):125–152.

Etling, Arlen. 1975. "Characteristics of Facilitators: The Ecuador Project and Beyond." Amherst: University of Massachusetts, Center for International Education, School of Education.

Everett, Jana, and Mira Savara. 1987. "Organizations and Informal Sector Women: Social Control or Empowerment." Unpublished paper presented to the Association for Women in Development, Washington, D.C., April.

Fals Borda, Orlando. 1988. *Knowledge and People's Power: Lessons with Peasants in Nicaragua, Mexico and Colombia.* New Delhi: Indian Social Institute

FAO/FFHC. 1980. "Resources for Rural Development in Africa:The Information Activities of INADES." *Ideas and Action,* no. 13.

———. 1984. "Nijera Kori: 'We Will Do It Ourselves.' " *Ideas and Action,* no. 157.

———. 1985. "India: Are We on the Right Track?" *Ideas and Action,* no. 161.

———. 1985a. "NGOs in Latin America." *Ideas and Action,* no. 162, pp. 6–9.

———. 1985b "FFHC/AD in Africa" and "Towards a Latin American Programme." *Ideas and Action,* no. 162.

———. 1985–86. "NGO Partnership and the Challenge of the Rural Poor: The Third International FFHC/AD Consultation." *Ideas and Action,* no. 165.

———. 1987. "Alternative Agriculture: An Experience from the Grassroots in Latin America." *Ideas and Action,* no. 175.

———. 1987a. "How Peasants in Burkina Faso Reacted to the Food Crisis and Their Views on Aid." *Ideas and Action,* no. 177.

———. 1987b. "NGOs in Latin America: Their Contribution to Participatory Democracy." *Development: Seeds of Change,* no. 4, pp. 100–105.

Fatima, Burnad. 1984. "Rural Development and Women's Liberation: Caste, Class and Gender in a Grass Roots Organization in Tamil Nadu, South India." *Bulletin* 15, Institute for Development Studies, Sussex, England, pp. 45–56.

Fausto, Ayrton. 1988. "La Cooperacion al Desarrollo en un Proceso de Fundacion Democratica: El Caso de Brasil." *Cooperacion Internacional al Desarrollo* No. 33, Taller de Cooperacion al Desarrollo, Santiago, pp. 11–13.

FCI (Family Care International). 1989. *NGO Participation in Improving Women's Reproductive Health in Africa*. Unpublished manuscript, New York.

Felsenthal, Mark. 1985–86. "The Small Farmers of Nepal: Group Strength." In *Ideas and Action*, no. 165.

Fernandes, Cesar Rubem. 1988. "Sems Fems Lucrativos." In Landim, pp. 8–23.

Fernando, Marina. 1986. "Sri Lanka:The Kirillapone Project." Unpublished paper, Save the Children.

Ferrin, Cynthia. 1987. "When the Price Is Right: Cooperative Marketing in Uruguay." *Grassroots Development* 11, no. 1:10–17.

Fishel, John T. 1979. "Political Participation in a Peruvian Highland District." In Booth and Seligson, eds., 1979b, pp. 51–61.

Fisher, Julie. 1977. "Political Learning in the Latin American Barridas: The Role of the Junta de Vecinos." Ph.D. dissertation, The Johns Hopkins University.

———. 1984. "Development from Below: Neighborhood Improvement Associations in the Latin American Squatter Settlements." *Studies in Comparative International Development* 19, no. 1:61–85.

———. 1986. "Colombia: When Women Are United." In *Already I Feel the Change* Lessons from the Field 1, Save the Children.

———. 1989. *Agrarian Reform in Peru and El Salvador: Technoserve's Experience*. Technoserve, Replication and Policy Analysis Division, Norwalk, Connecticut.

Flora, Jan L., and Cornelia Butler Flora, with Humberto Rojas and Norma Villareal. 1988. "Community Stores in Rural Colombia: Organizing the Means of Consumption." In Annis and Hakim, eds., pp. 117–131.

Foweraker, Joe. 1990. "Popular Movments and Political Change in Mexico." In Foweraker and Craig, 1990: 3–10.

Foweraker, Joe, and Ann L. Craig. 1990. *Popular Movements and Political Change in Mexico*. Boulder, Colo.: Lynne Rienner.

Fowler, Alan. 1988. "Non-Governmental Organizations in Africa: Achieving Comparative Advantage in Relief and Micro-development." Discussion Paper No. 249, Institute of Development Studies, Sussex, England.

———. 1990. "Political Dimensions of NGO Expansion in Eastern and Southern Africa and the Role of International Aid." Ford Foundation. Unpublished paper.

Fox, Jonathan, and John Butler. 1987. "Research Project Preview: Membership Organization Dynamics: Lessons from the Inter-American Foundation Experience." IAF Memorandum, May 18.

Fox, Jonathan, and Luis Hernandez. 1989. "Offsetting the Iron Law of Oligarchy." *Grassroots Development* 13, no.2:8–15.

Fox, Thomas. 1987. "NGO's from the United States." *World Development* 15 (Supplement, Autumn).

Frantz, Telmo Rudi. 1987. "The Role of NGO's in the Strengthening of Civil Society." *World Development* 15 (Supplement, Autumn).

Freire, Paulo. 1970. *The Pedagogy of the Oppressed*. New York: Herder and Herder.

Friedmann, John. 1989. "Collective Self-Empowerment and Social Change." *IFDA Dossier* 69 (January-February):3–14.

Fruhling, Hugo. 1985. "Non-Profit Organizations as Opposition to Authoritarian Rule: The Case of Human Rights Organizations and Private Research Centers in Chile." Working Paper No. 96, Program on Non-Profit Organizations, Institution for Social and Policy Studies, Yale University.

FUNDESA (Guatemalan Development Foundation). 1989. *Directory of Private Voluntary Organizations Serving the Guatemalan Community.*

GADIS (Grupo de Analisis y Desarrollo Institutional y Social). 1989. *Directorios de Organizaciones No-Gubernamentales Argentinas de Promcion y Desarrollo.* Buenos Aires.

Gahlot, Deepa. 1991. "SPARC of Hope for India's Slum Dwellers." IDRC Reports, April : 8–10.

Gain, Philip. 1991. Case Study Done for Beyond Boundaries: Issues in Asian and American Environmental Activism. April 24–26, Asia Society, New York.

Gamer, Robert E. 1982. *The Developing Nations: A Comparative Perspective.* Boston: Allyn and Bacon.

Ganmei, Wu. 1990. "How Does a Non-Profit Organization Carry Out Its Activities in The Socialist China?" In Independent Sector, pp. 587–595.

Ganuza, Mario. 1988. "Development NGOs in Guatemala." Unpublished paper for Technoserve, Norwalk, Connecticut.

Garilao, Ernesto. 1987. "Indigenous NGO's as Strategic Institutions: Managing the Relationship with Government and Resource Agencies." *World Development* 15 (Supplement, Autumn):113–120.

Garrison, John. 1989. "Computers Link NGOs Worlwide." *Grassroots Development* 13, no. 2:48–49.

Gaytan, Austreberto. 1991–92. "Por un Capital en Manos del Pueblo?" *La Otra Bolsa de Valores,* no. 11, pp. 7–8.

Ghai, Dharam, and Anisur Rahman. 1981. "The Small Farmer's Group in Nepal." *Development,* no.1.

Ghose, Ajit Kumar, ed. 1983. *Agrarian Reform in Contemporary Developing Countries.* New York: St. Martin's Press.

Goertzen, Donald. 1991. "Sweet and Sour: Planters and Peasants Battle It Out." *Far Eastern Economic Review,* August 8, p. 24.

Goff, Brent. 1990. "Mastering the Craft of Scaling-Up in Colombia." *Grassroots Development* 14, no. 1:13–22.

Goldsworthy, David. 1984. "Political Power and Socio-Economic Development: Two Polemics." *Political Studies* 32, no. 4:551–569.

Gomes, P. I., ed. 1985. *Rural Development in the Caribbean.* New York: St. Martin's Press.

Gonoshasthaya Kendra. 1980. "Progress Report No. 7," August.

Gorman, Robert F., ed. 1984. *Private Voluntary Organizations as Agents of Development.* Boulder, Colo: Westview Press.

Goulet, Denis. 1988. "Development Strategy in Sri Lanka and a People's Alternative." In Attwood, Bruneau, and Galaty, eds., pp. 61–83.

Grameen Dialogue. 1990. Vol. 1, no. 5 Dhaka: Grameen Trust.

Gran, Guy. 1983. *Development by People.* New York: Praeger.

Gran, Guy. 1987. *An Annotated Guide to Global Development: Capacity-Building for Effective Social Change.* Olney, Md.: Resources for Development and Democracy.

Grzybowski, Candido. 1990. "Rural Workers and Democratisation in Brazil." *The Journal of Development Studies* 26, no. 4:19–43.

Gueneau, Marie Christine. 1984. "Analyse Economique d'un Echantillon de Petits Projets de Developpement-Evaluation Ex-Post de 30 Projets situes au Senegal et en Haute-Volta." Centre d'Etudes du Developpement, Universite de Paris I, Paris.

———. 1988. "L'Emergence des O.N.G. du Sud." *Croissance de Juenes Nations* 310 (November):16–18.

Gueneau, Marie Christine, and C. Morrisson. 1985. "Economic Survey of a Sample of Small Development Projects." DAC meeting on Aid Agency Cooperation with Non-Governmental Organizations. Paris: OECD.

Gupta, Anil. 1990. "Initiative, Innovation and Institutions: The Study of Emerging Trends in Voluntarism in Rural Development in India." In McCarthy, 1992, pp. 422–437.

Guyer, Jane. 1986. "Women's Role in Development." In Berg and Whitaker, eds.

Harazim, Dorit. 1990. "A Civil Society in the Making." *Kettering Review* (Winter): 23–30.

Harvey, Neil. 1990. "Peasant Strategies and Corporatism in Chiapas." In Foweraker and Craig, 1990, pp. 183–198.

Haubert, Maxime. 1986. "Adult Education and Grass Roots Organisations in Latin America: The Contribution of the International Co-operative University." *International Labour Review* 125, no. 2 (March-April):177–192.

HAVA (Haitian Association of Voluntary Agencies). 1991. *Liaison*, no. 13:3.

Healy, Kevin. 1987. "From Field to Factory: Vertical Integration in Bolivia." *Grassroots Development: Journal of the Inter-American Foundation* 11, no. 2:2–12.

Helmore, Kristin. 1985. "Working for Survival." Part 3 of "The Neglected Resource: Women in the Developing World." *The Christian Science Monitor*, December 19.

Herman, Robert D. 1990. "Methodological Issues in Studying the Effectiveness of Nongovernmental and Nonprofit Organizations." *Nonprofit and Voluntary Sector Quarterly* 19, no. 3:293–306.

Herrera, Xochitl, and Miguel Lobo-Guerrero. 1988. "From Failure to Success: Tapping the Creative Energy of Sikuani Culture in Colombia." *Grassroots Development* 12, no.3:28–37.

Hinnebusch, Raymond A. 1984. "Syria: The Role of Ideology and Party Organization in Local Development." In Cantori and Harik, eds., pp. 99–124.

Hirabayashi, Lane Ryo. 1986. "The Migrant Village Association in Latin America: A Comparative Analysis." *Latin American Research Review* 21, no.3.

Hirschman, Albert O. 1963. *Journeys Toward Progress: Studies of Economic Policy-Making in Latin America.* New York: The Twentieth Century Fund.

———. 1984. *Getting Ahead Collectively: Grassroots Experiences in Latin America.* New York: Pergamon Press.

Hollnsteiner, Mary Racelis. 1979. "Mobilizing the Poor Through Community Organization." *Philippine Studies* 27:387–416.

Horrigan, Alice. 1986. "Terror in Brazil." *The New Haven Advocate*, November 24.

Hsiao, Hsin-Huang Michael. 1990. "The Rise of the New Reformism: Toward an

Understanding of Private Philanthropy in Taiwan in the 1980s." In Independent Sector, pp. 661–673.

Hulme, David. 1990. "Can the Grameen Bank Be Replicated? Recent Experiments in Malaysia, Malawi and Sri Lanka." *Development Policy Review* 8, no. 3:287–300.

Hunt, Robert W. 1984. "Voluntary Agencies and the Promotion of Enterprise." In Gorman, ed.

———. 1985. "Private Voluntary Organizations and the Promotion of Small-Scale Enterprise." AID Evaluation Special Study No. 27, U.S. Agency for International Development, July.

Hunter, Guy. 1974. "Indigenous Development and the Developing World." *Overseas Development Institute Review*, no. 2, pp. 61–74.

Huntington, Samuel P., and Joan M. Nelson. 1976. *No Easy Choice: Political Participation in Developing Countries*. Cambridge, Mass.: Harvard University Press.

Hyden, Goran. 1981. "Modern Cooperatives and the Economy of Affection in Sub-Saharan Africa." Paper presented at IUAES Symposium on Traditional Cooperation and Social Organization in Relation to Modern Cooperative Organization and Enterprise, Amsterdam. April 23–24, Cited in Esman and Uphoff, 1984.

———. 1983. *No Shortcuts to Progress: African Development Management in Perspective*. Berkeley: University of California Press.

Ibrahim, Yousef. 1987. "Mosque and State: As Moslem Zeal Rises, Egypt Under Mubarek Avoids Confrontation." *The Wall Street Journal*, August 10.

———. 1987a. "Mosque and State: Revolutionary Islam of Iran Is Neutralized by Policies of Bahrain." *The Wall Street Journal*, August 7.

———. 1990. "An Affluent Kuwait Joins an Arab Trend Toward Democracy." *The New York Times*, March 11, p. 1.

IDRC. 1992. Special issue on "Children: Agents of Change." *IDRC Reports* 19, no. 4.

IFDA Dossier. 1984. "Lokayan, Dialogue of the People." No. 41, pp. 37–50. Nyon, Switzerland: International Foundation for Development Alternatives.

———. 1984a. "The Chingleput Rural Women's Social Education Centre," no. 42.

———. 1985. "India: Samakhya and the Cooperative Movement," no. 48.

———. 1985a. "Phillippines: Mindanao Community Theatre Network," no. 50.

———. 1986. "Ecuador: CATER, Centro Andino de Tecnologia Rural," no. 53.

———. 1986a. "Philippines: PROCESS (Participatory Research, Organization of Communities, and Education Towards Stuggle for Self Reliance)," no. 54.

———. 1987. no. 57/58:"A Sarvodaya Project," pp. 15–24; "Paraguay:Base /ISEC," pp. 93–95; and "Chile: El programa campesino del Centro el Canelo de Nos," pp. 96–97.

———. 1987a. No. 59: "ANEN—The African NGOs Environment Network," pp. 31–41; "Philippines: Cordillera People's Alliance," pp. 63–65; "India: Centre for Human Development and Social Change," pp. 66–67; "Argentina: Accion Popular Ecumenica," p. 68; "Peru Mujer," pp. 69–70; and "Italy: IDOC," pp. 75–77.

———. 1987b. No. 61: "ALOP-Trabajando por Latinoamerica," pp. 65–67; "Philippines: Pamalakaya, Small Fishermen's Movement," pp. 68–69; and "Netherlands: A New Environment and Development Service for Third World Citizen's Groups (ENDS)," pp. 73–74.

———. 1988. "Philippines: Fisherfolk Demand Genuine Reforms," no. 65, pp. 73–74.

———. 1988a. "Pakistan: Rural Development Foundatin," "The African Centre for Technology Studies," and "The Institute of Cultural Affairs," no. 66, pp. 69–76.

———. 1989. No. 69: "Honduras: Servicios Tecnicos, Legales y Economicos (SETELEC)," pp. 69–70; "Senegal: Federation des Organisations Non Gouvernementales (FONGS)," pp. 73–74; and "Caribbean: Graduate Theatre Company," p. 82.

———. 1989a. "Phillipines: NORLU," no. 70, pp. 71–72.

———. 1989b. No. 71: "Philippines: Community Information and Planning Systems," pp. 70–72; and "Trinidad and Tobago: Community Media for Development," p. 81.

———. 1989c. No. 72: "Indonesia: Usaha Bersama Arisan Manjung," pp. 15–23; and "Zaire: CADIC," p. 70.

———. 1989d. "India: Institute for Integrated Rural Development," no. 73, September-October.

———. 1989e. "India: Some SLARTC Activities in 1988"; "Brazil: The Institute of Technology for the Citizen;" "India: Equations, Equitable Tourism Options;" and "South West Asian Ocean: A Directory of Activists," no. 74, pp. 81–96.

———. 1990. No. 75/76: "Bolivia: Accion un maestro mas," pp. 99–100; and "El Salvador: CESTA-ECOBICI," p. 109.

———. 1990a. "Latin America:CLADES". No. 77, pp. 99–103.

———. 1990b. No. 78: "Philippines: Friends of the Wilderness for Tropical Rainforest Campaign," pp. 102–103; and "India: Development Alternatives," pp. 115–117.

———. 1990c. No. 79: "Bangaldesh: Antarjatik Beshamarik Sheba Sangstha," p. 106 and "Solomon Islands: SIDT," p. 107.

———. 1991. No. 80: "Liban/Palestine: L'Association Najdeh," pp. 102–103; "Sri Lanka: The National NGO Council," p. 110; and "Jamaica: The Association of Development Agencies," p. 111.

IHERC (Inter-Hemispheric Education Resource Center). 1988. "Private Organizations with U.S. Connections: Honduras;" "Private Organizations with U.S. Connections: Guatemala;" "Private Organizations with U.S. Connections: El Salvador."

IMPACT. No. 12, Fall 1990, pp. 5–6.

Inda, Caridad. 1980. "Honduran Organization Involves Community in Curriculum Reform Project." *Development Communication Report* No. 31. Clearinghouse on Development Communication, Washington, D.C.

Independent Sector (Washington, D.C.). 1990. *The Non-Profit Sector (NGOs) in the United States and Abroad: Cross Cultural Perspectives*. Working papers, Independent Sector, Spring Research Forum, Boston, Massachusettes, March 15–16.

International Tree Project Clearinghouse. 1987. *A Directory: NGOs in the Forestry*

Sector. 2d Africa ed.. Non-Governmental Liaison Service, United Nations, New York.

IRED. 1985. IRED Forum, no. 17. Geneva: Innovations et Reseaux pour le Developpement.

————. 1986. IRED Forum, no. 18.

————. 1986a. IRED Forum, no. 21.

————. 1987. IRED Forum, no. 22.

————. 1987a. IRED Forum, no. 23.

————. 1987b. IRED Forum, no. 24.

————. 1987c. IRED Forum, no. 25.

————. 1988. IRED Forum, no. 27.

IWRAW (International Women's Rights Watch). 1987. The Women's Watch, no. 1.

Jacoby, Erich H. 1972. "Effects of the 'Green Revolution' in South and Southeast Asia," Modern Asian Studies 6. Cited in Goldsworthy, 1984, pp. 63–69.

Jahan, Rounaq. 1987. "Women in South Asian Politics." Third World Quarterly 9, no. 3.

Jamela, Sibongile. 1990. "The Challenges Facing African NGOs: A Case Study Approach." Voices from Africa, no. 2, United Nations Non-Governmental Liaison Service, Geneva, pp. 17–27.

James, Estelle. 1982. "The Non-Profit Sector in International Perspective: The Case of Sri Lanka." Journal of Comparative Economics 6:289–318.

Jaquette, Jane S. 1986. "Women, Feminism and the Transition to Democracy in Latin America." Paper presented to the 20th Anniversary Meeting of the Latin American Studies Association, Boston, Massachusettes, October 23–26. Forthcoming in Abraham Lowenthal, ed., Latin America and the Caribbean Contemporary Record (New York: Holmes and Meier).

Jatoba, Jorge. 1987. "Alternative Resources for Grass Roots Development: A View from Latin America." Development Dialogue 1:114–134.

Jorgensen, Jan, Taieb Hafsi, and Moses Kiggundu. 1986. "Towards a Market Imperfections Theory of Organizational Structure in Developing Countries." Journal of Management Studies 23, no. 4:417–442.

Joseph, Suad. 1984. "Local-Level Politics and Development in Lebanon: The View from Borj Hammoud." In Cantori and Harik, eds., pp. 142–165.)

Jung, Ku-Hyun Jung. 1990. "Corporate Philanthropy in Korea." In Independent Sector, pp. 675–687.

Kabarhuza, Hamuli. 1990. "Development NGOs in Zaire: Experiences and Challenges." Voices from Africa, no. 2, United Nations Non-Governmental Liaison Service, Geneva, pp. 29–37.

Kannan, K. P. 1981. "A People's Science Movement," Development, no. 1, pp. 37–40.

Karim, M. Bazlul. 1985–86. "Rural Development Projects-Comilla, Puebla, and Chilalo: A Comparative Assessment." Studies in Comparative International Development 20, no. 4.

Khan, Mafruza. 1991. "Participatory Management of Local Resources: Proshika's Inititives in Forest Management," Dhaka, Proshika.

Khan, Nighat Said. 1987. "Together We Are Stronger: Report of a Women's Workshop in Pakistan." Ideas and Action, no. 172, pp. 11–16.

Khan, Nighat Said, and Kamla Bhasin. 1986. "Role of People's Organizations." *IFDA Dossier*, no. 53, pp. 3–15.

Kinzer, Stephen. 1987. "The Hunger for Land Feeds the Crisis in Central America." *The New York Times*, September 7.

Klenner, Arno, and Humberto Vega. 1989. "Support for Income Generation in an Economy of Poverty." In Downs et al., pp. 149–167.

Knapp, Martin, and Jeremy Kendall. 1990. "Defining the British Voluntary Sector." In Independent Sector, pp. 23–34.

Koldewyn, Phillip. 1986. "Mexican Voluntary Associations: A Community Study." *Journal of Voluntary Action Research* 15, no. 1:46–64.

Korten, David. 1990. *Getting to the 21st Century: Voluntary Action and the Global Agenda*. Hartford, Conn.: Kumarian Press.

Korten, David, and Felipe Alfonso, eds. 1983. *Bureaucracy and the Poor*. Hartford, Conn.: Kumarian Press.

Korten, David, and Rudi Klaus, eds. 1984. *People Centered Development: Contributions toward Theory and Planning Frameworks*. Hartford, Conn.: Kumarian Press.

Korten, Frances F. 1983. "Community Participation: A Management Perspective on Obstacles and Options." In Korten and Alfonso, eds., pp. 181–200.

———. 1986. "The Policy Framework for Community Management." In David Korten, ed. 1986. *Community Management: Asian Experience and Perspectives*, Hartford, Conn.: Kumarian Press, pp. 275–291.

Kramer, Ralph. 1981. *Voluntary Agencies in the Welfare State*. Berkeley: University of California Press.

La Forgia, Gerard. 1985. "Local Organizations for Rural Health in Panama: Community Participation, Bureaucratic Reorientation and Political Will." Ithaca, N.Y.: Rural Development Committee, Cornell University. Cited in Uphoff, 1986, p. 208.

La Gra, Jerry, Larry Leighton, and Susan Oechsle. 1989. *Profiles of Farmers Organizations in Saint Lucia*. Interamerican Institute for Co-Operation on Agriculture, Castries.

Lance, L. M., and E. E. McKenna. 1975. "Analysis of Cases Pertaining to the Impact of Western Technology on the Non-Western World," *Human Organization*. 34, no. 1:87–94.

Landim, Leilah. 1987. "Non-Governmental Organizations in Latin America." *World Development* 15 (Supplement, Autumn):29–38.

———. 1988. *Sems Fins Lucrativos: As organizacoes nao-governamentais no Brasil*. Rio de Janeiro: Instituto de Estudos da Religiao.

———. 1988a. "A Servico do Movimento Popular: As Organizacoes nao-governamentais no Brasil." In Landim, pp. 24–52.

———. 1988b. "Catalogo de ONGs no Brasil." In Landim pp. 54–61.

———. 1992. "What Is an NGO? Notes on the Nonprofit Organizations in Brazil." Third International Conference of Research on Voluntary and Nonprofit Organizatins, Indiana University, Center on Philanthropy, March 11–13.

Langer, A. 1985. "Is Development a Risk?" *Reporter* (Italian daily), July 5. Reprinted in *Compass*, no. 24/25.

La Otra Bolsa de Valores. 1991. No. 9, Promocion de Desarrollo Popular, Mexico City.

Lara, Francisco, and Horacio R. Morales. 1990. "The Peasant Movement and the

Challenge of Rural Democratisation in the Philippines." *The Journal of Development Studies* 26, no. 4:143–162.

Larson, Barbara K. 1984. "National Seeds in Local Soil: Will Development Grow?" In Cantori and Harik, eds., pp. 193–211.

Leach, Mark, Jeanne McCormack, and Candace Nelson. 1988. "The Tototo Home Industries Rural Development Project." Case study prepared for the Synergos Institute.

Lecomte, Bernard J. 1986. *Project Aid: Limitations and Alternatives.* Paris: OECD Development Center Studies.

Ledesma, Cesar R., and Cesar Decena. 1992. "Political Science Activism among NGO's in the Philippines." Paper submitted to the Third International Conference of Research on Voluntary and Nonprofit Organizations, Indiana University, Center on Philanthropy, March 11–13.

Leet, Glen, and Mildred Robbins Leet. 1989. "Trickle Up Program: 1988 Global Report." New York: Trickle Up Program.

LeMoyne, James. 1987. "Tenancingo Journal: Village Where Peace Fears to Tread." *The New York Times.*, August 29.

Leonard, David K. 1982. "Choosing Among Forms of Decentralization and Linkage." In Leonard and Marshall eds., pp. 193–226.

Leonard, David K., and Dale Rogers Marshall, eds. 1982. *Institutions of Rural Development for the Poor: Decentralization and Organizational Linkages.* Berkeley: University of California, Institute of International Studies.

Lewis, Flora. 1990. "The Right to Credit." *The New York Times*, September 26, p. A25.

Lewis, John P. 1986. "Development Promotion: A Time for Regrouping." In Lewis and Kallab, eds.

Lewis, John P., and Contributors. 1988. *Strengthening the Poor: What Have We Learned?* U.S.- Third World Policy Perspectives No. 10, Washington, D.C.: Overseas Development Council.

Lewis, John P., and Valeriana Kallab, eds. 1986. *Development Strategies Reconsidered.* U.S. Third World Policy Perspectives No. 5, Overseas Development Council. New Brunswick, N.J.: Transaction Books.

Liamzon, Tina. 1990. "Strategizing for Relevance: Trends and Roles for NGOs in the 1990s." *Phildhrra Notes* 6, no. 4:3–5.

———. 1990a. "Philippine NGOs in the 1990s: Six Trends." *Monday Developments* October 29: 8.

Lipnack, Jessica, and Jeffrey Stamps. 1984. "Creating Another America: The Power and the Joy of Networking." In Korten and Klaus, 1984:288–296.

Little, Peter D., Michael M. Horowitz, and A. Endre Nyerges. 1987. *Lands at Risk in the Third World: Local Level Perspectives.* Boulder, Colo.: Westview Press

Logan, Kathleen. 1990. "Women's Participation in Urban Protest." In Foweraker and Craig, pp. 150–159.

———. N.d. "A Tale of Two Women NGOs." *Lokniti: The Journal of the Asian NGO Coalition* 4, no. 3.

Lopezllera Mendez, Luis. 1988. "The Changing Role of NGOs in Latin America." Society for International Development, Nineteenth World Conference, March 25–28, New Delhi, India.

———. 1988a. *Sociedad Civil y Pueblos Emergentes: Las Organizaciones Auton-*

omas de Promocion Social y Desarrollo en Mexico. Mexico City: Promocion del Desarrollo Popular.

———. 1990. "The Struggle of the Indigenous People and the New 'Reservations.' " *Fenix*, pp. 6–7. (A single issue published by the Friends of the Ideas and Action Foundation, Hoofddorp, Holland)

Loveman, Brian. 1991. "NGOs and the Transition to Democracy in Chile." *Grassroots Development* 15, no. 2:8–19.

Ludwig, Richard L., and G. Shabbir Cheema. 1987. "Evaluating the Impact of Policies and Projects: Experience in Urban Shelter and Basic Urban Services." *Regional Development Dialogue* 8, no. 4:190–209.

Macdonald, Theodore. 1987. "Grassroots Development: Not Just Organic Farming and Good Faith." *Cultural Survival* 11, no. 1:41–45.

MacDougall, John James. 1986. "Indonesia: Economic Growth and Political Order." *Current History* 85, no. 110: 72–75, 78–79.

Maeda, Justin. 1983. "Creating National Structures for People Centered Agrarian Development." In Korten and Alfonso, eds., pp. 136–162.

Mainwaring, Scott. 1985. "Grassroots Popular Movements and the Struggle for Democracy: Nova Iguacu, 1974–1985." Working Paper No. 52, The Helen Kellogg Institute for International Studies, University of Notre Dame.

———. 1986. "Grassroots Popular Movements, Identity, and Democratization in Brazil." Working Paper No. 84, The Helen Kellogg Institute for International Studies, University of Notre Dame.

Malamah-Thomas, David Henry. 1989. "The Telu Workshop Experience." *IFDA Dossier*, no. 70 March-April, pp. 3–14.

Martinez Nogueira. 1987. "Life Cycle and Learning in Grass Roots Organisations." *World Development* 15 (Supplement on Development Alternatives: The Challenges for NGO's):169–178.

Massoni, Vittorio. 1985. "Nongovernmental Organizations and Development." *Finance and Development* 22, no. 3:38–41.

Mathai, Wangari. 1992. "Kenya's Green Belt Movement." *The UNESCO Courier*, March, pp. 23–25.

Mathews, Jessica. 1991. "A New String on Third World Loans." *Washington Post*, October 25.

Matos Azocar, Luis Raul. 1986. "Hacia Otra Venezuela?" *IFDA Dossier*, no. 54.

Max-Neef, Manfred. 1985. "Another Development Under Repressive Rule," *Development Dialogue*, no. 1.

McCarthy, Kathleen D. 1989. "The Voluntary Sector Overseas: Notes from the Field." Working Papers, Center for the Study of Philanthropy, City University of New York.

———. 1992. *The Nonprofit sector in the Global Community*. San Francisco: Jossey-Bass Publishers.

McClelland, David C. 1970. "The Two Faces of Power." *Journal of International Affairs* 24, no. 1:29–47.

McCord, William, with Arline McCord. 1986. *Paths to Progress: Bread and Freedom in Developing Societies*. New York: Norton.

McKee, Katharine. 1989. "Microlevel Strategies for Supporting Livelihoods, Employment, and Income Generation of Poor Women in the Third World: The Challenge of Significance." *World Development* 17, no. 7:993–1006.

McRobie, George. 1983. "We're Not Talking about Revolution but about Changing the Rules." *Ceres* 16, no. 3:33–38.

Mead, Margaret, ed. 1955. *Cultural Patterns and Technical Change*. New York: Mentor Books.

Mendez Lugo, Bernardo. 1988. "Artesanos y Alfareros, Apoyados por la Investigacion: Una Experiencia Regional en Mexico." *IFDA Dossier*, no. 65, pp. 11–15.

Merschrod, Kris. 1980. "Participation in Program Evaluation at the Regional Level in Honduras." *Rural Development Participation Review* (Rural Development Committee, Cornell University, Ithaca, N.Y.) 2, no. 1:18–22.

Messerschmidt, Donald A. 1987. "Conservation and Society in Nepal: Traditional Forest Management and Innovative Development." In Little, Horowitz, and Nyerges, pp. 373–397.

Michels, Robert. 1915. *Political Parties*. New York: Dover Publications (1959 ed.).

Millet, Richard. 1987. "The Honduran Dilemma." *Current History* 86, no. 524:409–412, 435–436.

Millwood, David, and Helena Gazelius. 1985. *Good Aid: A Study of Quality in Small Projects*. Swedish International Development Authority.

Moen, Elizabeth. 1991. *Voluntary Sector Grass Roots Development in Tamilnadu*. Gandhigram Rural Institute, Deemed University, Tamilnadu, India.

Moita, Luis. 1985. "NGO Production of Training Materials: The Brazilian Experience." *Ideas and Action*, no. 161, pp. 3–8.

Montgomery, John D. 1972. "The Allocation of Authority in Land Reform Programs: A Comparative Study of Administrative Process and Outputs." *Administrative Science Quarterly* 17, no. 1:62–75.

Moore, Barrington. 1966. *Social Origins of Democracy and Dictatorship*. Boston: Beacon Press.

Moreira Alves, Maria Elena. 1984. "Grassroots Organizations, Trade Unions, and the Church: A Challenge to the Controlled Abertura in Brazil." *Latin American Perspectives* 11, no. 1:73–102.

Morgenthau, Ruth. N.d. "International Liaison Committee for Food Corps Programs." Waltham, Mass., Brandeis University. (Booklet)

Muchiru, Simon. 1986. "NGOs and African Development: Contributions, Capabilities and Needs." Nairobi: African NGOs Environmental Network, April (mimeo). Cited in Berg, 1987, p. 21.

Mulwa, Francis W. 1987. "Participation of the Grassroots in Rural Development: The Case of the Development Education Programme of the Catholic Diocese of Machakos, Kenya." *Development*, nos. 2, 3.

Mulyungi, Josphat. 1990. "On the Role of African NGOs." *Voices from Africa*, no. 2, United Nations Non-Governmental Liaison Service, Geneva, pp. 45–58.

Murray, Gerald F. 1986. "Seeing the Forest While Planting the Trees: An Anthropological Approach to Agroforestry in Rural Haiti." In *Politics, Projects, and People: Institutional Development in Haiti*, D. W. Brinkerhoff and J. C. Garcia-Zamor, eds. New York: Praeger Publishers. Cited in Uphoff, 1986, p. 259.

Muttreja, Poonam. 1990. "Private Social Action Groups in India: Their Role in Enhancing Capabilities and Social Action." Unpublished paper.

Mwangi, Jacob. 1986. "Towards an Enabling Environment: Indigenous Private Development Agencies in Africa." Paper presented at the Enabling Environment Conference, Nairobi, Geneva: The Aga Khan Foundation, 1986. Cited in van der Heijden, 1987, p. 111.

Myrdal, Gunnar. 1970. *The Challenge of World Poverty*. New York: Pantheon Books.

Ndjonkou, Djankou. 1986. "Cooperatives and Other Craftsmen's Associations in Rural Areas." *The Courier*, no. 99, September-October, pp. 81–83.

Neumann, Franz L. 1950. "Approaches to the Study of Political Power." *Political Science Quarterly* 65, no. 2 (June). Reprinted in Roy C. Macridis and Bernard E. Brown, eds., *Comparative Politics: Notes and Readings* (Homewood, Ill.: Dorsey Press, 1972), pp. 49–59.

NGLS News (U.N. Non-Governmental Liaison Service). 1987. September.

Nielsen, Waldemar. 1979. *The Endangered Sector*. New York: Columbia University Press.

Nyoni, Sithembiso. 1987. "Indigenous NGOs: Liberation, Self-Reliance and Development." *World Development* 15 (Supplement): 51–56.

OAS (Organization of American States), Inter-American Commission of Women. 1990. *Non-Governmental Women's Organizations and National Machinery for Improving the Status of Women: A Directory for the Caribbean Region.*

Oberg, Keith L. 1989. "Confronting Violence Against Women." Annual Report, Inter-American Foundation, pp. 32–33.

OECD (Organization for Economic Cooperation and Development), Development Cooperation Directorate. 1988. *Voluntary Aid for Development: The Role of Non-Governmental Organizations*. Note by the Secretariat, September 14.

OECD (Organization for Economic Cooperation and Development), Development Centre. 1984. *Directory of Development Research and Training in Latin America.*

———. 1986. *Directory of Development Research and Training in Africa.*

———. 1988a. Development Cooperation Report by Joseph C. Wheeler.

———. 1991. Development Cooperation Report by Alexander Love.

Okoli, F. C. 1982. "Organizing for Community Development in Anambra State of Nigeria: Toward a Strategy of Development Humanism." *The African Review* 9, no. 2:62–77.

Olson, Mancur. 1965. *The Logic of Collective Action: Public Goods and the Theory of Groups*. Cambridge: Cambridge University Press.

Organski, A.F.K. 1965. *The Stages of Political Development*. New York: Knopf.

Ouedraogo, Bernard. 1986. " 'Development Without Damage'—The Naam Groups Tackle Drought." *The Courier*, no. 99, September-October, pp. 88–90.

Oxby, Clare. 1983. " 'Farmer Groups' in Rural Areas of the Third World." *Community Development Journal* 18, no. 1: 50–59.

Oxfam America. 1984. *News*, Winter.

———. 1986. "The Philippines." *Project Report.*

PACT (Private Agencies Collaborating Together). 1989. Asian Linkages. *NGO Collaboration in the 1990s: A Five Country Study.*

———. 1990. "Green Forum, Philippines, Take Up Community-Centered Activism." *Impact*, no. 12, pp. 5–6.

Padron, Mario. 1983. "Third World PDA's Meet in Lima." *IFDA Dossier*, no. 37, September-October.

———. 1986. "The Third World NGDO's Task Force: Origin, Aims, Evolution and Present Status." *IRED Forum*, no. 18, January-March.

———. 1986a. "NGDO's and Grass Roots Development in Latin America." Paper presented at the Thirteenth Annual Congress of the Latin American Studies Association, Boston, Massachusetts, October 22–26.

———. 1987. "Non-Governmental Development Organizations: From Development Aid to Development Cooperation." *World Development* 15 (Supplement):69–77.

———. 1988. "Los Centros de Promocion y la cooperacion internacional al en America Latina: El caso Peruano." In Padron, ed., pp. 24–87.

Padron, Mario, ed. 1988. *Las Organizaciones no gubernamentales en el Peru.* Lima: Desco (Centro de Estudios y Promocion del Desarrollo).

Panini, M. N. 1987. "India." *Ideas and Action*, no. 3, pp. 20-21.

Pardo, Lucia. 1990. *Instituciones de Fomento y de Apoyo a Talleres Productivos y Pequenas Empresas o Negocios.* AID, FINAM, and Departamento de Economia, Universidad de Chile.

Partners of the Americas. 1988. *Natural Resources Directory: Latin America and the Caribbean.* Julie Buckley-Ess and Mark Hathaway, eds.

Paul, Samuel. 1987. *Community Participation in Development Projects: The World Bank Experience.* World Bank Discussion Papers No. 6. Washington, D.C.: The World Bank.

Pavard, Claude. 1986. "Rural Structures as Agents of Development—the Bafut Experimental Project." *The Courier*, September-October.

Peng, Khor Kok. 1983. "Whose Felt Needs?" *Ceres* 16, no. 3: 28–32.

Peterson, David. 1991. "Whither Afrocommunism?" *The Foreign Observer*, April 4.

Peterson, Stephen B. 1982. "Alternative Local Organizations Supporting the Agricultural Development of the Poor." In Leonard and Marshall, eds., pp. 125–150.

Pettit, Jethro. 1987. "Farm Co-ops Grapple with Adversity." *Oxfam America News*, Fall.

Pezzullo, Caroline. 1986. "For the Record . . . Forum '85: The Non-Governmental World Meeting for Women, Nairobi, Kenya." International Women's Tribune Center, New York.

Pollnac, Richard B. 1985. "Social and Cultural Characteristics in Small-scale Fishery Development." In Cernea, pp. 189–223.

PONPO (Program on Non-Profit Organizations). 1986. "Coordinating the Development Efforts of PVO's in Africa: Nigeria, Senegal, and Togo." *Research Reports* No. 6, Yale University.

Population Institute. 1987. "Bangladesh Determined to Lower Its Fertility." *Popline* 9, no. 7: 7–8.

———. 1987. "World Bank Turning to NGO's for Support," *Popline* 9, no. 2: 1–2.

Postel, Sandra, and Lori Heise. 1988. "Reforestation with a Human Touch." *Grassroots Development* 12, no. 3: 38–40.

Population Institute. 1988. *The Nairobi Challenge: Global Directory of Women's Organizations Implementing Population Strategies.* Washington, D.C.

Powell, John Duncan. 1970. "Peasant Society and Clientelistic Politics." *American Political Science Review* 64, no. 2.

Powell, Walter W., ed. 1987. *The Nonprofit Sector: A Research Handbook.* New Haven, Conn.: Yale University Press.

Pradervand, Pierre. 1988. "Afrique Noire: La Victoire du Courage." *IFDA Dossier,* no. 64, pp. 3–12.

———. 1990. *Listening to Africa: Developing Africa from the Grassroots.* New York: Praeger.

———. 1990a. "Colufifa: 20,000 Individuals Fighting Hunger." *African Farmer,* no. 4, July, p. 81.

———. 1990b. "Bartering Helps Farmers Find New Markets," *African Farmer,* no. 5, November, pp. 38–39.

Prijono, Onny S. 1990. "Voluntarism and Voluntary Organizations in Indonesia." In McCarthy, 1992, pp. 438–453.

Proterra. 1990. "Peruvian Environmental Network." Lima. (Directory)

Rahman, Anisur. 1981. "Reflections," *Development,* no. 1.

Rahnema, Majid. 1990. "Swadhyaya: The Unknown, the Peaceful, the Silent yet Singing Revolution of India." *IFDA Dossier,* nos. 75, 76 pp. 19–34.

Ralston, Lenore, James Anderson, and Elizabeth Colson. 1983. *Voluntary Efforts in Decentralized Management.* Berkeley: University of California Press.

Ratnapala, Nandasena. 1980. "The Sarvodaya Movement: Self-Help Rural Development in Sri Lanka." In Coombs, pp. 469–523.

Reed, Richard. 1987. "Federations of Indian Communities: Strategies for Grassroots Development." *Cultural Survival Quarterly* 11, no. 1: 16–20.

Reilly, Charles. 1989. "The Democratization of Development: Partnership at the Grassroots." Annual Report, Inter-American Foundation, pp. 16–20.

———. 1990. "Helping the Poor to Save the Planet." *Grassroots Development* 14, no. 2:42–44.

Riding, Alan. 1986. "Cuzco Journal: In the Inca's Land, a War for the People's Hearts." *The New York Times,* November 18.

Ritchey Vance, Marion. 1991. *The Art of Association: NGOs and Civil Society in Colombia.* Country Focus Series No. 2. Washington, D.C.: Inter-American Foundation.

Ross, Thomas. 1990. "See, Understand, Learn." *Grameen Dialogue* 1, no. 5. (December): 1–2.

Roth, Gabriel. 1987. *The Private Provision of Public Services in Developing Countries* New York: Oxford University Press. Published for the World Bank.

Rouille D'Orfeuil, Henri. 1984. *Cooperer Autrement: L'engagement des organisations non gouvernementales aujourd'hui.* Paris: L'Harmatton.

Rubin, Jeffrey W. 1987. "Election, Repression, and Limited Reform: Update on Southern Mexico." *LASA Forum* 18, no. 2. Latin American Studies Association.

Ruiz Zuniga, Angel, and Daniel Morgan Ball. 1989. "El Estado, La Sociedad Civil y la Tecnologia Apropriada en la Produccion de Vivienda Popular." Universidad de Costa Rica. (Unpublished manuscript)

Rush, James. 1991. *The Last Tree.* New York: The Asia Society (distributed by Westview Press).

Salmen, Lawrence F., and A. Paige Eaves. 1989. "World Bank Work with Nongovernmental Organizations." Working Papers, Public Sector Management and Private Sector Development, Country Economics Department, World Bank.

Samarasinghe, L. M. 1992. "Historical Development of the Non Profit Sector in Sri Lanka." Paper submitted to the Third International Conference of Research on Voluntary and Nonprofit Organizations, Center on Philanthropy, Indiana University, March 11–13, 1992.

Santana, Pedro. 1983. *Desarrollo regional y paros civicos en Colombia*. Bogota: Centro de Investigación y Educación Popular (CINEP). Cited in Brian Smith, 1990, p. 243.

Santiago, Asteya M. 1987. "San Martin De Porres: A Case Study of Squatter Settlement Upgrading in Metro Manila." *Regional Development Dialogue 8*, no. 4: 86–107.

Saouma, Edouard. 1985. "Issues in Rural Poor Organizing." *Ideas and Action*. no. 162, pp. 18–21.

Sawadogo, Alfred. 1990. "The State Counter-Attacks: Clearly Defined Priorities for Burkina Faso." *Voices from Africa*, no. 2, United Nations Non-Governmental Liaison Service, Geneva, pp. 59–64.

Schkolnik, Mariana. 1985. "Las Organizaciones Economicas." Review of L. Razeto, A. Klenner, A. Ramirez, and R. Urmeneta. *La experiencia de las nuevas organizaciones economicas populares en Chile* (Santiago: Academia de Humanismo Cristiano, 1983). In *IFDA Dossier*, no. 47, May-June.

Schmidt, Ozzie, and Gerry Toomey. 1987. "Sorghum's Knight in Shining Armour." *The IDRC Reports*, 16, no. 4:4–5.

Schneider, Bertrand. 1985. *La Revolution des Pieds Nus-Rapport au Club de Rome*. Paris: Fayard.

Schteingart, Martha. 1986. "Social Conflicts and Environmental Deterioration." *Development*, no. 4, 56–60.

Schuh, G. Edward. 1987. "PVO Role in Influencing Agricultural Policy: A View from the World Bank." Paper presented at the Quarterly Meeting of the Advisory Committee for Voluntary Foreign Aid, U.S. Agency for International Development, Washington, D.C, June 24–25.

Secretariat ONG/Zaire. 1988. "Recontre Euopeene ONG operationelles au Zaire, Septembre 22. Brussels.

Seibel, Hans Dieter, and Andreas Massing. 1974. *Traditional Organizations and Economic Development: Studies of Indigenous Cooperatives in Liberia*. New York: Praeger. Cited in Uphoff, 1986, p. 117.

Seva Mandir. 1988–89. *Annual Report*. Udaipur, India.

Shadab. 1987. Bimonthly Pulbication of the Rural Development Foundation of Pakistan, Islamabad, vol. 5, no. 8.

Shaw, Timothy M. 1990. "Popular Participation in Non-Governmental Structures in Africa: Implications for Democratic Development." *Africa Today 37*, no. 3:5–22.

Sheth, D. L. 1983. "Grass-roots Stirrings and the Future of Politics." *Alternatives 9*, no. 1 (Summer): 1–24.

Shiva, Vandana. 1986. "Ecology Movements in India." *Alternatives 9*, no. 2 (April).

Simons, Marlise. 1986. "With a Fiery Pen Bush Pilot Fights for Amazon." *The New York Times*, November 11.

Sivaramakrishnan, K. C. 1977. "Slum Improvement in Calcutta." *Assignment Children*, no. 40, pp. 87–115.

Smith, Brian H. 1990. *More Than Altruism: The Politics of Private Foreign Aid.* Princeton, N.J.: Princeton University Press.

Smith, Carol. 1990. "Cisma: A Mayan Research Organization." *Cultural Survival Quarterly*, no. 4:80–81.

Smith, Emily. 1992. "Reaping the Spoils—Without Spoiling the Earth." *Business Week*, June, 1992, pp. 12–14.

Smith, Richard C. 1987. "Indigenous Autonomy for Grass Roots Development." *Cultural Survival Quarterly* 11, no. 1:8–12.

———. 1987a. "Bolivia: Aid Reconsidered." *Oxfam America News*, Spring.

Smith, Robert J., Maria Rehnfeldt, and William M. Barbieri. 1988. "Indian Colonization in Paraguay." In Annis and Hakim, eds., pp. 58–64.

Somjee, A. H. 1979. *The Democratic Process in a Developing Society.* New York: St. Martin's Press.

Stein, Alfredo. 1990. "Critical Issues in Community Participation in Self-Help Housing Programmes. The Experience of FUNDASAL." *Community Development Journal* 25, no. 1:21–30.

Stremlau, Carolyn C. 1987. "NGO Coordinating Bodies in Africa, Asia and Latin America," *World Development* 15 (Supplement) (Autumn):213–226.

Swartz, Carl. 1990. "Experiments in Partnership Research." *Grassroots Development* 14, no. 2:21–23.

Taal, Housainou. 1989. "How Farmers Cope with Risk and Stress in Rural Gambia." *IDS Bulletin* 20, no. 2:16–22.

Tendler, Judith. 1983. *What to Think About Cooperatives: A Guide from Bolivia.* The Inter-American Foundation.

———. 1987. *What Ever Happened to Poverty Alleviation?* A report prepared for the Mid-Decade Review of the Ford Foundation's Programs on Livelihood, Employment and Income Generation, March.

Terrant, James, and Hasan Poerbo. 1986. "Strengthening Community-Based Technology Management Systems." In Korten, 1986, pp. 172–182.

Thiele, Graham. 1986. "The State and Rural Development in Tanzania: The Village Administration as a Political Field." *The Journal of Development Studies* 22:540–557.

Thompson, Andres. 1990. "Democracy and Development: The Role of NGOs in the Southern Cone (Argentina, Chile and Uruguay)." In McCarthy, ed. 1992, pp. 389–405.

———. 1992. "The Nonprofit Sector in South America." Paper submitted to the Third International Conference of Research on Voluntary and Nonprofit Organizations, Center on Philanthropy, Indiana University, March 11–13.

Thomson, Randall J., and Michael Armer. 1980. "Respecifying the Effects of Voluntary Association on Individuals in a Traditional Society," *International Journal of Comparative Sociology* 21, nos. 3–4:288–302.

Thoolen, Hans. 1990. "Information and Training in an Expanding Human Rights Movement." *Development*, no. 2, pp. 86–90.

Tinker, Irene. 1986. "Feminizing Development—for Growth with Equity." *Care Briefs on Development Issues*, no. 6, pp. 1–11.

Tolles, Robert. 1981. "Special Report: Grass Roots Development." *Ford Foundation Letter*, no., 12 June 1.

Tongsawate, Maniemai, and Water E. J. Tips. 1985. *Coordination Between Governmental and Non-Governmental Organizations in Thailand's Rural Development.* Monograph No. 5. Bangkok: Division of Human Settlements Development, Asian Institute of Technology.

Towle, Judith, and Bruce G. Potter. 1989. "Organizational Profiles of Who Is Doing What in Support of Programs for Sustainable Development and Environmental Management in the Eastern Caribbean: A Guide to Donor Assistance Agencies." Island Resources Foundation, St Thomas, U.S. Virgin Islands.

Trejos, Marta. 1992. "Homes, Not Slums." UNESCO Courier, March, pp. 34–35.

Tutwiler, Richard. 1984. "Ta awun Mahwit: A Case Study of a Local Development Association in Highland Yemen." In Cantori and Harik, eds., pp. 166–192.

Twose, Nigel. 1987. "European NGOs: Growth or Partnership?" *World Development* 15 (Supplement):7–10.

———. 1988. "The Role of Indigenous NGOs in Africa." *Panoscope 5* (March):23–24.

UNICEF, Inades Formation Rwanda. 1985. *Inventaire O.N.G. 1985.* Kigali. (B.P. 445)

United Nations. 1988. "Africa: Four Years On." Final Report, UN-NGO Conference, April 23–27.

United Nations, Non-Governmental Liaison Service. 1988. *Non-Governmental Organizations and Sub-Saharan Africa,* July.

United Nations, Non-Governmental Liaison Service/New York and Advocates for African Food Security. 1987. *Case Studies from Africa: Towards Food Security.*

Uphoff, Norman. 1986. *Local Institutional Development: An Analytical Sourcebook With Cases.* Hartford: Kumarian Press.

———. 1988. "Assisted Self-Reliance: Working With, Rather than For, the Poor." In John P. Lewis and Contributors, pp. 47-59.

———. 1992. *Learning from Gal Oya: The Possibilities for Participatory Development and Post-Newtonian Social Science.* Ithaca, N.Y.: Cornell University Press.

USAID (U.S. Agency for International Development), Bureau for Food For Peace and Voluntary Assistance, Office of Private and Voluntary Cooperation. 1989. "Accelerating Institutional Development." PVO Institutional Development Evaluation Series.

Valenzuela, David. 1989. "Searching for New Frontiers in Microenterprise Development." Annual Report, Inter-American Foundation, pp. 49–50.

van den Akker, Piet. 1987. "Savings Clubs (Jam'iyyat Iddikhar): The Egyptian Experience." *Development*, nos. 2/3, pp. 145–147.

Van der Heijden, Hendrik. 1985. "Developmental Impact and Effectiveness of Non-Governmental Organisations: The Record of Progress in Rural Development Co-Operation." Paper prepared for the Symposium of the Royal Tropical Institute in Amsterdam on "Effectiveness of Rural Development Cooperation," October 2.

———. 1987. "The Reconciliation of NGO Autonomy, Program Integrity and Operational Effectiveness with Accountability to Donors." *World Development* 15 (Supplement): 103–112.

Van Nieuwenhuijze, C.A.O., M. Fathalla Al-Khatib, and Adel Azer. 1985. *The Poor Man's Model of Development.* Leiden: E. J. Brill.

Van Orman, Jan R. 1989. "Leadership and Grassroots Development." *Grassroots Development* 13, no. 2:3–7.

Velarde, Federico. 1988. "Las ONGs en el Peru: Algunas Notas." *Cooperacion Internacional al Desarrollo,* no. 3, Taller de Cooperacion al Desarrollo, Santiago, pp. 15–18.

Vetter, Stephen. 1986. "Building the Infrastructure for Progress: Private Development Organizations in the Dominican Republic." *Grassroots Development* 10, no. 1:2–9.

———. 1989. "The Elements of a Grassroots Development Strategy." Annual Report, Inter-American Foundation, pp. 10–13.

Vozza, Giuseppe. 1987. "Ecuador: The Crisis of Rural Cooperatives and the Quest for Alternatives." *Cultural Survival* 11, no. 1:38–40.

Wali, Alaka. 1990. "Living with the Land: Ethnicity and Development in Chile." *Grassroots Development* 14, no. 9:12–20.

Wanyande, Peter. 1987. "Women's Groups in Participatory Development: Kenya's Development Experience Through the Use of Harambee." *Development,* nos. 2/3.

Weber, Ron. 1984. "Political Democracy, State Strength and Economic Growth in LDC's: A Cross-National Analysis." *Review of International Studies* 10:297–312.

———. 1990. "Water for the People: The IAF Experience." *Grassroots Development* 14, no. 2:pp. 8–9.

Wells, A. F., and D. Wells. 1953. *Friendly Societies in the West Indies.* London: Her Majesty's Stationery Office, Colonial Research Publications. Cited in Craig, 1985.

Weyers, Helmut. 1980. "Co-operation between Non-governmental Volunteer Services and the United Nations Volunteers Programme." *International Journal of Comparative Sociology* 21, no. 5 (September-December):75–92.

Wheeler, Joseph et al. 1988. "Strengthening the Poor: What Have We Learned?" Overseas Development Council.

Whiting, Susan. 1989. "The Non-Governmental Sector in China: A Preliminary Report." The Ford Foundation, Beijing.

Williams, Aubrey. 1990. "A Growing Role for NGOs in Development." *Finance and Development,* December, pp. 31–33.

Williams, Dave. 1991. "Prospects for Change in South Africa." *Impact* (Fall), p. 11.

Williams, John Hoyt. 1987. "Paraguay's Stroessner: Losing Control?" *Current History* 86, no. 516, pp. 25–28, 34–35.

Williams, Paula. 1989. "Zimbabwean Women's Groups." Letter to the Institute of Current World Affairs, Hanover, New Hampshire, February 28.

World Bank. 1988. "Operational Manual Statement: Collaboration with Nongovernmental Organizations." Washington, D.C.

———. 1989. "Cooperation Between the World Bank and NGOs: Progress Report for 1989." Preliminary draft for discussion at the the 1989 Meeting of the World Bank–NGO Committee.

———. 1989a. "Strengthening Popular Participation in Development: World Bank Experience." Strategic Planning and Review Department, October.

———. 1990. "How the World Bank Works with Nongovernmental Organizations."

World Council of Credit Unions and International Cooperative Alliance. 1988. "Geographical Affiliations of International Cooperative Organizations in Developing Countries." Washington, D.C. and Geneva.

Yudelman, Sally. 1987. *Hopeful Openings*. Hartford, Conn.: Kumarian Press.

Zambrano, Angel Enrique. 1989. "Las Asociaciones de Vecinos en Venezuela." IFDA Dossier, no. 72, pp. 25–36.

Zamosc, Leon. 1990. "The Political Crisis and the Prospects for Rural Democracy in Colombia." *The Journal of Development Studies* 26, no. 4:44–78.

Zeuli, Kim. 1991. *Solving the Problems of the Third World Through Women*. Unpublished senior thesis, Vassar College.

Zhang, Junhai. 1990. "The Voluntary Sector in the People's Republic of China: An Overview and New Challenges." In McCarthy, 1992, pp. 466–484.

Index

About the Author

JULIE FISHER is a Scholar in Residence, Program on Non-profit Organizations, Yale University. She has been a consultant to UNICEF, Save the Children, Technoserve, World Vision, the Asia Society, Lutheran World Relief, and Interaction.